Beloved Infidel

Beloved Infidel

BY SHEILAH GRAHAM

AND GEROLD FRANK

Quality Paperback Book Club
New York

When I am dead, my dearest,
    Sing no sad songs for me;
Plant thou no roses at my head,
    Nor shady cypress-tree:
Be the green grass above me
    With showers and dewdrops wet;
And if thou wilt, remember,
    And if thou wilt, forget.

—*Christina Georgina Rossetti*

Dear Scott:

You wanted me to write the story of my life and now, so much later, here it is. I have always wondered whether I should tell it. I thought it an interesting story, yet I was afraid. I have made up so many fantasies about my beginnings, I lived a life of pretense for so long, I could not bring myself to reveal the truth. But you who alone knew my whole story were fascinated by it all—by the background I had created, the parents I invented, the name I gave myself—and so I was encouraged. "You must do your story," you told me, and you brought a ledger and showed me how to begin by making notes of all I remembered. I might have written it then, with your help, had you lived. But you died and I had neither the heart nor mind for it. I went to London full of self-pity, almost hoping that I would be killed in the war. But instead of being killed, I lived. I married and made a new life, and to my two children I have tried to pass on something of what you taught me.

When they were younger, Wendy and Robbie, I pondered again the question of writing this book. I was still not ready—and I was frightened. What would they think of me? Of us? Would they understand how two people can be deeply in love and yet find they cannot marry? How would they feel to learn that their mother was not born to the wealth and social distinction she pretended, that her childhood photographs had been altered to show her as she had never been, that even the photographs of uncles and aunts on the walls were frauds. . . .

But the most significant part of my story is your story, too, and this helped me resolve my dilemma. As the years passed and I read increasingly about you in books and magazines, I found myself thinking, "This is not the Scott I knew." From those pages there emerged a man who was often a stranger to me. The man they put together from your correspondence, your books, the quick, fugitive glimpses they caught of you toward the end—this was not Scott Fitzgerald as I knew him. And others should know, too, that though Scott Fitzgerald had a demon, a terrifying demon, he had fought it and conquered it before death came to him. He did not die a defeated man.

As for my own fears, I have been able to push them aside. Little by little I have told the truth about my background to my children. They have always known about you: they know that you are something very precious in their mother's life. Only the other day Wendy, coming upon your name, asked, "Would he have liked me, Mother?" I tried to explain to her why we were never married. I said, "I could not marry him because his wife was very ill in a sanitarium and there was a daughter he loved very much, and he could not abandon them." I told her of your relationship to Francis Scott Key and once when she sang the "The Star-Spangled Banner" she turned to me and said, quite proudly, "I'm kind of related to F. Scott Fitzgerald, aren't I?" And then Robbie asked, "I'm related to him too, aren't I, Mom?" I said, "Yes, you are, both of you—in a kind of a way." I told them that you would have liked them. Very much.

Now that they are old enough to understand and now that I have brought myself at last to face all of the truth, I can tell it. I know that I need not be afraid.

Sheilah

Book I

CHAPTER ONE

I WAS BORN Lily Sheil, a name which to this day horrifies me to a degree impossible to explain. I have not pronounced that name for twenty years. I have written it here for the first time since my childhood. My children have never heard it, nor has anyone who knows me today: they will read it on this page for the first time. Is this hard to believe? It is true. The sound of it still sends the blood rushing to my cheeks, I break out in cold perspiration, I want to flee. . . .

The fact is that the whole of my childhood has been something dark and secret to me, and the name I was born with is tied up with the years I have kept hidden for so long. I have looked upon it as some sorcerer's dread incantation: if I forget myself so much as to utter it, in a flash everything I have so carefully built up will be destroyed, the present will vanish and I will be once again what I was. Even now it is a struggle to tell the truth about my past. . . .

It begins with a bus ride. It is an open bus, in London, and we are atop it, Aunt Mary and I. I had never ridden in a bus before. I was six, and excited, because I was bound for my new school.

"You're so lucky to be going there," Aunt Mary was saying. "They do treat little girls so nicely—"

I nodded but I was not listening. It was late afternoon of a wintry London day in 1914 and I drank in hungrily the sights and sounds of the city, the people moving in the streets, the flashing signs on the huge buildings as we roared by. I stared at one, transfixed: it was a very carnival of color, spelling the word BOVRIL, letter by letter, first red, then blue, then white. When it flashed on, it painted all the street in red, then blue, then white; and when it blinked off, the street, the houses, the roofs all whisked back into mysterious shadow.

I thought, I'm going to a place where I'll have a proper bed, I am. And I was thinking of that when the bus stopped. I clutched my wax doll in one hand and with the other in Aunt Mary's, we descended from the bus and walked toward a sprawling gray-brick building. As we neared the door Aunt Mary bent down. "Now remember," she whispered, "Don't ever tell them your daddy died of consumption or they'll send you away. And try not to cough—ever!"

Then we were in a long corridor and Aunt Mary led me before a table behind which presided a tall woman in black. I stared up at her in awe.

" 'Ere's Lily Sheil," Aunt Mary said.

The woman fixed her eyes on me and suddenly I was appalled. I shrank back but Aunt Mary's hand held me firmly and before a moment passed, the woman waved us on. Then, unexpectedly, I found myself in a large room with other girls and Aunt Mary was nowhere to be seen.

With the others I did as I was told. I placed my clothes in a pile on the floor. I watched, not understanding and so not ashamed as an older girl gingerly lifted my clothes with a pair of tongs and dropped them into a huge vat of boiling water. Then I was in another room, seated on a hard chair, a sheet about my naked shoulders and someone was running cold clippers through my hair, again and again, until it was cropped down to the skin. I watched my hair fall about me, ash-blondish and very thick. I did not cry then—I don't know why—but a week or so later when my head was clipped again and I reached up and felt my bristly, all-but-naked scalp, I wept bitterly.

A girl led me upstairs. I gazed, astonished, at a long room full of little white toilets. I'd never seen shining white toilets and, enchanted, I began to try them, one after another, but a voice called sharply, "Come here, child!" and I was in another enormous room filled with tubs of hot water and the acrid odor of carbolic soap. I was given a hot bath, soaped and scrubbed thoroughly from head to foot and then toweled dry just as vigorously.

Dressed in woolen bloomers, black stockings, and a dark serge dress with sleeves buttoned to the wrist, I lined up with half a dozen other newcomers—all with our heads cropped—and we marched by twos down a stairway into a cement courtyard.

Suddenly Aunt Mary was at my side, staring at my cropped head. I turned in time to see the look of horror fade from her face. She knelt down and kissed me. "Goodby, Lily," she said. Her blue eyes were bigger than ever and full-sized tears squeezed from them. "Remember, you're a lucky child to be here. They'll take proper care of you. Now, mind your manners, you hear!"

I was in The East London Home for Orphans. I was to remain there until I was fourteen.

When I look back on my early years, it's hard not to think that perhaps they never happened—that I read it all in Dickens or in some penny-dreadful novel of the time. I was born in London's East End, not far from Limehouse, in a poverty-stricken tenement neighborhood comparable to New York's Lower East Side. My mother was a cook in an institution. I never knew my father. He died in Berlin of tuberculosis when I was eleven months old. Why he went there, what he was doing there, I never learned. My mother told me little about him; and when I was old enough to be curious, she and I were like strangers to each other. To me she was always a small, tired lady who bore the title, Mother. I knew that for other girls this word held a kind of magic, a warmth and tenderness I yearned for but could not feel.

Until I was six, my mother and I boarded in a basement room with a woman who took in washing. There was a bed and sofa in the room. We rented the sofa from her: That was ours; during the day we lived on it; at night we slept on it. In the room there were always high piles of laundry and always the stinging smell of soap mixed with the pungent one of boiled potatoes, upon which it seemed we existed. I see myself perched on an empty packing case and Mother taking several spoonfuls of potato soup and then me sharing her spoon, eagerly taking several spoonfuls, each of us dipping chunks of bread into the soup to fill our stomachs.

When my mother was out working, I kept busy. While the washwoman toiled over her board, keeping an eye on me, I played on the floor amid the laundry or crouched on the stone steps leading to the street, lost in games I invented with sticks and bits of string.

Out of the vagueness of those first years, the day I was taken to the orphanage emerges sharply. My mother was unable to leave her job and the neighbor I had been taught to call Aunt Mary—"You have no real aunts, Lily, so we'll make believe she's your Aunt Mary"—did her that service. My mother kissed me, gave me my doll, Aunt Mary took my hand in hers, and we left.

In the orphanage that night I went to sleep in a huge dimly-lit dormitory. It was high-ceilinged with a cold wooden floor and row upon row of iron cots. In a woolen nightgown I crawled under my blanket. A lady came into the dormitory. She was tall, with eyes the color of rain. She said, "We're going to turn off the lights now, and you must behave. Now, no talking. Be sure you go to the lavatory. Does everyone know where the lavatory is?"

There was a small chorus of "Yes, mum's" and the lights went out.

I lay in the darkness feeling the tears well up. I was in a proper bed but I missed my mother. I didn't want to talk to anyone or have anyone talk to me. I felt strange. I couldn't express how I felt. Only now I know that it was a sense of coldness and wide space, of belonging to nothing but the bed upon which I lay.

Lying there, I suddenly remembered. Aunt Mary had left me a little bag of toffees. It had not been taken away. I fell asleep sucking them.

The place in which I found myself was no better nor worse than other institutions of that kind in England. During my eight years there I was not cruelly treated: two hundred of us were handled correctly, sternly, and with complete impersonality. We were fed regularly: bread dabbed with margarine, watery cocoa, and stew twice a week, but the portions were small, there were no seconds, and we were always hungry.

We lived by bells. A gong awoke us at 6:30 A.M., another marched us down to breakfast at 7:00, a third sent us to our daily chores at 8:00—scrubbing floors, polishing woodwork, cleaning pots and pans—still another signaled classes, then lunch, then recess, and so throughout the day until a final gong announced lights out.

We knew we were different. Our heads were cropped every two weeks until we were twelve, both as a hygenic measure and to make us identifiable if we ran away. We were Wards of Charity. We were taught love of God, King, and Country and gratitude toward the trustees, those kind, mysterious ladies and gentlemen who took poor children like us off the streets and prepared us for service as domestics, or if we proved very bright, typists and even secretaries. We knew we were not like other children. For we were inside, living behind high walls and locked gates, while they were outside, free to play as they wished, to walk with their mothers and fathers. We watched them day after day from the barred windows of our dormitory. And none of them had cropped heads.

Yet I was puzzled. Didn't I belong to somebody? I had a mother. If I had a mother, why was I here? I asked Jessie Duchard, a girl who came a year before me. She was snub-nosed and pert, with wide-apart eyes and a carefree disposition. Like me, she had one parent—a father.

"He didn't want me," Jessie explained. "He said I was in the way and nobody else wanted me so they put me here." And then, "That's why they put you here, too. Your mother didn't want you."

I could believe that. Once, I faintly remembered over-hearing my mother and Aunt Mary. Aunt Mary had said, "It's a pity she's so plain." I had waited, breathless, for my mother's reply. She had only sighed, heavily.

So it was true. I was plain. And they didn't want me.

Each time I ventured to look into a mirror only confirmed my plainness. My face was pale as marble. I was thin and scrawny. I had a perpetual cold. My eyes were red, my nose was always running. My ears and neck itched with eczema. I knew I was unattractive; when the trustees came, they never patted me on the head as they went by.

Who would want a girl like *me?*

If it was Jessie who helped me realize that I was undesirable, she also taught me there were ways to get what you wanted.

On Saturdays during the summer a group of us were taken to a small park and left there to amuse ourselves on the swings or to gorge ourselves with wild berries while our teachers stole a few hours off. One Saturday, as soon as our teachers left, Jessie led me out of the park. I was aghast: this was breaking rules. I followed her nervously down a side street until we came to a movie. On the marquee I spelled out WILLIAM S. HART IN THE GUNFIGHTER. "Do what I do," Jessie whispered.

We took a stance between the ticket window and the entrance so that anybody going in had to pass us. Each time someone approached the window Jessie began to sigh as though her heart would break. I followed suit. We must have made an odd appearance, identical with our bald heads, our calico pinafores, our faces turned up in eager yearning. Two or three persons passed us before we were rewarded. Then a middle-aged couple, tickets in hand, came by. Jessie looked beseechingly at the woman, then at the ticket window, and heaved a tragic sigh.

The woman melted. "Do you children want to go in and see the picture?"

"Oh yes, madam," Jessie breathed. "We like William S. Hart ever so."

I was speechless. My eyes were on the woman's face, too, and I was literally willing her to take us in. The words ran over and over in my mind: *Oh give us the money, give us the money, please give us the money.*

The woman opened her purse. "Here's a penny each." She smiled down at us. "Now buy your tickets and enjoy yourselves."

We ran to the window, reached up and plunked down our money, received our tickets and trooped in. It was pure bliss to sit in the darkness, our eyes glued to the screen, while William S. Hart galloped across the plains of far-off America to the stirring music pounded out by the pianist down in front. Then we stared awe-struck at what I now know were modest little comedies played out on the tree-lined streets of Los Angeles. But we thought we saw heaven. We gaped at the story-book homes with their perfect well-kept lawns, at the elegantly dressed children with their ponies, at the unbelievably sumptuous interiors of the houses. It seemed such a beautiful, such a *warm* life where children were free to play without bells ordering them through the day, who had smiling parents who spanked them so lovingly when they were cheeky or disobedient.

We came out into the bright daylight.

"Cor!" said Jessie, somehow expressing it in one word all we felt. We sighed. This time we meant it.

The following Saturday we begged our way into the movie again. On the way back to the park we passed a fish-and-chips shop. It had only the lower half of a glass window—painted a checkerboard red and black. Abo· : it, from the interior of the store, there wafted out the most heavenly odors on wings of steam. We watched as men and women emerged carrying their fish and chips in little funnels of paper, eating as they walked.

Jessie and I looked at each other. Without a word we took our places in front of the checkerboard window, put our heads up and began sniffing hungrily, loudly, and looking appealingly at every passer-by. This paid off, too. "All

right, little girls," a burly man said as he walked past.
He tossed us a coin.

We ran inside. Behind a long counter on which were
chained large canisters of salt and bottles of vinegar, a man
in an apron was busy serving up penny portions of fish and
chips. He scooped a dipperful of chips into half a sheet
of newspaper, twisted it with a flick of his wrist and presented it to us. Jessie salted our chips, doused them ex-
pertly with vinegar, and flushed with victory we floated
out and down the street, our cheeks bulging.

I learned quickly now. I began to forage for myself.
Other girls were hungry. I was always ravenously hungry.
One day, wandering aimlessly down a long corridor in the
orphanage, I found myself in a dark room surrounded by
huge barrels of cocoa, sugar, and flour. Suddenly I was inspired. Sugar and cocoa, chewed together should be almost
as good as a chocolate bar. I began scooping handfuls of
sugar and cocoa into my bloomers kept tight above each
knee with strong elastic. I was barely able to waddle away.

In the darkness of the dormitory that night Jessie and I
munched sugar and cocoa until our mouths were too dry
to talk. Jessie managed to whisper, "Lily, you *are* clever.
And you wouldn't think it to look at you."

But I didn't need Jessie to tell me that. My mind was
quick: I was an excellent student. When a prize of sixpence was offered for memorizing a poem, I did it in two
readings. By the time I was twelve I was first in my class.
My composition, "Why England Defeated the Hun," was
read aloud to the entire school. To pit myself against
others—and win—was enough to keep me glowing for days.
Miss Walton, my teacher, watching me throw myself
strenuously into every game, every contest, would say, "It's
do or die with you, Lily, isn't it?" She was right. To be
second in anything drove me to tears: I had to win. I was

quick to insult, quick to lash back blindly at anyone who struck me. Once I was actually haled before Miss Mead, the matron, for striking a teacher who had slapped me. I could not explain it. It was pure reflex. Then—and in years to come—at any challenge, I fought back as though fighting for my life.

Eagerly I looked forward to any break in our routine. Once a year, at Christmas, we were taken to the pantomime. Once every three months there were visiting days. Sometimes my mother came to see me. She was a stranger, someone whose hands were warm and who kissed me lingeringly. Invariably she brought me a bag of broken biscuits. I bolted them down while she asked me questions. It was always a lame, unsatisfactory meeting. "Have you been all right? No coughing? You're not making trouble?" I would nod or shake my head, my mouth full, embarrassed by her attention, wanting her to stay, yet wishing she would go now that I had my biscuits.

One visiting day, Jessie came running in great excitement. Her father had unexpectedly appeared, and she wanted me to meet him. I was afraid. She had once told me he hardly ever came because he drank so much he was sleepy all the time. Out of the past a memory haunted me. I saw a large street crowd: I peeped through to see a man on his hands and knees, groaning, floundering in his own filth, and a policeman throwing pails of water on him to clean him off. Someone said, "That bloody drunk!" My flesh crawled—I fled. But Jessie's father turned out to be a thin, apologetic little man with a wispy mustache who said only, "Blimey, wot a fine plyce they've got you in!" Jessie brimmed over with pride. Now no one could doubt that she really *had* a father.

But my greatest excitement came with the trustees' annual visits. For days we were put to work polishing brass, waxing floors, cleaning and scrubbing every corner. Then, upstairs, we would press our noses to the windows, waiting. Presently the enormous black limousines drove up, the chauffeurs ceremoniously opened the doors of the cars, and the trustees stepped out.

Except in movies I had never seen people so elegantly dressed. My heart pounded. What I waited to see—what my eyes yearned to look upon each year—was a little blond girl who descended daintily from a magnificent automobile. She was a trustee's daughter. The first time I saw her she could have been no older than I—perhaps eight or nine. She was a vision out of a fairy tale. She had long golden curls falling down her back, she was dressed all in white—a white frock, a white coat, and a hat tied in a bow under her chin, white slippers and white gloves—and I stared at her, spellbound. Everything about her burned into my memory. She seemed to glide, not walk, at her father's side and as she moved I made out just the edge of a fragile pink petticoat. Her skin was pink and white and she looked so cared for, so well tended, even to the white muff into which she put her small gloved hands.

I do not know if the full contrast between us struck me, and how sharply, but I knew how I looked. My hands were rough and red, the knuckles split with chilblains, my head was bald, my nose was red from sniffling, my black stockings were bunched and lumpy on my broomstick legs, my shoes were black and clumsy, my bloomers reeked of cocoa — Oh, the trustee's daughter! How wonderful, I thought, to be a girl like that. It was not envy; you cannot envy what lies hopelessly beyond your reach. I could no more envy her than I could have envied a royal princess. She represented everything the outside world could be. I thought simply, fervently, how nice it would be to be like that.

Was it then that I promised myself, without being aware of it, that someday *I* would become that girl, live as she lived, and be as she was? I do not know. I only remember how little I thought of myself, how worlds apart I knew we were, when I saw that lovely little girl with the golden curls, so well-tended, so pink and white, so beautiful and elegant, the trustee's daughter.

CHAPTER TWO

SUDDENLY, at fourteen, my days at the orphanage ended. Word came: my mother had had an operation and needed me at home. Fourteen was the earliest age under the law at which I could be taken out of school. Miss Mead, telling me the news, shook her head. "I had hoped to see you go on to win a shorthand-typing scholarship," she said. "You have a good brain, Lily. You deserve something better. I do hope that someday you will make up the education you must miss now."

I left her office curiously numb. Even the loss of the scholarship—the dream of every girl at the orphanage—seemed unreal. What excited me was the overwhelming fact that I was at last going into the outside.

For the next week I sewed on my "trousseau"—a complete set of clothes that the orphanage gave to every departing girl. And presently I said good by to Jessie, to Miss Walton, to Miss Mead, and walked out through the high, front gate. I was dressed in my new clothes. My hair, allowed to grow for the past two years, was now almost shoulder length, blond and thick; I wore my first hat, a navy-blue straw with a sailor ribbon hanging down the back. I carried a little tin suitcase packed with my belongings which included thick gray bloomers, black woolen stockings, and two high-necked calico nightgowns.

I had the directions to my mother's flat written on a sheet of paper. For the first time I took a bus by myself. Again I rode on top, as with Aunt Mary. I was consumed with excitement, with anticipation, with a sense of do or die. The wind blew on my hot face and sent the ribbon of my hat fluttering straight out behind me: I put a firm hand on top of my hat and rode on, face forward, into the wind.

The flat in which my mother now lived was in the back of a row of identical slate-gray tenements. Small and dark, it consisted of a tiny sitting room with a horsehair sofa and chair, a cubbyhole of a bedroom, and a small kitchen with a two-burner coal grate which served for both heating and cooking. During the first days at home I actually enjoyed the smallness of the rooms. After the enormous dormitory, it was cozy: you could actually *feel* the four sides. I was enclosed, protected. My mother, recuperating slowly from her operation, was grayer than when I last saw her, but when she took me in her arms her body was warm as I remembered it. We tried, in the months that followed, to know each other but it was difficult. There was no communication. Though I am sure she loved me, we felt awkward and far apart. I was grateful when I made a friend of Mildred Bannock, who lived in the neighborhood and worked for her sister in a dress shop.

Mildred was a plump girl with muddy brown hair who limped—and lived for dancing. She taught me how to dance and I became almost hysterical over it. This was action, excitement—this was almost as good as food! I loved to whirl and swing, to follow intricate steps as we hummed the tunes from two popular musicals, *Head Over Heels* and *Little Nelly Kelly*. At home I did the housework in fox-trot time. I'd dance over to the broom in the corner, sweep it up, bow deeply and dance with it about the kitchen, sweeping as I went. It made me forget the drudgery of housework.

One day, when I was visiting Mildred in her shop, her sister invited us to lunch. Gratefully I trotted along with them to an Express Dairy around the corner. In the tea shop we took a small table. To the waitress Mildred said, "I'll have toad-in-the-hole." I sat quietly, looking about the room wondering idly, what does toad-in-the-hole mean? Then I became aware of a silence. The waitress, pad and pencil in hand, was looking at me, and so were the others. "What would you like, miss?" the waitress repeated, impatiently. I stared at her blankly and began to stammer. No one before had ever asked me what I wanted to eat. My food had been placed in front of me and I had eaten it. In desperation I finally blurted out a hoarse, "The same," and pointed to Mildred. I let my purse slip to the floor so I could bend down and hide my crimson face. Could these girls know that this was the first time I had been in a restaurant? But now they were chatting gaily and when the food arrived—toad-in-the-hole turned out to be a sausage baked in batter—we all fell to.

Then, over our tea, Mildred told me of Saturday-night dances at The Cottage, a small dance hall in nearby Bow. She knew all the boys there. Now that I danced well, she'd take me next time she went. It cost only sixpence.

When I broached this to my mother for the first time, she said no. "I don't want you to go to a dance hall, Lily." And then reluctantly: "Bad men go to dance halls."

I knew what she meant. A few days before, *The News of the World* had a story about three English girls who had been abducted by a South American white-slave ring. I had shown the story to her. Did this really happen?

Oh, yes, my mother had said solemnly. She went on to warn me. I was getting pretty. Men would bother me. I was taken aback. Pretty? I did not believe her. But she continued. Bad men might try to do something with me and no one would want to marry me. I'd be an old maid. They might even inject me with a drug that made you unable to distinguish right from wrong and you'd become their willing slave and follow them everywhere. This terrified yet thrilled me, to think I'd become some man's willing slave. But I checked with Mildred, and Mildred confirmed it. My mother was right. Not only that, but a husband would always know if a man had had anything to do with you before you were married. He would *always* know. Mildred and I promised ourselves no matter what the temptation, we would be pure when we went to our husbands.

"But Mother," I protested now. "Mildred goes to that dance hall all the time. If bad men went there she wouldn't go. She's a good girl."

We quarreled until my mother finally agreed that I could go to the dance if I brought Mildred home so she could judge Mildred's character for herself. Mildred came over. My mother took one look at her and gave me the sixpence for the dance. Mildred was simply too homely to be bad.

When we walked into The Cottage that Saturday night I stood there, overwhelmed. The bright, rhythmic beat of the music made my pulse tingle. Mildred, waving and calling to friends, grabbed my hand and pulled me after her. The three sides of the floor were lined with girls sitting on benches while the boys wandered about studying and choosing at their leisure. "Sit here," Mildred said, indicating a place on a bench, and she went limping across the floor. When I glanced around later, she was happily dancing.

I sat primly on the bench, hardly daring to look up lest my eyes catch those of a boy and I start blushing. I had never known a boy: I wouldn't know what to say to one. In the orphanage there had been a boys' section, but they lived in a separate building which was a world apart. I had had a secret romance with a boy, but we had never spoken. Our eyes had only met in the mirror above the organist's head each Sunday at chapel. Each time this happened, my face had flamed, and I had looked away. Now and then, as we filed out of the room, he would cast a bold glance at me, but I dared not meet his eyes. I learned his name was Albert. At night I pretended the ceiling above my cot was a magic mirror and Albert, lying in his dormitory across the courtyard, could see me. I lay there, not a skinny, long-legged girl, but a beautiful and fascinating creature, while he watched me with adoration in his eyes, not knowing that I knew he watched me. I turned, I twisted sinuously, I raised my arms languidly over my head, I fell into all the poses of all the sirens I had seen on the screen. And night after night, thinking of Albert secretly watching me, I would smile mysteriously, promising him unimaginable delights though I had no idea what those delights might be. How he adored me, how wonderful it was to be admired, to be wanted. . . .

My reverie was interrupted. A shadow fell on me as I sat on the bench at The Cottage and I saw a pair of dark trousers ending in sharply pointed shoes in front of me. I looked up. A tall young man, about seventeen, with ginger-red hair slicked back until it gleamed, was looking down at me. There was absolutely no expression on his face. "Dance?" he said, casually.

I stood up, terribly nervous, terribly grateful. We danced. The music stopped, we danced again. I had never had a boy's arms around me. He held me firmly, he led me with great skill, and I was in a golden haze as we turned and whirled. His hair smelled sweet and familiar, exactly like the cleanser we used on windows at the orphanage, and he danced beautifully. "What's your name?" he asked carelessly. I told him "What's yours?" I managed to ask. My voice came out hardly more than a whisper. "Call me Ginger," he said. "Everyone does." His aplomb, his self-assurance, made me weak.

In the middle of the dance he took my arm and led me off the floor. "Come into the garden," he said. It was not a request; it was an order. We walked down a dim path into a little green arbor with two benches in it. Here it was quite dark. My heart pounded. Was I going to be kissed? We sat down and Ginger promptly put his arms around me and kissed me.

I allowed myself to be kissed. I remained completely passive. I made not the slightest move. I was as limp and unresisting as a sack. Kissing was something a boy did to a girl. After a few minutes Ginger said, "Let's go back." We went inside and danced.

Now dancing became my life. Ginger was a catch, the boy most sought after at The Cottage, the most accomplished dancer there. The girls swooned in his general direction when he appeared, they treated him like a king and he returned their homage with the arrogance of a king. I went to The Cottage every Saturday night. Ginger danced with me. We'd have little to talk about to each other. Regularly he would say, "Come into the garden," and I would follow him dutifully, and there in the darkness, sitting in the arbor, he would begin kissing me as a favor to me. I took it as a favor. I was humble. I wondered how he could have time for a clumsy, undesirable girl like me.

When he kissed me I was all aglow. For a little while I

was transported far away from washing dishes and scrubbing floors, from wondering what was going to happen to me and whether I would ever be married. . . . It was better than any dream you could have, to be held so warmly and tightly and kissed by a boy.

Each time I came home from a dance, my mother and I quarreled. As the weeks went by, we grew more and more estranged. We fought about The Cottage, about her warnings that dancing and boys would ultimately lead to my disgrace. We fought about Mildred, who she decided was a bad influence on me; about my endless daydreaming; about my constant reading of *Pearson's Weekly* and other tuppenny periodicals. Once I tried to explain how much dancing meant to me: how gloriously free it made me feel. But she only looked at me suspiciously. We simply could not reach each other.

When she grew strong enough to resume her job, I could not endure staying at home. It had become a straitjacket. I detested the interminable scrubbing and cleaning, the marketing and cooking—everything I had to do when she was out. Why had she made me give up a scholarship for this? I might have gone on to be a typist, even a secretary.

Matters boiled over one day when I refused to put blacking on the coal grate. "I won't," I cried. "You don't want me to have any fun at all. You brought me here just to make me work! I wish I was back at the orphanage!"

It was the cruelest thing I could say to her. Hurt and furious, she advanced on me, her hand upraised: I warded off the blow and struck back blindly, as I had struck back at the teacher in the orphanage. I was horrified to feel the flat of my hand hit her stingingly across the cheekbone. I had never known my mother's face was so soft, her skin so smooth.

She backed away and burying her face in her hands, suddenly burst into tears. She sat down hard on a chair and wept, her hands still over her face. I was beside myself. "Don't cry, don't cry," I begged her. I put my arm around her. "Mother, I didn't mean it, oh, I'm so sorry—"

She flung my arm away. "Go away," she said, through her tears. "Leave me alone. Go away and get a job. I don't want you!"

I went to the orphanage. I told Miss Walton that my mother and I had quarreled. Could she find a job for me away from home? There was one available immediately— a position as an under housemaid—a skivy—in Brighton, fifty miles from London. It paid board, room, and thirty shillings a month—about seven dollars.

Though I hated housework, I took the job. I took it because I would be free, on my own, earning money, without teacher or mother to order me about. I could even underwrite my independence by sending a few shillings home every month—and at same time assuage the faint sense of guilt I felt.

The address to which I was sent in Brighton, which is a well-known seaside resort, turned out to be a stately, five-story house with gleaming brass fixtures and a basement gate of intricate wrought iron. I walked up the front steps and knocked timidly on the door. Presently it was opened by a plump middle-aged woman. "Yes?" she asked.

I said apologetically, "I'm the new maid."

Without a word she swung the door wide to let me in. "Come this way," she said. My feet sank into thick carpets as I followed her through a spacious reception hall and up what seemed endless flights of stairs to a small sitting room on the fourth floor. She looked me over doubtfully. How old was I? I told her, nearly sixteen. She went on: "Are you strong?"

"Oh, yes, madam, I'm very strong."

"Are you used to doing housework?"

"Oh, yes I've been doing it at home and I did it at the orphanage."

She looked at me for a moment. "Very well," she said briskly. "There'll be nothing for you to do tonight. You may go to the kitchen now and have your supper. You are to begin first thing in the morning. I will give you your uniforms and caps then."

Suddenly I realized I'd never thought of myself wearing a maid's cap. I'd seen maids in the films—somehow that piece of starched white lace perched on their heads was a badge of servitude. That really made you a servant. I blurted out, "Madam, I don't want to wear a cap."

She stared at me. "Why not? Good heavens girl, why not?"

"I just don't." I would work as a skivvy, I would work hard, but I felt once I permitted myself to wear a cap I'd be a servant for the rest of my life.

"I've never heard of anything so silly," she said, annoyed. "If you want to stay here, my girl, you'll wear the cap like every maid does."

"No, madam," I mumbled, miserably, looking at the floor. "I won't." I stood before her, head down, saying to myself, *if she makes me wear it, I'm leaving. I'll go home and make it up with my mother.*

"Oh," she exclaimed, impatiently. "You're a tiresome girl. I really think I shall have to send you back and be done with it."

I was silent.

Finally: "Well, for the time being, we'll let the cap go."

Now she was all business. "We'll have to get you blue dresses to do the scrubbing in. And a black serving dress with a white apron." When I said nothing, she asked, suspiciously, "You'll wear the apron?"

I said, "Yes, madam, I'll wear the apron."

"Good," she said. She had one more matter to settle. She led me downstairs to the basement and into a small, gloomy room. It was furnished with a round wooden table, a wicker rocking chair and a table lamp. "You'll sleep on the fifth floor, but this is your sitting room," she said. "Once you come down in the morning you're not to go upstairs again except to change. I don't want you going up and down the stairs at all hours of the day."

She outlined my work. Each day before breakfast I was to water the plants, scrub the basement floor, clean and put whiting on the front steps, and polish the brass fixtures. I was to do all the cleaning, serve breakfast, lunch, and dinner, and wash the dishes. I would take my meals in the kitchen. I was to have no visitors. When I left or entered the house I was to do so by the basement gate. I would have every Thursday off, after washing up the lunch dishes, and must be in the house by ten o'clock.

As she explained my duties I glanced about my sitting room. Daylight came from a single high, narrow window, with an iron grating on the outside. The window was below the pavement level and I could see feet hurrying past. As I watched, a dog trotted by, paused, and left his message on the grating. My employer followed my glance and she made a grimace of distaste. "The grating is to be cleaned thoroughly every day," she said. "Now, you may go to the kitchen and have your supper."

In my spare time, those first few days, I sat in my sitting room, watching the feet go by—high-heeled shoes, flat-heeled shoes with walking sticks, tightly rolled umbrellas—

to whom did they belong, and where were they going so busily? Everybody but me, it seemed, had a place to go. I shouted at the dogs who made the grating a regular port of call. Sometimes I read. There were few books in the house but I found copies of *Peg's Paper,* a penny weekly, and eagerly I read about the mill-owner's noble, handsome son. Usually the mill foreman, an evil, unscrupulous type, would try to get the innocent working girl in the family way, but it all ended happily because the mill-owner's son fell in love with her and married her. I read romances about aristocratic girls whose lives were preordained; they went to Roedean, one of England's most exclusive schools and, after attending a French finishing school, were presented at court and invariably married peers of the realm. This was the course of their lives—always. I loved these stories.

It was Thursday afternoon, three P.M.—my first day off. I strolled on the promenade, wearing my best: my black sailor hat, a white blouse and blue skirt, a little blue coat. My blond hair, tied in back with a black bow, hung below my shoulders. I came upon a bench facing the street and I sat down, dreaming. I had seven precious hours. What would I do with them? There was always food to look forward to, ham in a roll with a glass of hot milk—that would cost a shilling. Then, sixpence for a movie . . . I juggled my hours of freedom in my pocket, fumbling with the money I had there and feeling very happy. This was the moment for which I lived, my little green oasis of independence in the great desert of housework. To work so hard and then to have seven hours of absolute freedom— it was like seven years!

The promenade was all but deserted. From my bench I could see the bandstand, empty now but alive with music on Saturday and Sunday nights when I had to stay in. A man walked slowly by and looked intently at me. I averted my face until he passed. I was excited and a little frightened. Suppose he spoke to me? I might wake to find myself on a ship bound for South America, a willing slave. *The News of the World* would print my picture, my mother would cry, "Oh, I warned her, I warned her—"

The put-put-put of a motorcycle broke into my thoughts. I looked up to see a young man with dark hair slowly riding by on his cycle. As he passed he smiled at me. It was a charming, contagious smile. I half-smiled back, hardly aware of what I was doing. He continued on for a few yards, then, with an ear-splitting roar of his motor, made a wide, swooping U-turn and was at the curb opposite me. Now I could see him clearly. He was handsome, and about twenty.

"Hello," he said, with his smile. "Care for a ride?"

I thought, he certainly doesn't look like a white slaver. The easiest thing was to nod. If I shook my head I might have to explain and I wasn't sure what I would say. I gave the faintest kind of a nod.

"Righto!" he said. "Come on—" He instructed me how to sit sideways and how to place my arms around him. "Now, hold on tight because you might fall off—" I dutifully locked my arms around his waist. The warmth of his body, the sense of strength there, comforted me. I liked holding him. And off we went. We careened around corners and I held on, thrilled. I wasn't afraid. I wasn't afraid of falling off and I wasn't afraid of this strange man. We rode until we reached the Sussex Downs, about two miles away, a vast stretch of green, rolling grass.

"Let's walk a little," he suggested. We strolled in silence for a few moments. Did I live nearby? I said, yes, I lived with my rich aunt in a big house and I told him where it was. And I chattered on: "I love to take little walks, to get the air, it's so healthy here by the sea. That's why I was on the promenade. I get so bored doing nothing, because we have three servants who do all the work."

He listened, smiling. Then he asked, gently, "How old are you?"

"Eighteen," I said.

He laughed, put his arm around me and as we walked, bent down and kissed me. His kiss was gentle. We walked, until we came to grassy knoll. We were utterly alone. We sat on the Downs, the fresh, fragrant wind blowing, and he kissed me. I enjoyed being kissed and murmured to, there on the Downs, not a soul around us for miles and strangely without fear because he was kind to me and I could not distrust anyone who was kind to me. He told me about himself. His name was Ralph. He was a bank clerk, and he hoped someday to be manager, perhaps even chairman of the bank.

I said, "And when I get my inheritance won't it be grand if I bring all my money to your bank?"

He laughed, and kissed me again, gentle kisses, and then said, "I have an appointment—I must go now." As we walked back to his cycle I dared to ask, "Will I see you again?" I could meet him at the same time a week later. Good, he said. I must wait for him on the same bench— our lucky bench.

"I'll take you home," he said, and before I could think of what to say he had deposited me in front of the house. I stood there knowing I dared not use the front door. For an anguished moment I thought he would wait until I went in. But he jumped on his machine, waved and was gone. When he was out of sight I turned on my heel and went to a movie. I hardly knew what I saw on the screen, thinking, this will be my secret life, meeting charming men, bank chairmen-to-be, making them adore me, kiss me until they expired on my lips.

Was I getting pretty, as my mother had said? I remembered the ornate, full-length mirror in one of the bedrooms. Each time I cleaned the room I had stood in front of the mirror and looked at myself. I saw a rather anxious face, round and pale, with greenish eyes and straight blond hair. I was no longer so scrawny. Slowly I lifted the shapeless blue work dress to reveal my legs. They weren't so skinny now. My stockings hadn't bunched for a long time. My legs aren't bad at all, I said to myself. Could my mother have been right?

The hours dragged until Thursday. At three o'clock I was on our bench waiting. And I sat there through the long afternoon until darkness fell. He never appeared. When I rose I felt wretched and more unattractive than ever. My mother was wrong, the mirror lied. What had made him change his mind? I reviewed every word of our conversation, how he had looked and laughed, how he had kissed me, how he had said, "Good. And you'll be waiting on our lucky bench. . ." Utterly miserable, I had my sandwich and milk and went to the cinema. The film was Gloria Swanson in *Male and Female*. It lifted my spirits a little. I walked out, thinking, I could have been Gloria Swanson. In the darkness I walked sensuously, slinkily, as Gloria Swanson walked. I whispered, "Oh, Reginald, I do love thee. I do. I do!"

CHAPTER THREE

How long I might have stayed in Brighton—how long I might have remained a skivy—I will never know, for after several months I had to give up my position and hurry back to London. My mother had been taken desperately ill.

When I saw her again in our little flat I was appalled. She had become gray and shrunken. She walked with difficulty and was bedridden most of the day. Only later I learned that her illness was cancer.

Our arguments were forgotten and I threw myself into the task of nursing her. I cooked, I shopped, I did the housework. I bathed my mother daily. A visiting nurse came twice a week and I followed her directions painstakingly.

Yet I was consumed with impatience and boredom. It did not help that Mildred came over often to help me pass the time. As one day merged into another, my unhappiness and discontent overflowed. I wanted to get away—away from the tiny flat, the duties, the frustration of trying to make my mother comfortable and knowing that she was in constant pain. It was not easy to take care of her, and my resentment was only underlined by her resignation, her lack of complaint.

I felt trapped, hemmed in, and wretched because I knew I should not feel this way. I rose each morning bitter, knowing only, I want to escape, I don't know where.

My mother slept badly at night but usually, in the evenings, she grew drowsy and fell asleep. Then I would escape. I would put on my best—a blouse and skirt, my high-heeled slippers, and my special pride, a black taffeta hat with a huge brim which I had bought for my sixteenth birthday. It was a magic hat for I could make it match my moods. If I wanted to look mysterious, I turned the brim down to hide my eyes. If I wanted to look windblown, like Colleen Moore, I turned it up. I had begun to wear lipstick, but no rouge. Sometimes I let my hair hang long, tied behind with a black ribbon. If I wanted to look older, I put it up in a bun, under the black hat with its brim shadowing my eyes.

I stole out of the flat and clattered to the top of the street, a little awkward in my high heels, and waited for the No. 25 bus. This took you down Bond Street, through the fashionable West End, through the heart of London. I would be hard put to explain what I was seeking. I wanted to go where wealth and elegance were, to see the fine shops and restaurants, the strolling ladies and gentlemen, watch the glittering limousines swish past carrying beautifully gowned women and top-hatted men—this was the West End at night to me, a place of wonder and enchantment, a place to dream in.

As I waited for the bus, the smell of hops was strong in the air. It came from a huge black brewery across the street. It nauseated me and I shuddered—the grayness, the drabness of the street, the men in sweaters and caps, some

of them drunk, reeling from the pubs, the smell from the
public houses.

When the bus came I climbed to the top. I rode past
the great industrial and banking houses, their enormous
offices all lit up. I looked in as we went by. Through the
windows I saw typists and secretaries moving about with
papers in their hands. I envied them, laughing in the glow
of the lights inside the offices. Sometimes I saw girls standing together, chatting, sometimes a young man, his black
hair slicked back so sharply, talking and laughing with
them. I thought, *how glamorous, what an enchanted life
that must be, how I'd love to be part of it—how sad that I
had to miss it!*

At Bond Street I dismounted. Now the luxury of walking slowly, enjoying each moment, looking in the shop
windows, strolling down Piccadilly. I did not know that
Piccadilly meant danger, that in Piccadilly strange, foreign
gentlemen said hello to girls who walked alone.

Here were the rare-book shops, one after another. I
looked at the lovely bindings, the maroon and gold leather.
Here was an engraver's shop and the sign: WE RENO-
VATE YOUR ANCESTORS. I stared at the photographs
and engravings of grandparents and great-grandparents in
their antique frames, the "Before," and "After." *If only I
had ancestors.* I remembered how I had envied Jessie because she had a locket with a picture of a little brother who
died before she was born. I had nothing: no uncles or
aunts, no cousins, no brothers or sisters, no ancestors—*I'm
related only to me.*

As I sauntered on, my eye was taken by the exquisite
dresses in the fashionable women's shops, then up Bond
Street by the glittering jewelry in Cartier's window. I
stood before Cartier's window, dreaming. How would I
feel if a gentleman said as he handed me a magnificent

diamond-and-ruby necklace, "Little girl, would you like this?" If I were a great beauty there'd always be a peer of the realm to say, "You're so beautiful, my dear, but you'd be even more beautiful if I could put this diamond necklace around your neck." "Oh, I'm not the kind of a girl you think I am, really I'm not," I'd protest. "I'm a good girl. But if you want to buy me that necklace anyway—" And he would put it around my neck and I would let him kiss my lips.

Now it was growing dark. In the dusk I played a game. Men were passing. When they looked at me I looked away. But now and then I dared return their glance with the slightest smile—to see what would happen. They stared at me boldly; they appeared to me to be extremely wicked men, their eyes sharp and piercing. I did not know that I was walking on a street where prostitutes walked.

I wanted the men to look at me. I played my game. Once a deep voice said clearly, "Good evening." I gave a faceless man what I thought was a very mysterious smile and averted my eyes and walked on. It was deliciously frightening. A few minutes later I heard footsteps behind me. I walked faster. The steps kept pace. I was not too fearful for people were all about me. I stole a quick glance behind: a clean-cut young man in a gray suit was at my heels. He caught up with me. "Where are you going?" he asked, in a pleasant voice.

"Oh, just taking a walk," I said airily, though my heart thumped wildly.

He asked, walking at my side, "May I walk with you?"

"I don't mind."

Wasn't I bound anywhere at all, he asked? Charing Cross Station was directly across the street. I said "Charing Cross, to catch my train." At the station we talked—I have no idea what about. I was in a fever. *This was happening.*

I had gone to catch a fish and I had it—it was in my net!
I had found a gentleman! Of all these teeming people
going backward and forward, nobody knowing the other,
suddenly I knew a face!

He would see me the following night, he said. He'd
meet me here, by this pillar, in Charing Cross Station, and
we'd go to the cinema.

Next night I waited in Charing Cross Station. But it
was Brighton all over again. The clean-cut young man
never appeared. Oh, the agony of waiting when people are
bustling to and fro, people who have destinations, who
have homes and friends and loved ones to go to! I stood,
wretched, not knowing in what direction to look. As
crowds of people flowed about me, I tried to look as though
I, too, had a destination—and I had no destination. And
the awful dawning, finally, that I was not to have one. I
waited for an hour, an hour and a half, then disconsolately took the bus home. What is life? I thought. Is it this
dreary waiting for something to happen? To wake each
morning full of hope, sure that something tremendously
extraordinary will happen this day, and to have nothing
happen. . . .

Thus, in the evenings while my mother slept, I walked
on the edge of adventure. Once the footsteps behind me
quickened, and I slowed down until a tall man was in step
at my side. I dared not look up. When we came under a
lamp I stole a glance at him out of the corner of my eye.
A great pang of fear shot through me. I was walking with
a coffee-colored gentleman. But he smiled at me with great
sweetness and said, quietly, "You look very young. How
old are you?"

I said, "Nineteen."

He looked at me thoughtfully.

"You know," he said, "you really ought to be home. You shouldn't be walking here."

I said, "Oh, no, I like it here. This is nice."

He shook his head. "I think you should go home." He hailed a taxi, placed a ten shilling note in my hand, helped me into the cab and asked, "Where shall I tell him?"

I was so astonished I could think only, "Charing Cross Station. I can get my train from there."

I sat in the back of the taxicab. I looked at the ten shillings, then I looked out the window at the people who had to walk, then at the back of my chauffeur. *I'm riding in a taxi,* I said to myself, over and over. I couldn't quite believe it. When we reached the station I caught my bus and went home.

Then, one night shortly after seven o'clock, a middle-aged man, dapper in a gray Homburg and spats, and carrying a cane, tipped his hat and said, "Good evening." I smiled timidly at him. He asked me if I lived in that district. No, I said, I was in London for a visit. We walked together silently for a moment. "I'm about to have dinner," he said, unexpectedly. "Would you like to join me?"

We had passed a restaurant with curtained windows concealing the magnificence within. The menu, in French, was framed ornately on the window. If only he would take me to a place like that.

I nodded. "I don't mind if I do."

The restaurant into which he took me was elegant, with waiters in tails moving around the ladies and gentlemen at the dining tables. I thought, there'll be no toad-in-the-hole here. But his hand was at my elbow and we were walking away from the tables. "We are going upstairs," he said easily. A little thrill ran through me. I had read about private dining rooms above restaurants. Edward the Seventh always took his favorites there. Upstairs we were shown into a lovely little room with a table set with gleaming silver, and a settee at one side. A waiter appeared and deferentially presented us with a menu. It was in French.

My escort turned to me. "Shall we start with soup?"

I was enchanted. No peer of the realm could have conferred more flatteringly with his lady. "And, after soup," he said, "would you care for roast chicken, or perhaps lamb chops?" I chose lamb chops. I'd never had lamb chops because they had too little meat on them to be bought by any but the rich.

It was a beautiful dinner. I ate fast and with all my might. He questioned me about myself. I said I was a companion to a rich old lady who lived in Brighton, in an enormous five-story mansion. "I simply have to get out every little while and I love to come to London." I spoke feelingly, from experience, and I thought he listened with great attention, smoking a cigarette in a holder and now and then tapping it gently on an ash tray. When I had finished eating, I sat back.

"Would you like coffee? he asked. I nodded. We would take it on the settee, he said. He pulled my chair away when I arose and we sat down on the settee. The waiter returned with our coffee, which he served us on a small table, and then left.

My escort poured the coffee for me. As I drank it, I asked timidly, "What do you do?" "I'm an importer," he said. I learned no more, for now that I had my coffee and he his cigarette, he put his arm around me and kissed me. I didn't want to kiss him, but I didn't wish to offend him, either, for he had bought me such an expensive dinner. "You're a very pretty girl," he said. Then he kissed me again. I turned my face away when he tried to kiss me a third time, and his grip tightened on my arm. "What's the matter?" he asked, annoyed, and he pulled me roughly to him. I was panic-stricken. With all my strength I broke away and found myself on my feet, trembling.

"You let me go!" I burst out. "You let me out of here!"

He remained on the settee, looking at me. "Why did you come with me?" he asked. There seemed more curiosity than anger in his voice.

I felt ashamed of myself. I wanted to say, I'm not that kind of a girl and I'm sorry I made you think I was. Instead I said, "I thought how nice it would be to have a good dinner."

He looked at me coldly. "Then go," he said, "You've had your dinner." I opened the door and ran down the stairs and out into the cool air. I would not tell anyone about this. I would tell no one.

When I slipped back into our flat that night, I heard my mother's voice, weakly, from her room. "Lily? Where did you go?"

"To the pictures, Mother," I replied.

Even now, I wonder, who looked after me? What protected me? I played with fire. I was so vulnerable, and yet I was protected.

Sometimes I prevailed on Mildred to come to the West End and window-shop for glamor, but the fine stores and restaurants, the strolling ladies and gentlemen, did not excite her. Only once was she caught in the dream.

Wandering along the Mall, the long, tree-lined avenue that leads to Buckingham Palace, we came upon a procession of waiting limousines. Inside were the daughters of the aristocracy, about to be presented at court. The Palace was lit up and spectators were milling about excitedly. Swept up by the crowd, we peered inside the cars and exclaimed aloud at the young ladies in their magnifi-

cent court gowns, at their mothers and aunts in diamonds
and tiaras. Mildred gaped, too, but she was content in the
East End. For Mildred, Saturday nights at The Cottage
were enough.

It was Mildred, one Saturday, who introduced me to a
brown-eyed boy with sandy hair, slow spoken and sincere,
who worked in a shirt factory. His name was Leslie, and
he was twenty. Leslie liked me; he became a steady caller.
On Sunday nights, after my mother fell asleep, he took
me to a movie. But until she dozed off, we would sit on
our ancient horsehair sofa and kiss. Every little while we
talked so that my mother would know we were behaving
properly.

I enjoyed Leslie's kisses. I wanted love badly—I wanted
to be as close as I could to somebody else. But I had been
taught that the consequences were frightening. To me,
love meant babies, and Mildred had told me the most
horrifying stories about women in labor who shrieked
until they went mad or were found dead. Each time I
kissed Leslie I was torn by this conflict—how far to kiss,
not to kiss too much.

But Leslie took no liberties with me. He respected
me, and he wanted to marry me. It was nice for someone
to want to marry me but I didn't want it to be Leslie. He
was kind, he was dependable, but he was not exciting.
He was not the West End.

My mother grew steadily worse now. She developed
excruciating bedsores and sometimes when I woke at
night I heard her turning and tossing. She was very brave,
very uncomplaining. I had no idea how she suffered. I
was so full of dreams, and my mother lay dying and I did
not know it.

I had no inkling how dreadful her last days were. I
had never been close to her. From my sixth to my four-

teenth year there had been the orphanage, and now in
her extremity there was no warmth between us. I did
what I had to do, but with poor grace. I washed her
clothes. I helped care for her, while all I could think of
was, there must be a better life for me than this. And
when she fell asleep I escaped to the West End or tried to
forget myself by going to a movie with Leslie.

One night when Leslie and I returned from the cinema,
there was a note on the table. My mother had been taken
to the hospital. I rushed there guiltily, and tiptoed into
her ward. She lay in a bed behind screens, pale as chalk.
She apologized for frightening me. I was permitted to
see her only a few minutes, and then I went back to our
flat. A neighbor, a Mrs. Barton, looked in on me several
times a day.

I went to see my mother every morning. In a week she
was brought home. Two men carried her on a stretcher
to her bed. As she came through the sitting room I saw
her eyes: she looked about the room as best she could,
but so piercingly—at the sofa, at her clock, at the little
wicker armchair—as though she knew she was seeing them
for the last time and wanted to fix everything in her
memory forever.

And within a week she died.

Why could I not have been more sympathetic in her
illness? She knew she was coming home to die. Why could
I not have understood! But I was indifferent to her in her
dying days. Years later I thought, perhaps this was how I
punished her for placing me in an orphanage. But, poor
woman, there was nothing else she could have done. She
was ailing, and poverty stricken, and uncomplaining, all
her life.

I was alone with her when she died. I sat in the sitting
room, my nose buried in the pages of the *News of the*

World, when I heard a small sigh. Almost incuriously I wandered into her room. She was half out of bed. She had fallen out. I lifted her up—it was very hard to do so—and put her back on her pillow and she was gasping.

Mrs. Barton, who had been sitting with her and had gone out for groceries, walked in as I struggled to make my mother comfortable in her bed.

"Oh, my God!" Mrs. Barton screamed. Then I saw that my mother's eyes were closed. All at once the room was full of neighbors. Where they had come from, how they knew so quickly, I do not know. But I had the strangest feeling of being a spectator, dry-eyed, not a part of what was happening. . . .

Then suddenly I found myself sobbing heartbrokenly, not for my mother's death but for the death of this poor, good, uncomplaining woman who was the mother of the girl in that room.

CHAPTER FOUR

Now look, young ladies," the florid-faced man said carefully. He held before us a small, U-shaped brush, about two inches across, with a short wooden handle. "You will note that this fits the inside of your teeth. You place it in your mouth—" he suited action to word—"and rub vigorously up and down. That's all there is to it." He was demonstrating a novel tooth brush that reached the backs of the teeth as no other on the market could do.

With a dozen girls I stood in a half-empty loft watching him with great attention. We had all come in answer to the advertisement in the *Daily Telegraph*

WANTED, GIRLS WITH GOOD TEETH. NO EX-PERIENCE NECESSARY. TO DEMONSTRATE NEW TOOTH BRUSH.

Leslie had shown me the advertisement in the terrible week of my mother's funeral. He had been my rock and anchor, comforting me because now I had no one.

I was alone and felt sorry for myself. Yet with my sorrow came a subterranean excitement that almost broke to the surface despite my shame that I could feel this way. *I was free!* There was no one now to stop me from doing what I wanted, going where I wished.

Leslie had said, "I ought to marry you now so you'll have someone to look after you." But to be married to Leslie meant the end of adventure, and I wasn't ready for that. Not yet. Leslie, I was sure, would always be there if I wanted him.

It was obvious I must find a job. My mother had left not a penny. My only inheritance turned out to be a small, faded snapshot found in her purse. It was of me, taken when I was about two. Dressed in a high-necked apron, and wearing little black boots, I was seated on a table, a woebegone expression on my face. My right hand was clutching a wooden spool. When I looked at it, I cried. My mother must have carried the photograph with her all the time.

I had set out a few days after the funeral wearing my siren hat and a coat Mildred's sister had made for me— a knee-length black satin with beaded fringes trailing from cuffs and elbows. I swished when I walked and I thought it the height of elegance.

I was not seeking a job as a skivy. If I had a good brain, why not use it? I would find a good job—and directly I found a job I would leave Leslie. I would leave the East End. I would leave the sweetly sickening smell of the brewery, the sight of the drunken men reeling out of the pubs. I'd leave the sound of people fighting and screaming at each other, the cries of women being beaten by their husbands, all the frightening, depressing, horrifying, shameful sounds of poverty. Oh, how gladly I would leave the East End!

I chose Oxford Street, London's busiest shopping district, and summoned up courage to try one shop after another. But I had no sales experience; I had no employment references; I could not bring myself to admit that my only other job had been as a skivy. At the end of two days without success I was in tears when Leslie, faithful Leslie, found the *Daily Telegraph* advertisement. "Lily," he cried, "It's perfect for you. You have wonderful teeth!"

Leslie was right. I had excellent teeth for an English girl. I could thank the orphanage for looking after them and for raising me on a diet of few sweets and no candy.

I kissed Leslie gratefully, washed my face and answered the ad.

Now, after solemnly examining our teeth, the florid-faced man had weeded us down to six. We were hired on the spot. He was dispatching us to six fine shops, he explained. We were to start next morning. Each of us was to stand at the shop's cosmetic counter and demonstrate this amazing new tooth brush. Salary was a pound a week— five dollars—and commission. We were given a counter display showing a beautiful girl using our tooth brush. Our employer rehearsed us carefully in a little sales speech, which, he assured us, would make our stock melt away in a few hours.

I had my job. It was at Gamage's, a department store in Holborn, not far from the West End. I wasted no time. That afternoon I found a room in a once-fashionable section of the West End. It was small and musty, over-looking a narrow side street; bed and breakfast was ten and sixpence a week, more than half my salary—a room in the East End could be had for one-third as much. But I took it. Though it wasn't Mayfair, the heart of the West End, it was far from the East End. I was content.

I said nothing to Leslie. I said nothing to Mildred. I simply vanished. I cut off the East End with a knife as sharp and ruthless as I could make it.

Next morning before Gamage's opened for business I was at my post. I set up my cardboard display on a corner of the beauty corner, and practiced my sales talk. "Good day, sir, or madam." (Smile.) "Have you tried this new and different tooth brush that cleans the *backs* of the teeth and prevents decay?" (Wide smile.) "If you examine it, you will see that it is altogether different from ordinary tooth brushes which never reach the *backs* of the teeth." (Place tooth brush in prospect's hand and smile.) "We have a special price during this demonstration period, sir, or madam."

I turned, still smiling, to find a very thin, elderly woman with frizzed hair standing behind the beauty counter, watching me. She laughed. "Must you go through all that to sell a tooth brush?" she asked in friendliest fashion. She extended her hand. "My name is Ruth Houghton and I'm in cosmetics, so I'm your neighbor."

I said, "I'm Lily Sheil." Miss Houghton was so outgoing I couldn't be angry. She immediately began calling me "Sheilsy," and lent me her little black feather duster to dust my wares.

The doorman unlocked the front door and the store's first customer of the day, a woman with a large handbag, bustled in. I stepped forward two paces as she approached —"You must not be too aggressive," the florid-faced man had warned us—planted myself in her path and beamed at her. "Have you tried this new and different tooth brush—" I began. She swept past me. My confidence suddenly rocked. I thought, maybe this will be harder than I think.

A middle-aged man strode in. I waited, took two paces forward, smiled brightly and launched into my speech. He stopped and listened—a grin on his face—to every word. When I placed the brush in his hand he took it.

"Well, my dear, how much is this?" he asked.

"Two and six, sir." I added hurriedly, "But it's so

much better than the others and you'll really save in dentist's bills." Most tooth brushes, I knew, sold for half the price.

He said, "All right, I'll take one."

I returned to my post flushed with triumph. Miss Houghton winked at me. I winked back. I *could* sell!

Two women entered, deep in conversation. They seemed annoyed when I interrupted them. They did not buy. Then a man entered. He bought a tooth brush. A second man bought one, too. It was clear that men were more concerned about reaching the backs of their teeth than women, and I pondered this for a little while. As the morning progressed I sold five brushes—to men. By the end of the day I had sold nine—to men. I decided next day I wouldn't even try to sell to women. Let their teeth decay. It would serve them right.

I learned how to banter with my customers, but I was wary. When one well-dressed gentleman in a bowler hat said, "My dear, a beautiful girl like you is wasting her time selling tooth brushes. Wouldn't you like to work for me?" I dimpled and smiled but I wasn't taken in. Yet time and time again men paused to talk with me when they made a purchase. I was pretty, they said; they could make use of a girl like me. They would leave me their business cards. I'd look at Miss Houghton, smile, and drop the card in a cigar box in which I kept change.

One rainy, gusty December morning the door swung open and a man dashed in. He was slim, in a trenchcoat and soft hat. He came in briskly, almost as though the wind and rain had blown open the front door and blown him in. He hurried by me and I ran after him—he was the first customer in an hour—and almost shouted, "Sir, have you tried this new tooth brush that cleans the *backs* of the teeth?"

He wheeled around and stared at me. His eyes were deep blue, his skin was tanned, and his dark hair grew low on his forehead. He seemed about forty. His face suddenly broke into a beautiful smile. "By Jove!" he exclaimed. "You're a damned pretty girl!" I was struck by his voice, so low, so musical. Without waiting for another word he took the tooth brush and examined it. "By Jove!" he exclaimed, "this is a weird thing—if you can sell this you can sell anything." He turned to me and said with almost boyish eagerness: "I'm in iron and steel but I have a fancy-goods department and I could find a place for a girl like you. Why, you're so pretty you'd sell everything I have!"

I'd heard all this before. I didn't propose to be cheated out of a sale. "Sir, it reaches the *backs* of the teeth where decay—" He wasn't listening. "Splendid," he said. "Splendid. I'll take one. Just the girl I'm looking for. Here—" He gave me a pound note and extracted a visiting card from his vest pocket—"Here's my card. Now, telephone me, you will remember?"

"Oh, thank you, sir," I said triumphantly. I wrapped the tooth brush and gave him his change. He pocketed his purchase and hurried out, apparently completely forgetting what he had dashed in to buy. I glanced at his card, winked at Miss Houghton, and dropped it into the cigar box.

That night I studied myself in the mirror, as I had done so often before. Was I really so pretty? Could I believe the compliments men paid me? The face that looked back at me was no longer round, but heart-shaped. My ash-blond hair, always so straight and dull, had taken on a natural wave. My nose had evolved from a tiny snub into a feature of respectable length. With gray-green eyes, a mouth that was a fashionable cupid's bow, and a perfect English complexion, creamy, pink and white. . . . I *was* pretty.

I began to clothe myself in the belief that I had that mysterious quality—whatever it was—that lured men. The other girls on the floor didn't quite have it. Miss Weymouth, in stationery, was pretty but somehow she didn't have it. Women, not men, spent their time talking to her. Miss Knight, in gloves and bags, was attractive and petite and wore her hair in provocative bangs, but she didn't have it. Whatever it was, it was something I had and I was grateful that I had it.

Three weeks passed—and my job ended. The florid-faced man, looking doleful, appeared unexpectedly one Monday morning. The company was going out of business. The cash commissions which were to be calculated at the end of each month could not be paid, although I had done well. He could manage a week's pay. He was terribly sorry.

I was shattered. My voice trembled when I told Miss Houghton. "What are you going to do, Sheilsy?" she asked. I didn't know. How would I eat? Pay my enormous rent of ten and six? In my hand was my week's wages of a pound, in my purse a few shillings I had saved. I must find another job. My heart sank at the prospect of going through that ordeal again. Yet the thought of returning to the East End, perhaps to be the wife of Leslie who worked in a shirt factory, terrified me.

Then I remembered the man in the trenchcoat. "By Jove—" he had said. His voice had been so gentle, his smile so boyish. He had seemed sincere. Now which card was his?

With Miss Houghton's help I went through the contents of my cigar box. I fingered each card, reading the

name aloud, pondering: is this it? Then I remembered
what he had said, "I'm in iron and steel but I have a
fancy-goods department—" We rummaged through the
cards, perhaps ten of them.

Here it was:

THE JOHN GRAHAM CO.
Iron and Steel Manufacturers
Major John Graham Gillam, D.S.O.
Managing Director

On the other side had been scribbled a telephone
number. I waited two days before calling Major Gillam.
Miss Houghton, most impressed, had told me that D.S.O.
meant the Distinguished Service Order—second only to
the Victoria Cross, England's highest decoration for military bravery. His Majesty, George V, himself, had pinned
the medal on Major Gillam at Buckingham Palace! I
couldn't quite believe that a D.S.O. would want me to
work for him. When I called, a girl's voice said excitedly,
"Miss Sheil, he's been trying everywhere to find you. He
even got in touch with the tooth-brush company." A
moment later I heard a low, musical voice: "Oh, Miss
Sheil, I went to Gamage's yesterday and they said you'd
gone and left no address. You promised to call—why
didn't you?"

I blurted out, "Do you still want me?"

He laughed. "How long will it take you to get here?"

An hour later I was sitting opposite him in his office.
By Jove, of course he'd meant his offer. He wanted me
to work for him.

I tried to be businesslike. "What are the wages?" I asked
primly.

How much had I been getting at Gamage's?

I lied. "One pound, ten."

"I'll give you two pounds and commission."

"That will be fine," I replied sedately, but my heart beat fast. Two pounds—and commission! Commission that would be paid! He looked at me for a moment, then jumped up from behind his desk. "Let me show you the office."

The John Graham Company occupied two large rooms and a storeroom. In the storeroom were his fancy goods—lacquered trays, polishes and cleansers, costume jewelry, travel kits, clocks for automobiles, stamp boxes and wallets. And, against one wall, carton after carton of foot-high table lamps.

"I want you to look at these," he said, and brought one out. "This is a Lite-o-lamp. Watch." He lifted the lamp—it lit—and put it down. "Very simple," he said, "To turn it off, lift it again. Ingenious, isn't it?"

I was impressed.

"This will be one of the major items I'll want you to sell. I'll give you a list of stores to call on," he explained. "Of course I'm just starting to distribute these, but you are in charge of this division. This is your department. Pretty soon you'll have other people working under you. You should do very well for yourself."

I felt pangs of conscience. "Major Gillam, I really haven't had too much experience—"

He waved that aside. "I told you anyone who can sell that absurd tooth brush can sell anything. I'm not worried about you, Miss Sheil." He led me to the door. "All right?" he said. His face brightened. "By Jove, I'm so glad you called! Now, you'll be in early tomorrow morning?" I smiled and nodded and left.

I walked back to my room thinking, If this keeps up, I'll be in Mayfair before I know it. Here I am getting twice as much as before. I looked about my room—always dark, a sleazy yellow scarf over the sofa to hide a jagged tear, a cracked little wash basin— I marched downstairs and knocked on my landlady's door. "I want a front room," I said. She gave me one at twelve and six, with a window overlooking the avenue. I moved my belongings into the new room, thinking, all her life my mother had never managed to live in the front, where the sun came. I had done it in three weeks.

That evening I sat in an armchair and looked out of the window at the traffic. How gentle Major Gillam had been, how kind his manner, how sweet his smile! This was not a man who wanted to clutch and grab. He treated me with respect and courtesy. And he was a grown man, not a Ginger or a Leslie—a man of the world. I knew it by the elegance of his clothes, the courtliness with which he had led me to the door. I thought, he is handsome, brave, charming—he is the most attractive man I have ever known!

CHAPTER FIVE

NEXT MORNING when I arrived for work, Major
Gillam was reclining comfortably behind his desk, reading
The Times.

"Good morning, good morning," he called out. He
put his paper down and watched me smilingly as I removed my black satin coat and hung it carefully in a
closet. "I want you to take your time and become accus-
tomed to the job," he said. "Now, let's see." He looked
about. In the storeroom were several gross of artificial-
pearl necklaces selling for the equivalent of fifty cents. I
might try taking a few samples around to the shops. He
gave me a list of stores to try.

With my goods packed in a small brown suitcase, I
went forth on my first tour as a representative of the
John Graham Company, fancy-goods department. The result was appalling. At the end of three days I had failed
to sell a single necklace. "Costume jewelry? Not in January, miss. You should have called before Christmas."

It was the same story everywhere.

"Never mind," said Major Gillam. "Perhaps we are off
on our timing. We'll try placing them before Easter." He
smiled. "Just put them back where they belong. I have

something else, here, Miss Sheil, that I think is really first rate."

This turned out to be a new automobile polish called "Suji-Muji." "Has an Oriental ingredient in it that's said to be most effective," Major Gillam explained. "You could try Great Portland Street—dozens of car showrooms are there—and I'm sure you'll do splendidly." He patted me on the arm. "Just smile," he said. "No one can withstand your smile."

In my big picture hat and trailing coat I fancied I cut a stunning figure, but the salesmen in the showrooms were extremely sophisticated young men who were not easily impressed. I felt conspicuous as I entered the first showroom, smiling brightly, and asked, "May I see the manager, please?"

I beamed at the handsome man with a finely waxed mustache who approached me. "I have a new polish for cars, the famous Suji-Muji Oriental Paste. I would like to show you how much better it is than what you are using now."

The manager, rubbing a finger delicately along his mustache, looked at me with an amused glint in his eye. "Suji-what, miss?" he asked.

I repeated the name with dignity. "Suji-Muji. May I demonstrate it, sir?"

By now three or four salesmen, each with bright tie and white handkerchief overflowing his breast pocket, had joined us. They listened with considerable interest.

The manager smiled broadly. "Well," he said, "there's a car over there you might use." Followed by the men, I walked to the car. The manager said, "Would you mind trying it on the lower fender?" He explained that he could not risk spotting an area easily visible.

There was nothing for me to do but get down on my

knees and apply the polish where he indicated. I set to work. "You see, only a small amount is required," I enunciated carefully. I looked up to see my audience exchanging glances. "And with this cloth which comes in the tin—you take a small amount and gently rub back and forth, back and forth—" I looked up as I rubbed, smiling hopefully. Some of the men had changed positions and were now studying my work from the rear. They ogled me shamelessly as I polished, on my hands and knees: I felt my clothes were all but transparent, but I plunged on doggedly. "And now—you see how clean and sparkling it is!"

I scrambled to my feet. The corner of the fender shone like a mirror. The men looked at me, nodding appreciatively. "Beautiful stuff," one said, with a wink.

The manager said, "If you'll come over here, miss—" He bought one tin of polish. As I gave him his change, he lowered his voice. "What are you doing later on?"

I was most indignant. "I'm sorry," I said icily. "I shall be selling Suji-Muji elsewhere, thank you." I stalked out. How dared he not treat me seriously as a sales representative!

It took only a few days to prove a distressing lack of demand for Suji-Muji Oriental Paste. When I informed Major Gillam, he was as unperturbed as before. "Timing is most important, as you'll learn," he explained. "We'll try selling them after a rainy spell when cars need a wash and polish." He went on, "Please don't let this upset you. I told you I'll have all sorts of things you can help me with." I said to myself, this is the *sweetest* man!

"One duty I haven't told you about," he said. "As you know, I have a large mail-order business, and I am obliged to get out an enormous number of letters each week.

Would you mind staying a little later tonight and helping me?"

I was so grateful for the salary he continued to pay me, for his lack of concern over my failure as a sales-woman, for his gentleness, that I was his willing slave. "Oh yes, I'd be happy to."

At five-thirty, I sat opposite him at his desk. He was busy signing letters the girls had typed for him. As he finished one he passed it to me, with the envelope. I inserted the letter, licked the flap and sealed it. Then I licked a stamp and fixed it on. Every little while he looked up. "Are you tired? You sure you don't mind doing this?"

I licked an envelope happily and shook my head. "Oh, no, I enjoy it."

One envelope called for extra postage. It was bound for Paris. "Oh, I know that name," I exclaimed. "It's Channel!" I had recognized it, for Chanel was a famous perfume.

Major Gillam smiled at me. "That's a French name, Lily. You pronounce it Shan—el." I was mortified. I thought, if I'd been of gentle birth and sent to a French finishing school, I would not be caught making a humiliating mistake like that. A little later, as I glanced through *The Times*, waiting for him while he caught up with his letters, I remarked, "It's so interesting what it says in the papers about the debuntees being presented at court—"

He roared. I looked up, startled. "Forgive me, Lily," he said. "But you pronounce it debū-tantes—not de*bun*-tees." And he laughed again. "Good Lord, how amusing!" I reddened but laughed with him. I couldn't get angry at Major Gillam. Sitting there opposite him, I was all in a warm glow. For now I was in a brightly lit office, laughing and chatting with a kind and charming gentle-

man, and working girls from the East End who might be
going by on buses looking longingly into the windows—
why, it was *me* they were seeing and envying. I thought,
I owe this man so much.

One night, as he finished signing the last letter, he sat
back and sighed. "By Jove, it's been a long day," he said.
"Nearly seven o'clock. How would you like to have dinner with me?"

I blushed. "Sh . . . you mustn't talk like that."

He looked surprised. "Why not?"

I tried to explain that it would not be proper, because
I worked for him. Though I couldn't envision him as one
of the gentlemen following me in Piccadilly, I knew
that girls who allowed their employers to become familiar
with them invariably ended by losing their jobs. And
while Major Gillam fascinated me and I adored him, two
pounds a week and commission were too precious to en-
danger.

A week passed before I agreed. Then it was a trip
abroad that seemed to make it permissible. Major Gillam,
I had learned, had offices in France and Belgium—at least,
business connections. One week end he was obliged to go
to Brussels. Would I like to go with him as far as Dover,
to see him off on the boat train?

I was enchanted. This was the role of a confidential
secretary, to accompany her employer to the boat train—
and it partook of great adventure, seeing a man off to the
Continent. It was vague, golden, mysterious—the Continent! I would be seeing a man off to Europe!

Once before I had been on a train, to Brighton. Then
I had been traveling third class. This time I was in a first-
class compartment. Major Gillam took me into the dining
car, with its oak paneling and richly upholstered seats.
A steward hovered over us and I munched cheese and

biscuits and felt utterly luxurious sitting with my distinguished employer amid the other first-class passengers.

Then I saw him off. He said good-by and put his face forward and automatically I kissed him on the cheek.

Returning to the train, I walked on air. I passed a telegraph office. On impulse I wrote out my first telegram —to Major John Gillam, in Brussels: I HOPE YOU ARRIVED SAFELY. LOVE LILY. I felt daring and sophisticated.

Now we had something between us. When Major Gillam asked me to dinner on the day he returned, I accepted.

He took me to The Mars, a pleasant little *café* in Soho. It was not as imposing as the curtained restaurant off Bond Street, but I loved the atmosphere. The maître d'hôtel bowed us to a table on which hummed an electric candle under a pink shade. Nearby were theater parties in evening dress: I was thrilled by their presence. The specialty of The Mars was sole. I enjoyed it so much that when Major Gillam looked the other way, I even popped the bones into my mouth.

The Mars became a once-a-week occurrence with us, usually when I stayed after hours to help with the mail. I always wore my one ensemble—my black satin coat, which I kept on through dinner. But each time I leaned forward for a roll, or to whisper a question to Major Gillam, I trailed fringe into the food.

"Oh dear," he said at one point. "You mustn't do that— really. You should remove your coat."

It was Major Gillam, then, who gently and with the greatest tact began to correct my table manners. I was astonished at what I did not know. How to use fish knives, so that I could bone the fish; how to use condiments—at the orphanage we'd never had salt or pepper on the table. He taught me to keep my elbows off the table, not to gesture with my knife or fork, to place them together on my plate when I had finished. He taught me how to wait patiently until all my food had been served—as far back as I could remember, the moment food was placed before me I began gobbling it down as though I feared it might be snatched away.

He taught me, when introduced, to say, "How d'you do," not as a question but as a statement. He said to me, gently, in almost fatherly fashion, "You're always sniffling, Lily—*do* blow your nose." I said unhappily, "We never had handkerchiefs at the orphanage." He taught me not to say, "Pardon?" when I failed to hear what had been said. "Just say, 'What?' I know it sounds rude but it's correct." He taught me to rise when an older woman entered the room, to remain seated and relaxed when a man approached the table to chat with us. And I took Major Gillam's words and was grateful because he was so kind.

He spoke to me about my clothes. We had been at The Mars perhaps three times when he began. "Lily, what I'm going to say to you may offend you but it isn't meant to. You really must change some of your clothes and I'm going to help you." I thought, in sudden dismay, oh, they haven't been as pretty as I thought!

"You see, you are my showcase," he explained. "You are the public representative of the John Graham Company, so you must be well dressed so that our customers will assume that we have a profitable business. You do understand, don't you?"

I said, not altogether understanding, "Oh, yes, certainly."

"Good," he said. "Please don't think there is anything behind this. I am going to send you to my tailor to make you a new coat. That will be the first thing." I looked up, startled, and he added hurriedly, "Now remember, you have no obligation to me whatsoever. I consider this simply a matter of sound business on my part."

I was not really startled. It was impossible for me to attribute evil intent to Major Gillam. I thought, only, isn't it amazing that a man of such aristocratic bearing, such charm and breeding would pay any attention to Lily Sheil, would even wish to talk to a girl like me who is so poor and uneducated and knows so little about anything. And I thought, isn't it wonderful that I'm pretty. This is the greatest gift I ever received, that I have become pretty.

I went to his tailor and chose a lovely dark red coat with a black velvet collar. "Beautiful," he said, approvingly. "Now you won't drip over everything." I laughed. "Now," he said, "you need a new hat. I don't think the one you wear is right for you. And you need shoes and a handbag and gloves to go with it."

Then: "Don't you think your hands are rather rough? I know young women who use glycerine and rose water every night on their hands. I will get you some." He told me about the care of my nails. I had never had a manicure. He bought me a manicure set.

He said, "Why don't you go to a hairdresser and have your hair done?" I was hurt. "Don't you like it the way it is?" He replied, "It is very nice—but I think a hairdresser might find a way to do you more justice."

Who could withstand that?

I began to learn a little about Major Gillam. He had won his D.S.O. at Gallipoli, but was reticent about his exploit. "Oh, some action I saw," he would say, dismissing it. He was a bachelor, about forty-two—twenty-five

years older than I. He was born in Birmingham. Before
the war he had been interested in writing and the theater,
had been one of the original members of the Birmingham
Repertory Theatre and acted briefly with Cedric Hard-
wicke, Melville Cooper, and others who were to make
names for themselves. Because his family frowned on a
stage career he joined H. M. Tennant & Sons, iron and steel
manufacturers. He had come, as I was to realize, from a
gentle, middle-class family, but knew his way about all
strata of society. I could have had no more knowledgeable
and devoted tutor.

I, in turn, was tremendously eager to learn, to know
good manners, to correct what were not only errors in
pronunciation but a Cockney flavor to my speech. I had
the orphanage, at least, to thank for taking me off the
streets from which I would have emerged speaking pure
Cockney. The more I was with Major Gillam the more
conscious I became of my speech. I told him everything
about myself. I was ashamed of my lowly beginnings, of
the orphanage, of the East End, but I trusted him. It was
as though he had decided to make me his protégé, to
mold me into a proper young lady whom he could display
as his representative or take to dinner at The Mars without fear that she would embarrass him.

One night when we worked late he said, "I have to go
to a regimental dinner tonight, Lily. Will you come to my
flat while I change?"

I accompanied him. A uniformed doorman, tipping
his hat, opened the lift for us; and as we went up I
thought, how grand to live in a building with a lift, not
stone stairs to climb, where you don't always come upon
poor, careworn women with shopping baskets and dirty,
tired men in caps.

Major Gillam opened the door with his key and

ushered me into a cozy apartment. There were two rooms
—a small, pleasant sitting room with deep, black leather
chairs and off it a bedroom and bath.

"I don't have a kitchen," he said, "but I can have food
sent in."

I sank into one of the leather chairs. Would I care for
a drink? I shook my head. Liquor had no appeal for me:
only food. As if reading my mind he said, "You must
have something to eat." He rang and when a boy appeared he sent out for biscuits and a bottle of ginger beer.
"Do the biscuits have rys'ns in them?" I asked. He laughed.
"Yes, but you'd do better if you pronounced it raisins."
I thought, *I have been saying ry'sns all my life. How much
I have to learn!*

Then he poured himself a Scotch and soda and we relaxed, he with his drink, I with my tray of food and
ginger beer. He told me more about himself. His heart
really wasn't in iron and steel, nor even in fancy goods.
He wanted to write. He spent hours in the reading
room of the British Museum studying military history
and antiquities, and sending articles about them to the
newspapers. He felt concerned because the John Graham
Company was not doing as well as he had hoped. An older
sister, quite rich, was financing him and he hoped not to
disappoint her. He showed me a photograph taken when
he came out of Buckingham Palace with his D.S.O. She
was on his arm and posed there, proudly. He spoke of
her with affection and, I thought, a note of apprehension.
But he was confident business would soon improve. He
had great faith in our fancy-goods department. With Easter
coming, he was certain I would sell every item in stock.
"I'll try," I said. "Oh, I will."

He came over and kissed me. He was very sweet, very
tender. He kissed me again, ardently, and I responded—I

was completely carried away. Anything might have happened. But Major Gillam rose abruptly. "I must bathe and dress now," he said. And he left me.

I didn't think it was wrong for me to be in his flat, or for him to kiss me. I was on my own, answerable to one but myself.

When he emerged from his room later, attired in full regimental dress, I gasped. He carried a sword and his chest gleamed with ribbons and medals. He cut such a handsome figure! He said, "We shall have to leave now."

Suddenly I didn't want to go. "Can I stay for a little while? I don't feel like going right away."

He said, with surprise, "Of course. Make yourself at home." He looked about. "Now, you have these biscuits, you have the ginger beer—is there anything else you'd like?"

I said, "No, thank you. It's just such a cozy flat. I'd love to stay a little longer."

I saw him to the door. He stood for a moment looking at me, a slow smile playing about his lips. "You're a very naïve girl, Lily." He kissed me and was gone.

Nibbling at my biscuits, I wandered about the room, touching his pipe rack, looking at the photographs on the wall. One, colored, was charming; it was obviously my employer at the age of two or three, attired in a blue and white sailor suit, with golden curls down to his shoulders, a skipping rope in his hand. What an elegant little boy he had been! I tried one easy chair, then the other. I peeped into his bedroom: on the dresser were a man's toilet accessories—razor, after-shave lotion, talc. I sniffed the lotion, and tried the talc on my cheek. I sauntered about and peered into the bathroom. It was palatial, with blue tile floor and walls. The tub was enormous, of gleaming white porcelain: a new cake of bath soap lay in the rectangular wire tray and nearby, a long wooden brush to reach the small of your back. I'd never used anything like that.

I thought of the ancient, spidery tub in my boarding house, and the impulse was irresistible. I took a bath. I undressed and got into the deep tub and luxuriated there for nearly an hour, in the fragrant suds, the scent of pine about them, and I thought of the antiseptic soap at the orphanage, the pungent, eye-stinging soap of the laundress with whom we had boarded. . . .

Then I dressed, put everything aright, and went home.

Major Gillam, as an eligible bachelor, attended two and three dinner parties and social affairs a week. Often I accompanied him home from the office, and while he bathed and dressed I munched on biscuits and ginger beer and read his magazines. Then, after he left, I took my bath. I didn't mind Major Gillam going off in the evening to his club. It was so pleasant, so luxurious to have the freedom of his flat: I admired Major Gillam, I enjoyed working for him. This was all so much more than I had ever hoped.

Sometimes, lying in the warm, scented water, dreamily massaging the small of my back with the long brush, I toyed with the idea: how would I like to be Mrs. John Graham Gillam?—and then I pushed the idea out of my mind. He was so much older; and why should he want to marry Lily Sheil? Now and then, in the office, he might say impulsively, "You're so beautiful" and if no one was looking, steal a quick kiss. Once he had added, half-teasingly, "I wish I could marry you but I owe my sister so much." I did not believe he meant it. He could not mean it. Major Gillam was a confirmed bachelor. I was his protégé: he found me pretty and amusing and eager to learn and terribly grateful. His protégé, that was all.

CHAPTER SIX

HE WAS SANDY HAIRED, pink faced and well dressed, and he had been watching me for nearly twenty minutes.

"Madam, will you try this Lite-o-lamp?" I was asking a stout, gray-haired woman. "You see, lift it—it lights. Lift it again—it turns off. Ingenious, isn't it?"

I was standing at the John Graham Company exhibit at the London *Daily Mail*'s Home Exhibition. Major Gillam had rented a small booth in an attempt to move our stock of Lite-o-lamps. The sandy-haired young man, about twenty-five, had bought a lamp, gone off a few yards, and hovered there, watching me. Now, apparently gathering courage, he approached as the stout woman walked on. He said hurriedly, "Miss, you may say no but I can't be hung for asking. Would you consider going out to dinner with me on Saturday night? And going to a cinema later?"

That was how I met George Nelson, who owned his own grocery store and on our second date introduced me to his mother, and sister, Helen. George knew of interesting places to go and he danced well. Now I had someone to take me out on the evenings Major Gillam dined with his sister or went off to his club. George's sister, Helen, was perhaps a year older than I. A millionaire was courting her, said George, proudly.

"A millionaire?" I asked, awed. "You really mean he has a million pounds?"

George nodded soberly. "Probably closer to two million. Name of Monte Collins. He owns property in the City and has so much money he doesn't know what to do with it. And he likes Helen—" He painted an intriguing picture of Mr. Collins, who had worked hard, but had played hard, too, and spent lavishly on his favorite ladies. Now, having marked his forty-seventh year, he was ready to settle down. He wanted to marry a sweet, respectable girl, rear a family and create a dynasty worthy of carrying on his name.

A few days later George brought exciting news. Mr. Collins had invited us to join Helen and him in his box at the Duke of York Theatre. Mr. Collins could call for Helen and George, then pick me up. George was jubilant: Mr. Collins had already met his mother and his invitation strongly suggested that he intended to become a member of the family.

I flew about getting the proper clothes. I rented a green evening gown and a black evening cape. I thought, as I fitted the dress, suppose Mr. Collins liked me instead of Helen? Suppose he falls madly in love with me and wants to marry me and make me his heiress? Major Gillam would be pleased if his protégé caught a real millionaire. Yet, for some reason, I said nothing to my employer.

I waited at my window. I heard the bell and stole a glance outside. There, in front of my boarding house, waited the longest, sleekest black car I had ever seen. It could only be a Rolls Royce. A uniformed chauffeur stood at attention at the car door. Down below, his finger nervously pressing the bell, waited George.

I swept down as gracefully as I could. George helped me into the car. In the enormous back seat, upholstered in luxurious gray, sat Helen, all in blue, and a fairly short, heavy-set man, his face pinkish and pouchy under the soft ceiling light, with small bags under his dark eyes. "Good evening," he said in a soft voice. He moved closer to Helen to make room for me. "Do come in."

George took a seat in front with the driver, Helen and I on either side of Mr. Collins who smelled strongly of talcum powder and cologne. There was little conversation on the way. Helen giggled and called Mr. Collins, Monte, while I sat in awed silence. At the theater Helen and I took our seats self-consciously in the front of the box, the two gentlemen arranging themselves behind us. I have no memory of the play. I only recall, almost as though it were a physical sensation, feeling Mr. Collins' dark eyes boring into my back. I dared not turn around because I knew I would find myself staring directly into his eyes.

In the car afterward Mr. Collins said, "Let's go to my flat and we'll have some champagne." When we arrived there, a butler opened the door to an enormous, heavily carpeted apartment decorated in black and gold. The furniture, the tables, the chairs, the rich brocaded hangings from ceiling to floor, were black and gold. Everywhere I had a sense of wealth.

The butler reappeared with an elaborate tray of small sandwiches, and champagne in a bucket of ice. George was doing his best to talk to me so Mr. Collins would pay attention to Helen, but Mr. Collins—as I was to learn is true of most rich men—did what he wanted to do. He talked to me. I felt sorry for Helen, who grew glummer and glummer, but I could not conceal my elation. A millionaire! And he was interested in *me*.

Now, as we stood about, Mr. Collins poured the champagne and solemnly handed us the glasses. I became very daring. I faced him, raised my glass and, looking directly at him with what must have been a shy look but which I thought was absolutely brazen, I said clearly, "To our friendship!" I caught a sick smile on George's face and utter consternation on Helen's. They had seen our eyes meet, and hold. Then everyone chimed in, "To our friendship," and we drank. But the magic moment had come—and I had seized it. Mr. Collins and I had *communicated*.

The next half hour passed like a dream. We drank champagne and devoured the exquisite sandwiches. I sat with legs crossed, my hands poised aristocratically. I knew that a middle-class woman would never dare cross her legs. Somewhere I had read this, perhaps in Charles Garvis' romances in which beautiful, high-born society women, wearing aigrettes in their hair, startled staid masters of industry with their unconventionality.

When it was time to go George tried to regain lost ground. "Lily lives closer," he said to Mr. Collins. "Let's drop her first."

"No," said Mr. Collins simply. "I'll drop you and Helen off first." George reddened, but said nothing.

Meanwhile, I was growing uncomfortable. I had never had champagne before. I wanted to go to the bathroom badly but I couldn't bring myself to say to a millionaire, "Where is the ladies' room?" I thought it immodest—or at least, in bad taste, to call such personal matters to a man's attention. Now, as we drove, I became increasingly distressed. When we dropped George and Helen at their flat in North London, I almost summoned courage to excuse myself and dart inside for a moment. But this would have been even more conspicuous. I thought, I'll use power of will. I'll forget it.

But I did not forget it. On the long drive back to my boarding house, sitting with Mr. Collins in the lovely car, on the lovely gray upholstery, I grew more and more desperate. He was talking to me: my predicament now made me breathless. I spoke in staccato bursts, I literally bounced in my seat as I tried to chat animatedly about the play.

Then nature took over. I couldn't help it. I knew what was happening. I struggled, in anguish and shame, but I could no longer control myself.

I thought, *Oh God, this light gray upholstery. Maybe it won't show. Maybe he won't notice. I want to die.*

The car arrived in front of the boarding house. Mr. Collins switched on the ceiling light. He got out and helped me out. As he did so I gave an agonized glance at where I had sat. There was a large black circle as big as the full moon. A wave of humiliation swept over me so that I almost fainted. That's what I had done to his lovely car. Not to mention—it flashed through my mind— the dress and cape I had rented.

I cried myself to sleep that night. I'll never see him again, I thought. He's a millionaire. I'll never see him again. I've spoiled the only big chance I'll ever have in my life. It could have come *true!* I *could* have been rich the rest of my life!

Next day there was a telephone call from Mr. Collins. Would I be his luncheon guest at Skindles, Maidenhead-on-Thames? I thought, he hadn't noticed!

At Skindles, Mr. Collins was the soul of thoughtfulness. He wanted to know all about me and I told him about Major Gillam and my job. He wanted to know if I had gone out often? What did I do with my time? He questioned me carefully and I told him what I thought he should know.

Just before we left, after he helped me on with my red coat, he inclined his head brusquely toward the end of the hall. "The ladies' room is down that corridor," he said.

I almost ran there. But I knew he knew—and everything was all right. The dream could still come true.

Apparently my contretemps was better proof of my character than anything I could have said. If I was too shy to ask to go to the ladies' room, I must be completely innocent. This was what he needed to be sure of: a beautiful, virtuous, and poor girl who would be grateful for the privilege of being his wife.

Mr. Monte Collins courted me. There was no question about it. Poor Helen fell by the wayside. Within a month he was seeing me twice a week, Sundays and Wednesdays. On other nights, I still saw Major Gillam. Several times a week I went to his flat for biscuits, ginger beer, and my bath. Sometimes we played a record and danced: he was a superb dancer; he kissed me and I clung to him, feeling warm and protected. I was always excited with Major Gillam.

One thing was certain. There was no excitement with Mr. Collins. Our routine was as prescribed as if I were his hired companion. On Sunday evenings, promptly at eight, his Rolls Royce called for me. There would be whispers from the boarders as I came down and entered the enormous car. I enjoyed the ride to his apartment but I grew gloomier and gloomier at the thought of seeing Mr. Collins.

He would open the door himself. Dressed in a black

velvet smoking jacket, he kissed me solemnly on the cheek, a gentle kiss, the faintest imprint, then drew me across the threshold. Carefully he took my coat and hat and led me to a black and gold settee. In front of us was a low gilt table, on which champagne stood in an ice bucket, and sandwiches.

I would notice now that he was not as heavy set as I had expected from his pouchy face: his feet were surprisingly small; his eyes were black and mournful; his hair always appeared wet but it was not wet, it was black and rather thin. He always smelled strongly of the powder with which he dabbed his cheeks after shaving. He spoke slowly and precisely and had a way—after making an apparently casual remark—of stealing a sudden sideways glance as if to catch me unaware.

Sitting with him in his luxurious apartment, I felt hemmed in. The heavy black and gold drapes that were always drawn over the long high windows, the deep pile carpeting with motif of black and gold, the black and gold décor everywhere, made me gasp for air. Major Gillam's flat was friendly, comfortable, inviting. This was formal and forbidding. Was this how the rich lived?

I listened while he talked. Usually it was about his childhood and his struggle for success, the need to be alert and shrewd to meet the challenges of everyday life. Or he spoke of a business deal that would bring him still more money. I tried to think, desperately, of what to say. I was drinking champagne with a millionaire who liked me—and I felt so stifled I could hardly breathe.

The butler refilled my plate with sandwiches. When I swiftly polished off a second plateful Mr. Collins put his hand over mine. "Ever hear the story about the two little boys, Lily? One was eating an apple. The other said, 'Gimme the core. Go on—gimme the core!' The first boy said, 'With this apple there ain't gonna be no core!' " And watching me, Monte laughed uproariously. I laughed politely, too, although I did not think it funny. I was learning that you laugh at a rich man's joke, even if the joke is on you.

Somehow the evening would come to an end. Mr. Collins would press his lips chastely against my cheek and send me home.

On Wednesday evenings he took me to dinner at the Café de Paris, one of London's most expensive dance restaurants. Now, when the Rolls appeared in front of my boarding house, Monte waited in the back seat. As he helped me in, he kissed me on the cheek. Then, after tucking the lap robe carefully about me, he would solemnly present me with a box of chocolates. "Oh, thank you, Monte," I'd say, and opening it, I would begin popping them into my mouth. "Better not take too many, Lily," he would say, jovially. "You'll spoil your appetite." I'd shake my head. "You know you don't have to worry about my appetite," I'd say archly.

When we arrived at the restaurant I ordered grilled turbot, which I loved. Monte ordered roast beef. And while I ate he looked at my face the way I looked at the grilled turbot. After dessert he offered me a cigarette and I accepted it and puffed languidly like a woman of the world. Always there was champagne.

"Would you like to dance, Lily?" he would ask.

I danced with him. He was a heavy-footed dancer, literally hopping from one foot to the other. As he hopped about, he sang the words of the latest musical hit in my ear:

> It had to be you,
> It had to be you,
> I wandered around and finally found

The somebody who could make me be true,
Could make me be blue. . . . .
With all your faults. . . . .
It had to be you.

He would pull his face away, look at me meaningfully with his dark mournful eyes, and then chant another song in my ear.

Dancing with Monte while he hopped and puffed and sang and nuzzled my ear, I could not help glancing about the floor at the other men, men who were slender, elegant, long-limbed, men who danced gracefully with beautiful, bored women. If only I were dancing with that tall, blond gentleman. If only I were dancing with Johnny Gillam!

I heard Monte's voice, sharp and harsh. "Are you flirting with that man?"

"Oh, Monte," I said. "Of course not. I just looked at him."

We danced a little while. I could not take my eyes away from the young bloods, the young lords so gay, so handsome on the floor.

"Now, Lily, I saw you smile at that man over there—"

"I didn't, Monte, really I didn't—" I wasn't flirting. I was looking longingly. I thought, Monte considers himself a great prize. If I play my cards right he will marry me and I will be rich and the whole world will be mine. But I thought, sadly, is this all there is? Will he be the end of the great yearning and the great adventure?

Monte never kissed me on the lips, never tried to caress me, never expressed tenderness toward me. I felt, he doesn't really love me. He wants to buy me as an adornment. And he is watching me, carefully, appraisingly, looking over the goods before he makes his purchase. Yet to have a rich husband—if only it didn't have to be Monte Collins!

I said nothing to Major Gillam about my millionaire suitor. I could not bring myself to tell him. Perhaps I feared he would be hurt, or perhaps—and I believe this was the truth—I was falling in love with him.

I knew now that he was deeply in debt to his sister—indeed, that the John Graham Company was far from a success. I knew that he had sold very little of the costume jewelry, the auto polish, the Lite-o-lamps, the dozen other items he always bought too dear and tried to sell at the wrong time. But I was falling in love with his sweetness, his tenderness, his acceptance of me as I was, his conviction that I was irresistibly beautiful and could succeed in anything I chose. I was falling in love with his unquenchable optimism, his eager, youthful attitude toward the world. Anything was possible with Major Johnny Gillam: life was an exciting adventure wherever he was and wherever he moved.

CHAPTER SEVEN

In the week of my eighteenth birthday, Johnny made an unexpected, breath-taking gesture. How would I like to go to Paris for him? To buy perfume? He had borrowed additional capital and was certain we could dispose of inexpensive French perfume at considerable profit. He could not spare the time to go himself. As a matter of fact, I might mix business with pleasure, and consider the trip a birthday present from the John Graham Company.

I was beside myself. Paris! Perhaps, even, a French finishing school flashed through my mind. How long could I stay? Oh, a fortnight, said Johnny, smiling at my excitement. I thought, even if I attended only a few days, no one could take from me the fact that I had *gone* to a French finishing school.

I hurried to tell Monte Collins. I had assumed a new importance in my own eyes. Monte, too, was impressed. "I really don't wish you to go, Lily," he said carefully. "But in a way I'm glad. It will give me a chance to do a great deal of thinking"—he paused and looked away— "which may alter your entire life." He stole a quick glance at me.

I let my face reveal nothing. I needed to do a great deal

of thinking, too. How was I to resolve my dilemma? I was almost sure I loved Johnny, but Johnny seemed to have no idea of how I felt, as he had no idea that I was being courted by an enormously rich suitor whom I might not have the courage to refuse.

I went to Paris. Immediately after registering at a hotel where Johnny had made my reservations, I set out for a well-known finishing school, the Coeur de Sévigné, at Neuilly. Monsieur le directeur was outraged. Enroll for two weeks? Impossible. When I asked helplessly what I could do, he could only suggest the Berlitz School. Perhaps they would accept a student for two weeks. I knew enough to know that Berlitz was not a finishing school—but it *was* a French school. I enrolled at Berlitz.

It took little time to carry out my mission for the John Graham Company. When I was not in class I rode the buses of Paris from Montmartre to Montparnasse, drinking in the lights and gaiety, or traveled by *Métro*, thumbing a French-English dictionary. I studied hard. No one would ever again hear me make a fool of myself saying Channel or de*bunt*ees or Champs Ilissees.

When I thought of Monte my mind revolved helplessly. His words could only mean that he was preparing, in his cautious, businesslike fashion, to propose marriage. And if he proposed, how dared I think of saying no? Who was I to turn down a chance to be rich, to have security for the remainder of my life, to push aside in one glorious stroke the deprivation, the helplessness and humiliation of the poor, the dreariness and hopelessness and squalor, the scraping, grasping, soul-chilling existence of the East End? Then I thought of Johnny. All sorts of outrageous fantasies flooded through my head. Perhaps Monte would die after I married him and then I would have two million pounds and I could marry Johnny and repay his sister and we would live happily forever after. But suppose Johnny, noble Johnny, were to spurn me for what I had done? Then my sacrifice would be in vain and I would be a widow, at eighteen, despicable and unloved—I could reach no conclusion.

At the end of two weeks I wasn't ready to return to London. If I could remain another two weeks at Berlitz I was sure I'd make tremendous progress. And I couldn't face what I had to face in London. Not yet. I wrote Johnny asking to stay another fortnight. I was studying at Berlitz to better myself. Perhaps, I wrote, I might stumble on a sensational bargain in fancy goods that would more than pay for the extra time.

The telegram I received was brief. "Impossible send you more money."

I remember folding it and placing it in my purse and slowly walking down the Boulevarde des Italiens, thinking miserably, I'll have to go back, I must go back.

When I returned to my room to pack, a special-delivery letter awaited me. It was from Monte Collins. When I opened it a bank draft fluttered out for one hundred pounds. "My dear Lily," he had written. "I am sending you this money because it occurred to me that while you are in Paris you may wish to buy some clothes. I should like you to use it all on clothes to please yourself. On your return I shall have a very important question to ask you."

From the lowest depths of despondency I was rocketed to ecstasy. One hundred pounds! Suddenly I saw Monte with new eyes. For a quick, infinitesmal moment, for the space of a heart beat, the door to the future had opened, only a fraction of an inch, to emit only the tiniest quiver of light—but how bright, how blindingly bright that future! I thought no more. I began buying clothes. I enlisted a girl in my Berlitz class to take me to fine shops where I spent every penny of what was then equivalent to five hundred dollars, today to more than three times that much. It was a fortune to spend selfishly.

I glutted myself. All my life I had been limited to dark shades, because they were more practical. The poor could not afford light colors. I bought a shimmering white evening gown flecked with silver, a pale blue dress, a beige coat with a lynx collar, and a light blue coat with gloves, hats, and shoes to match. I knew nothing about style or texture— away from cotton, flannel, and serge I was lost— but I knew enough not to clash colors.

My wardrobe complete, I marched into the Paris salon of Elizabeth Arden. I was terrified by the aloof attendants who seemed to wither me with a glance, to know instantly that I was Lily Sheil, orphan and skivy, but I spoke up. "I want my face massaged." I ordered every service available, from a pedicure to a facial guaranteed to remove wrinkles. Then I took a tremendous and, for me, daring step. I had my hair bobbed. I sat in the chair at Elizabeth Arden's and watched my golden hair fall to the floor about me. I suffered no panic. I thought how far I had come from the orphanage! I would return to London as a new glamorous personality, with new clothes, new face, new hairdo, with the new assurance of my Berlitz School background. To dazzle London. To dazzle Johnny. Above all, to dazzle Monte Collins, as only the future Mrs. Monte Collins could do.

When I finally saw Johnny again, I explained to him that I had used my own savings to remain in Paris. I simply had to complete one month of school. My bobbed hair made him forget any rebuke he might have had in mind.

A day later, dressed in my Paris clothes, I called on Monte. He drew me across the threshold and held me at

arm's length for a moment. Shyly I removed my new coat—
then the hat—and stood there, in my lovely blue dress.

His face lit up. "Very nice, the way your hair is cut," he
said. "Makes you look more grown up. I like it."

I was relieved. "And the dress?"

"Yes," he said. "Turn around."

I turned around.

"Yes, it suits you very much." Then: "My dear, sit
down." He led me to the settee and looked at me thoughtfully. Then, with a ghost of a smile, as he sat next to me,
he said, "I have something for you, Lily." With great de-
liberation he reached into his vest pocket and extracted a
small, square box. Watching my face, he opened it slowly.
I gasped. It was an engagement ring with an enormous
diamond. Still keeping his eyes on my face, he took my left
hand and solemnly, slowly, slipped the ring over the third
finger.

"You will be my wife, Lily," he said.

He did not ask me if I would marry him. There was no
question in his mind but that I would say yes. He was con-
ferring a great favor upon me. I was terribly excited. I
held my hand out, the ring up, and displayed it this way
and that to catch the light. The great square stone caught
fire even in that somber room. I thought, *Why, this must
have cost thousands!* "Oh, thank you, Monte," I breathed.
He put his face to mine and kissed me gently on the lips.
It was the first time.

I nestled against him on the settee, my head on his
shoulder, holding my hand up, watching the diamond
gleam and flash.

He pulled away. "Do you love me?" he asked.

"Oh, yes, Monte," I said. "I do."

"I love you, Lily," he said. He was still rather restrained,
and I was tense, for I had captured a millionaire. I stared,

hypnotized, at the diamond. No one would ever believe it was real.

I heard his voice, quite pleased. "At the same time, I bought you this—" With an effort I tore my eyes from the ring. Monte, watching my face and savoring every moment, was opening a long, narrow black velvet case. I stared—there, against a white satin background, glittered a diamond bracelet. A dozen diamonds, two dozen—I could not count the stones! He slipped the bracelet over my paralyzed hand. And suddenly I was not as excited. I thought—*but I must take him with all this.* My thank-you's sounded strained in my own ears as I exclaimed, "Oh, Monte, this is so wonderful, this is so lovely, I never dreamed—"

He was not finished. From an inside breast pocket, like a pleased Santa Claus, he produced still another narrow black velvet case. In it was a diamond brooch. I was speechless. I had never seen so much wealth before.

"Stand up, Lily," he said, gently. I rose like an automaton and carefully he pinned the brooch to my dress. I stood there emblazoned with diamonds and all I could think of was, *when am I going to see Johnny?* And, *How I wish I could be excited about this. I know it is fantastic, what is happening to me. Fantastic, fantastic, fantastic . . . !*

CHAPTER EIGHT

Eฎฌ sundฎฎ ฎfternoon my fiancé and I rode about the English countryside, looking at houses. He had set the date for the wedding: two weeks after Easter. I was like a woman in a spell. We wandered through huge mansions while agents droned in my ear. I was numb. I had been sentenced to a lifetime as Mrs. Monte Collins, a sentence I dreaded to serve but was powerless to escape. As we left each house Monte asked, "Did you like that? Did you like that?" and once he added, "Lots of room there"—he all but nudged me in the ribs—"for babies!" He chuckled in great good humor. I felt nothing. I was trapped.

Why, I asked myself, did he not sweep me into his arms, hold me tight and kiss me passionately? Perhaps then I might have seen the man through the powder, through the money, and fallen in love with him. But he was saving me; I know now that he who had been so dissolute, who had had so many women, was saving me for the wedding night so that his every touch was chaste and cold and discouraging. It was Johnny—Johnny, who I could not bear to tell about Monte—who kissed me ardently and bolstered

my spirits and made me breathless for love. I would tell
him after the marriage. Then it could not matter.

The denouement, however, came sooner than I expected.

"I'd like you to come to Brighton with me for Easter,"
Monte had said. He had added hastily, "It's perfectly
proper—we'll have rooms on separate floors, of course."

Brighton. This was poetic justice. I had left a skivy: I
would return a lady in silks and jewels.

I lied to Johnny. He was to spend Easter with his sister,
visiting relatives in Wales. What would I do over the holiday? I told him that Ruth Houghton of Gamage's had
asked me to go to Brighton with her for the weekend.

When Monte and I arrived in Brighton, we registered
at the resort's finest hotel, the Metropole, my room on the
third floor, his on the fourth.

We went down to dinner our first night. I dressed carefully. I wore my shimmering white evening gown flecked
with silver. My diamond brooch glittered on my left
shoulder; my diamond bracelet gleamed on my wrist: my
diamond ring flashed on my engagement finger. We entered the dining room and gracefully, regally, I followed
the deferential maître d'hôtel—with Monte bringing up the
rear—to a choice table at the edge of the small dance floor.
We sat down and ordered. I looked about at the dancing
couples. We knew no one. I thought, with a heavy heart,
I'm bored already and we have only begun our holiday.

Suddenly I felt a slow hot flush creep up my face. It was
incredible. I was staring directly at Johnny, seated alone
at a small table along the wall. He sat less than twenty feet
away and he was looking directly at us with an expression
on his face that was beyond description. What could he be
thinking! I sat, paralyzed.

At that moment Johnny rose deliberately and made his

way relentlessly to our table. He did not look at me. Courteously, in his low voice, he addressed Monte: "I know this lady. May I dance with her?"

Monte, taken aback, shot a sharp glance at me, then at Johnny. He was surprised, annoyed, suspicious. "All right," he muttered.

Johnny held out his hand to me. I turned to Monte. Hardly knowing what I was doing, I pulled off my ring and pressed it in Monte's hand. "Hold it! Hold it for me!" I blurted. "He doesn't know we're engaged!"

And I went into Johnny's arms.

He maneuvered me to the center of the floor. "Who gave you these jewels?" he demanded.

"That man did," I gasped. "We're engaged." I could only make a clean breast of it. "He wants to marry me."

Monte's table was still in sight as we turned on the floor. I saw him watching me as a cat watches a mouse, watching every movement of my lips, my eyes, watching Johnny as he held me, as he danced with me. Suddenly I knew that I could not marry Monte, millions or not. I clung to Johnny. "Do you really want to marry me?" I whispered in his ear.

He stopped for a moment, as though struck. Then he held me tighter.

"Yes," he said. "Yes, Lily!"

"When?"

"Right away!"

I nodded. "All right. Let's get married right away."

We stopped dancing. Johnny escorted me to my table, bowed to Monte, and walked out of the dining room. I was to telephone him in the morning.

I sat down, trembling.

Monte said, ominously, "Lily, what is this man to you?"

"He's Major Gillam, the man I work for," I faltered.

"The man you work for?" Monte ground the words out. He made them ugly. "Why, that man's in love with you. Anyone can see it." He grabbed my hand, hard. "What has been going on behind my back?"

It was too much. I exploded. "If you think there's anything between me and my boss—" I tore off the diamond bracelet and threw it at him. "I gave you back your ring," I cried. "Now you can have your bracelet, too!" My fingers shook so that I could hardly unfasten the brooch. "And this, too!" I shouted, sending it sliding across the table. "I never want to see you again!" I jumped up and rushed out of the dining room. I was too agitated to wait for the elevator. I ran about distractedly until I found the service stairs and dashed up to my room and locked the door. I sat on my bed, shaking. My mind was in a whirl. I was furious at myself for having been so greedy, at Monte for having tempted me, at Johnny for not having swept me off my feet long ago. Over and over I re-enacted the scene in the dining room. I had made such a tremendous gesture— throwing away a millionaire for a man I knew was going broke. Yet I was thrilled that I was going to marry Johnny. I was in love with him. It was as simple as that. I would marry the man I loved.

I did not undress that night. All night long I sat on the bed, excited, disturbed, swept by fits of trembling, alternately happy and frightened. I reviewed every word I had said, Monte had said, Johnny had said, but never once asked myself, am I doing the right thing? I had done it. The very audacity of my act, of what I had given up, took my breath away. I felt a little regret about the brooch. I couldn't have kept the ring or bracelet, but I might have kept the brooch. . . .

At one point in that long night I looked up to see dawn coming through the window. I had to talk to Johnny: I called him. He came to my room, we breakfasted and, so that I could tell him everything without interruption, we went for a long bus ride. Johnny listened sympathetically, shaking his head. "I never had any idea—why didn't you confide in me? You could never have married that terrible man!" But when I spoke of our marriage, Johnny said, a little uncomfortably, "I really should tell my sister first."

"No, Johnny," I said. I was afraid she would be furious and even stop the marriage.

We agreed that we would go at once to London, be married in a registry office, and immediately return to Brighton for our honeymoon—the remainder of our holiday.

How had he happened to be in Brighton? Why was he not in Wales?

He had been about to go. Suddenly the prospect bored him. He longed to see me. He came to Brighton, registered at the Metropole, and spent the entire day searching for Miss Houghton and me in every little pension and side-street hotel. Finally, utterly dejected, he had returned to the Metropole for dinner. He looked up from his menu just as I made my entrance—ablaze with diamonds, preceded by a bowing head waiter and followed by a shuffling, heavy-set man with bags under his eyes. "I was dumbfounded," Johnny said. "I was sure you were a fallen woman. Lost, ruined, gone forever from me—"

When we returned from the bus ride I found a note under my door. It was from Monte: "My dear Lily. I am very unhappy and deeply disappointed, as I do not need to tell you. If you have an explanation I am willing to hear it."

I could reverse it all now, I could make it up with Monte Collins.

I let the moment pass.

Ten minutes later Johnny and I were in a taxi bound for the station and the London train.

At eleven o'clock that morning we stood before the clerk in the Henrietta Street Registry Office near Covent Garden, with two charwomen as witnesses. They leaned their mops against the wall, dried their hands on their aprons, and stood smiling at our sides. I wore the pale blue suit I had bought in Paris with Monte's money. I felt a pang at the thought. Yet it was far more honorable for me to marry Johnny than to marry Monte without loving him.

At three minutes after eleven I was Mrs. John Graham Gillam.

I trembled as the clerk droned the words. But I was very happy. Until now it had been Lily Sheil alone against the world, a very uncertain world. Now it was the two of us, together, Johnny and me.

Book II

CHAPTER NINE

It was 8:00 a.m. The morning sun shone brightly through the bedroom window of the cozy service flat we'd taken in Oxford Street. Johnny slept peacefully. I rose, dressed, extracted two shillings from the loose change he had left on the dresser, and slipped out. I was a lady of leisure. For the first time I had nothing to do but enjoy myself. As his wife, Johnny made clear, he could not permit me to work in the office any longer.

I sauntered through the streets. *Mrs. John Graham Gillam!* I rolled the name on my tongue. Even after a month I was not used to it. *Wife of Major John Gillam, D.S.O.* A woman of position. I stepped into a candy shop, bought fourpence worth of toffee and strolled on, sucking on it.

I was happy. To be sure, there had been one difficult episode—Johnny had been reluctant to break the news of our marriage to his sister. I realized that he feared her far more than I had known. Yet she would never forgive us if she learned it elsewhere. Would I, Johnny had asked the day after we returned from our honeymoon, pay a call upon her and tell her? He was sure that I could win her over.

I had been afraid but, as always, when I had an unpleasant duty to do, I did it. I prepared carefully. I wore a conservative suit, little make-up, brushed my hair severely back, and armed with a discreet bag and quiet, elegant gloves, I called upon Mrs. William Gillam Ashton. Johnny rehearsed me, saying unhappily, "I shouldn't be sending you, you're so young, but I know that when she sees you she'll be captivated as I was—"

My heart pounded as I rang the bell of her flat in a quietly expensive apartment house in Knightsbridge. A prim little maid ushered me inside. I waited in the drawing room, sitting on the edge of my seat. Presently a door opened and I recognized the woman who had hung so proudly on Johnny's arm when he emerged from Buckingham Palace with his D.S.O. I rose. "I'm Lily Sheil from the office," I said.

She held out her hand. "Oh, yes. My brother has spoken of you." She told me to sit down and then took an armchair and looked at me inquiringly.

The speech I had rehearsed vanished completely. I didn't know how to begin. I said, falteringly, "I hope this won't—" I was stammering—suddenly all Cockney in my attempt to be elegant—so that I heard myself say, "I 'ope this won't come as too gryte a shock—" I saw her grow tense, her hands begin to grip the arms of her chair, "John and I were married last Saturday."

She exclaimed, "Oh, no!" and burst into tears. I didn't know what to do. I got up awkwardly and went to her as she wept. "Oh, well it isn't that awful, really it isn't—" I said, consolingly. I patted her on the shoulder as though she were a child. I had no idea what I was doing. "I'm going to make him a good wife, I am. Don't cry, please don't cry—"

She looked up at me through her tears. "I'll never see him again as long as I live and you can tell him that." She had control of herself now. She blew her nose. "I don't blame you, I blame him. You know he's going bankrupt, don't you? He won't get another penny from me."

I said, "He's very unhappy, Mrs. Ashton, he doesn't want to hurt you. He loves you very much."

She rose, near tears again. "You can tell him this for me"—by now her voice became a scream—"I will never see him, I am finished with him. If he wants money let him go bankrupt! He has made his bed, let him lie in it." She turned her back and hurried out of the room.

I picked up my bag and gloves and left.

Johnny was most upset. Now I had to comfort him. "Don't worry," I said. "Somehow we'll manage without your sister." He smiled at me. "Oh, I'll make it up with her sooner or later," he said. 'Of course we'll manage. It's spring, I expect a first-rate season—" He rose, full of vigor. "By Jove, you'll see!"

I kissed my Johnny.

Now, still sucking on my toffee, I passed a fruiterer's. Bunches of huge black grapes glistened in the window. I promptly bought half a pound and munched them as I walked. It was so glorious to indulge yourself. Fresh fruit— a delicacy we rarely received at the orphanage—still overwhelmed me. For the rest of my life I would never be able to get enough.

I stood looking into a familiar window. WE RENOVATE YOUR ANCESTORS. Johnny had many family photographs to decorate the walls of our flat. I had none. I remembered the faded snapshot of myself that had been found in my mother's purse. I recalled Johnny's adorable childhood photograph. Just then my eyes fell upon a pair of identically framed photographs, in color: someone's children. Suddenly I was inspired. Why couldn't I have my snapshot renovated, then colored like Johnny's?

Later that day I hurried to the engraver with both photographs. Could he renovate this little girl? And match her to this little boy? And instead of the cheap, high-necked apron, dress her in fashionable clothes of the time? And in color?

He nodded. "We'll keep the head, fix up the hair, put a nice dress on the body. We'll have her on a chair instead of a table—you just leave it to me."

I asked, "Wouldn't a rich little girl of that time be holding something more elegant than a wooden spool?"

He pursed his lips in thought. "How would you like a flower?" he asked.

A week later I emerged triumphantly from his shop. Here was a lovely, antique-framed photograph of Johnny, a blond-haired little prince of a boy. And here was a photograph, identically framed—to all intents taken by the same photographer—of me. I sat, not on a table, but an expensive elaborately carved chair. I wore a fragile blue frock with puffed princess sleeves, my hair was blond and in curls, my eyes were blue, and in my hand I held a daffodil. In the original photograph the corners of my mouth drooped unhappily: now, by the magic of dress and background, I appeared pouting and petulant, as might be expected of a disdainful and aristocratic little girl.

"A topping idea!" was all Johnny could say in admiration when I showed him the photographs. He watched as I hung them side by side. I gloated over mine. I still might not have photographs of my ancestors, but now proof hung on my wall, for all to see, that I had been a well-kept, well-tended, pink-and-white little girl of gentle birth.

Johnny thought it commendable of me to try to better myself. "There's no telling what heights you'll reach," he would say. "There's nothing you can't achieve if you set your mind to it."

I believed him. But what was it I wanted to achieve? Those first few months I was content to explore London, to buy on impulse whatever sweets I saw and, in the evening, to window shop with my handsome husband at my side.

One evening, as we passed a milliner's window, I stopped and exclaimed, "Oo—er! Wot an 'at!" Johnny actually winced. "Lily," he said, almost sharply, "We've got to do something about the way you talk." I was on the edge of tears. Was he ashamed? Was he humiliated by my speech, now that I was Mrs. Gillam? He had found it amusing before. "Look, darling," he began again, kindly, "You will be meeting people now and I don't want you to be embarrassed. Don't ever say 'oo-er!' or 'lum-me!' Say nothing unless you can start the sentence from the beginning. And if you say something, make a comment that reflects what you think. Not, 'Wot an 'at!' but, 'Isn't that a beautiful hat!' or,"—his good humor had returned—" 'I'd love to have a hat like that.' "

He was right. I thought, when I meet his friends, one wrong word and I'll give myself away. My renovated photograph will be ridiculous then.

I brooded about it, the more so because my idleness was suddenly beginning to bore me. Even unlimited toffee had begun to pall. Except for the weekends when we went to Brighton, where we hired horses and Johnny taught me to ride, my days seemed to pass with maddening slowness.

I tried to hide my dissatisfaction, but Johnny came home one day to find me crying. "I'm so lonely," I wailed. "I don't know what to do with myself."

So it was Johnny who came up with the proposal—again, one of his characteristically breath-taking gestures—suppose he were to enroll me in the Royal Academy of Dramatic Art? Kenneth Barnes, the director, knew Johnny from the Birmingham Repertory. A speech course would work wonders for me, Johnny went on enthusiastically; and though he failed to make a stage career, why couldn't I? "You're clever, you're beautiful," said my champion. "Why can't you be trained for the stage?"

I was thrilled. I could hardly believe him. Yet, if Johnny was so confident, perhaps I *could* become an actress. I might even earn some money to help my husband pay his debts. For though Johnny had avoided the bankruptcy his sister had predicted, he was still in financial straits. More than once I had come home to find an ultimatum from our landlord about the rent and a distressed Johnny: "You're so persuasive—will you go and see him?" I had gone to the landlord and won an extension.

I applied at the Academy the same day as a plump, clumsy man in his late twenties who seemed even more inept than I. In the anteroom waiting for his interview he sat down on his hat. Later, ready to leave, he suddenly clapped his hand to his head—where was his hat?—and began looking everywhere, only to find it, crushed, on his own chair. Red-faced, he snatched it up, glanced furtively this way and that and, apologetically, sidled out while everyone tittered. But after he gave his first reading in class none of us tittered at Charles Laughton. He was the Academy's star pupil.

Even today I do not know why I was accepted. I had no dramatic ability, I was inordinately self-conscious and absolutely terrified to open my mouth. I can only imagine that Mr. Barnes was obliging Johnny.

My most painful ordeal came in a drama course taught by Nancy Price, a distinguished character actress. Each student was to deliver a brief speech from *Romeo and*

Juliet. When my turn came I rose and launched into Juliet's lines:

> O, swear not by the me-uen, th' inconstant me-uen,
> That monthly changes in her circled orb—

Miss Price spoke up sharply. "Mrs. Gillam, please. It is not me-uen. It is *moon.* Say 'moon.' "

I said, "Me-uen." Under stress my accent grew worse.

Miss Price shook her head. "Say, 'It is noontime.' "

I said, "It is ne-uen time."

"Really!" Miss Price was growing annoyed although she knew that a Cockney accent is almost impossible to eradicate. She ordered me to stand before the class, made up of some thirty supercilious young men and women, many of them university graduates, and repeat, "Moo—moo—moo." I was on the verge of tears.

Later, in Johnny's arms, I wept. "Now, now—" he comforted me. "We'll practice." He had me stand in front of the mirror and go over my most troublesome vowels. Again and again he drilled me. "You open your mouth too widely," he said, finally. "Have you observed well-bred people when they speak? They hardly move their lips. Try it."

Though this helped, I had the greatest difficulty. Sometimes my speech became too refined. One day I heard myself say to Laughton, who had been away ill, "I do hoop you feel better—" I wanted to sink through the floor.

In one class I played the Queen to Laughton's King, in *Hamlet.* I was so impossible that I was replaced after one run-through.

The only course I did well in was miming. I played the rear end of a bucking horse and because no one saw my face and I had no lines, I managed to be quite funny.

At the Academy I learned about make-up. I learned

how to enter a room, and I did improve my speech. But it was a wretched time. After my *Hamlet* fiasco, one girl said, "Mrs. Gillam, with your pretty face you shouldn't attempt Shakespeare—you ought to be in musical comedy." I smiled and took it as a compliment but I knew she meant, "With your 'me-uens' and 'ca-ows' you're ridiculous trying to do Shakespeare." The farce ended after three months when I received a severe note from Mr. Barnes which closed with the warning, "It is imperative that you improve."

To Johnny I said, "I won't go back. It's better to quit than be thrown out." Maybe that girl was right, I told him. I might do well in musical comedy. After all, I was good at miming, I loved to sing and dance—and everyone said I was pretty.

My husband agreed. It would be most helpful if I could get a stage job and bring money in—most helpful. I took a long look at this man I had married. He was sweet, adorable, generous—but my future would be precarious if I trusted it to him. I must prepare for some kind of career to help us both.

Johnny optimistically borrowed more money from a loan company and I immediately enrolled for lessons in ballet, tap dancing, and voice. Furiously I studied and practiced all day, singing and dancing about the flat as I did my housework. I practiced ballet steps using the kitchen table as a bar, and squatting exercises with the bedpost as a support. At the end of the first month I announced, "Johnny, I think I'm ready for a job," and prepared to make the rounds of the musical-comedy shows. As I was about to leave he cautioned me, "Don't apply as Mrs. Gillam, Lily. It will hold you back. No producer wants to hire a housewife."

"But I can't go as Lily Sheil," I said. "I hate it. It's everything I want to forget." Not even Johnny knew how strongly I felt about my name—how unmistakably it seemed to blare to all the world the poverty and squalor of my childhood, the humiliation of my upbringing.

"Well," Johnny said thoughtfully, "we'll have to find another name for you." And in that moment, while I waited, he invented one. From Miss Houghton's Sheilsy he produced Sheila, and added, Graham, his middle name. I tried it on my tongue and liked it. He wrote it on a pad: "Sheila Graham."

We both studied it. I took his pencil and added an "h" to "Sheila."

"Why that?" asked Johnny.

"I don't know," I said happily. "It just looks more elegant."

But getting a job, even as a chorus girl, was harder than I thought. For a week I made the rounds without success. Then, at the Strand Theatre, I walked in at the right moment. Archie de Bear, whose show, *Punchbowl,* was to close in three weeks after a long run, had just lost a chorus girl through illness. He looked me over.

"Can you kick?"

"I can," I said.

"How high?"

"This high." I kicked with all my might.

"Well," he said, not enthusiastically. "All right, you go on, Monday." Salary: three pounds.

This was Friday. I had the week end to learn a dance routine. I rushed back. "This is it!" Johnny exclaimed jubilantly. "This is the beginning. You're going to be a star. All London will ring with your fame!"

"Oh, Johnny," I said, and we began practicing. At one point I had to be twirled on the shoulders of a chorus boy.

He was to stand with knees bent, hands cupped before him close to his body: I was to run, leap into his hands, he would twist me around and up and I'd be standing on his shoulders. We practiced it in our bedroom, Johnny and I. Time and again I bowled him over and we crashed to the floor, laughing and crying. But I learned it.

"Remember," said Johnny, as he brought me to the stage door. "Always smile. No one can withstand your smile."

I was terrified—actually trembling with fright—but Johnny's confidence buoyed me. He stood, a tower of strength, in the rear of the theater, where I could see him. On stage I tried to keep in step by watching the feet of the chorus girl next to me. I concentrated with great care. Suddenly I realized that my head was down and I was frowning. *Oh, I'm supposed to smile,* flashed through my mind. I looked up suddenly and beamed at the audience, then looked down—and never got back into step again. The dance mistress was merciless. Later I wailed to Johnny, "Oh, I was such a failure!"

"No, you weren't," he said stoutly. "That time you looked up and smiled, it broke the heart of the whole audience." I was touched, though I was sure all anyone noticed was a most inept girl out of step.

Three weeks later, as scheduled, *Punchbowl* closed, but not before I had a new triumph. At the annual Motor Show Ball held at the Albert Hall, I won the London Theatre Beauty Trophy—a silver cup—as the most beautiful chorus girl in London. Girls were entered from every show: we danced the Charleston and black bottom, then paraded before the judges. My cup was engraved with my name, Sheilah Graham, and the legend: BE FAITHFUL BE BRAVE AND O BE FORTUNATE. I walked home in a trance.

What now? My award filled me with confidence. *Anything* might be possible—if, as Johnny had said, I put my mind to it. Johnny, absolutely delighted, recalled that John Drinkwater, the playwright, whom he knew through the Birmingham Repertory, was a friend of C. B. Cochran, the noted musical-comedy producer. Cochran was the Ziegfeld of London: to be one of Cochran's Young Ladies was to be as glorified as a Zeigfeld Girl. Johnny, in a letter eloquently describing my beauty and talent, persuaded Mr. Drinkwater to write in my behalf to the producer. The result was an invitation to audition before Mr. Cochran himself at the London Pavilion, where he was preparing a new revue.

I hurried there bringing the music from *Rose Marie*, which I had been studying in my voice lessons, and my brief costume from *Punchbowl*. There, in the darkened theater, sat Mr. Cochran with three aides. Several other girls had just completed their auditions. When my cue came, I walked on the empty stage and launched into, "Rose Marie, I love you—"

After half a stanza one of Mr. Cochran's aides called out: "That's enough. Let's see you dance."

I danced several turns in thick silence and then, utterly dejected, almost stole off the stage. I had reached the wings when a high, thin voice which could only be Mr. Cochran's said, "Get the name of that last girl."

I wheeled and dashed back on stage and shouted into the dark expanse of seats, "Oh, Mr. Cochran, I'm the girl! I'm Sheilah Graham and you had a letter from John Drinkwater about me."

There was a silence. Then Cochran's voice: "Will you come down into the stalls, please?"

I went down into the stalls. Mr. Cochran was portly, with a red, cherubic face and bright blue eyes. He said,

"Sit down, my dear, next to me." He looked at me appraisingly. I was very round and firm and fully packed. "Well—" he began.

"I don't want to be just a chorus girl, Mr. Cochran," I interrupted him. "I want to be something better than that."

He looked at me again, slightly amused. I knew I was being brash, but I wanted him to know that though I might be the most beautiful chorus girl in London, I was not a chorus-girl type.

Mr. Cochran said slowly, "I shall have a small chorus— every girl will be able to show what she can do." On his face I recognized the look I'd seen on the faces of my customers at Gamage's.

He hired me at a salary of four pounds a week for the chorus line of *One Dam Thing After Another,* a new Rodgers and Hart show. I was on my way!

CHAPTER TEN

In her dressing room at the London Pavilion I sat at the feet of the great Mimi Crawford, star of *One Dam Thing After Another*. "How do you become a star?" I asked her, anxiously.

She was so sure of herself, this dainty, pale blond beauty with enormous blue eyes in a little heart-shaped face. She said, "Think of nothing else when you're on stage except your part. Just concentrate on that and you'll be a success."

I took her advice. I was third from the right in the chorus and I needed only to keep in step, smile, and pirouette at the right time, but every moment off stage I stood glued in the wings and studied Mimi Crawford. I followed her every movement, the turn of her head, the coquettish glance of her eyes, the twinkling toe, the seductive turn. I had convinced myself that I would be her understudy. I cannot explain why: no one had given me the idea. But it seemed to me then that my ambition would burst without something to cling to. Stardom was something to cling to. And I continued my furious lessons in dancing, ballet, voice.

My concentration on her part got on Miss Crawford's nerves. Finally she informed William Ring, the stage man-

ager, "If you don't get that girl out of the wings, I won't
go on." Mr. Ring allowed me to watch from another
vantage point. I memorized her entire part, learned her
songs, including one I loved to sing at home to Johnny:

Mary Make-Believe,
Dreams the whole day through,
Mary Make-Believe,
Cried a little up her sleeve,
Nobody claimed her,
They only named her,
Mary Make-Believe.

Johnny, as always, encouraged me. If there was no limit
to my ambition for myself, there was even less to Johnny's
ambition for me. He came to each show, to stand in the
rear of the stalls, applauding wildly, and to call for me
after the show at the stage door. Our marriage remained
a secret. To the girls, Johnny had been introduced as my
uncle, an affectionate elder relative who was my constant
escort and chaperone.

Concealing the truth, however, led to unexpected com-
plications. Presumed single, I was fair game for the young
men about town, by whom Mr. Cochran's Young Ladies
were highly esteemed. We all received dinner invitations
from London's gay blades and young peers. For the girls
this was their shining opportunity: more than one had
gone from a Cochran chorus to become mistress of a great
estate and possessor of a proud name. But invariably I
refused all invitations. Even when Elsa, a lovely brunette
who took a liking to me, asked me on double dates, I had
to say, no.

One evening Elsa, with a triumphant smile, passed a
calling card to me. It read Sir John Carewe-Pole, Bart. On
the other side was written in a fine hand:

It is said that you do not accept invitations and will make no exception. I have wagered with my regiment to the contrary! I shall be deeply honoured if you will have supper with me next Saturday.

J.C.-P.

Elsa watched me as I read it. I shook my head. "Now Sheilah, really," she exclaimed. "You can't turn him down. He's the handsomest man in the Guards! You can't spend the rest of your life with your uncle!"

Johnny and I discussed the matter seriously. Sooner or later I must accept an invitation—or else disclose our marriage. What should I do?

"I think you'd better say yes to Carewe-Pole," Johnny said finally. He spoke not as a husband but as a patron to a protégé. "It might be an excellent experience for you to be the guest of someone like Sir John Carewe-Pole. He'll undoubtedly take you to Ciro's and you'll have a topping time and dance to your heart's content. I'm sure he's an honorable fellow. You're young—why shouldn't you enjoy yourself?"

When Saturday came, waiting for me at the stage door was a tall, dark-haired man with a small clipped mustache. He was extremely handsome in white tie and tails. He bowed and announced, "Miss Graham, I'm John Carewe-Pole. Very sporting of you to accept my invitation." He conducted me to a taxi and helped me in.

We rode in silence. I was very ill at ease. I had never been with a Sir before. Did one speak or wait until spoken to?

My escort turned to me with a charming smile. "I enjoyed your show—very much."

I wanted to say something more gracious than, "Thank you," but I could think of nothing. "Thank you," I said.

"Your dance in the first number—" he went on smoothly. "You stood right out, Miss Graham. Quite."

I was silent. "It's nice of you to say so," I said. Johnny had once used that phrase.

He said, "You know, you're very pretty—but other men must have told you this." I nodded, uncomfortably.

"How long have you been on the stage?" "About three months," I murmured. Now apprehension was added to my discomfort. I did not like being questioned.

"Three months? Well." He smoothed his mustache. I felt his eyes on me. "Must be a fascinating life, what?"

I said, carefully, choosing words with vowels I was sure of, "Yes, it is. But it's not as easy as it looks. I must rehearse every day and take dancing and singing lessons—"

He listened courteously. "Never thought of it that way, you know." He was silent again. Then unexpectedly, "Did you do anything before the stage?"

I racked my brain, almost in panic. If only he would kiss me so I wouldn't have to answer any more questions! I managed to make some kind of reply.

When we arrived at our destination—it was Ciro's—I ordered grapefruit, which I had always associated with elegance, then sole and coffee and a chocolate éclaire. Sir John ordered champagne with dinner. I ate with painstaking care. Then we danced, mainly in silence. He saw people he knew and bowed to them. I saw no one I knew. Then he sat down again. The silence was agony.

The evening ended, we bid good-by to each other. I had had my dinner and dance at Ciro's. He had won his wager. I never saw Sir John Carewe-Pole, handsomest man in the Guards, again.

Mimi Crawford continued in excellent health and I bided my time. Just before the end of November all of

Cochran's Young Ladies were assigned to the lobby of His
Majesty's Theatre to sell programs for a charity show. I
took my place with the others. A man strolled by and I
accosted him: "Buy a program, sir?"

He was a thin, rangy man with a long nose, long face,
long chin. "I'd be happy to," he said. He shot a quick
glance at me. "Don't I know you? I'm sure I've seen you
before—"

I was sure that I had never seen him before. A little
distantly, I said, "I'm Sheilah Graham. I'm one of Mr.
Cochran's Young Ladies."

He said, still gazing at me thoughtfully, "I'm A. P.
Herbert." My haughtiness changed to awe. I had read
about this man. He was the well-known writer for *Punch*,
and author of comic operas on the London stage.

"I have it!" His face brightened. "I've seen you with a
man in the reading room of the British Museum. Now,
what on earth would one of Cochran's Young Ladies be
studying in the British Museum?"

I blushed. Mr. Herbert had seen Johnny and me. Johnny
had gone to research for a newspaper article he hoped to
sell. I had spent the time reading an unexpurgated edition
of *The Arabian Nights*, which I found naughty and fascinating.

"I read a great deal," I replied, evading his question.
"I'm preparing myself to be a star."

"Really?" He looked at me with interest. How was I
preparing myself? I began to tell him something of my
lessons, my desire to better myself, my dream of starring in
musical comedy. "Why don't you let me hear you sing," he
suggested. "Perhaps I can help you." He added that he
would drop in to see our show at the Pavilion.

"Oh, please do," I said. "You'll recognize me—I'm the
third from the right."

A few days later he sent a message backstage at the Pavilion asking if he might call on me one afternoon with a few of his songs. Johnny approved: A. P. Herbert was an excellent person for me to know. On the afternoon Mr. Herbert visited me, Johnny discreetly took himself to the cinema. I was proud to usher Mr. Herbert into our little flat. Somewhere I had read that black was fashionable and I had had our sitting room walls done in black wallpaper covered with little orange butterflies. It was busy and dreadful but I thought it very smart.

Mr. Herbert was the essence of charm. He sat at our rented upright and I sang his songs. "Very good," he said encouragingly. "By all means keep up your voice lessons." He looked at the photographs on the wall and seemed properly impressed. "Who is that?" he asked, indicating a hazy snapshot that Johnny had taken of me on our honeymoon.

Suddenly I had to have more of a family than just me.

"My sister Alicia," I said.

Mr. Herbert stared at it again, then at me. "Amazing! Is she your twin?"

"Oh, no, she's a little older than I am," I hastened to say. "But everyone remarks on the resemblance."

He gazed at my treasure, my renovated childhood photograph hanging in a place of honor side by side with Johnny's. "This is you, of course," he said, to my delight. "And this?" He pointed to Johnny's photograph.

For a moment I was nonplused. Then I thought of Jessie and her little brother.

"My brother David," I said. "He died before I was born."

"Ah, too bad," murmured Mr. Herbert, sympathetically. On a Sunday afternoon a few days later, he came over to play songs from his new operetta. After he ran through them on the piano, he looked at me mysteriously, and announced, "I have written a poem you might like to hear. I call it, 'The Third From the Right.'"

"Oh," I cried. "You've written something about me!"

He grinned, and began to recite:

The Third From The Right

> Mr. Mumjumbo's been telling my bumps,
> And it seems I'm a wonderful girl.
> I'm lovable, kind, ambitious, refined,
> And likely to marry an Earl.
> I've Culture well-marked in my forehead, I hear,
> And Talent for Business just over the ear,
> I'm sure to succeed in some brainy career—
> Well—but why am I still in the Chorus!

I listened, enraptured:

> They all like the third from the right,
> I'm filling the house every night;
> I could act if I once got a chance—
> Well, I've made people think I can dance;
> The public may wish us,
> Just merely delicious,
> But we want to play Desdemona.

> I could be tragic and husky and hoarse,
> Ophelia, perhaps is my part—
> If the manager thinks I'm a butterfly minx,
> I can tell him I live for my Art.
> Sometimes I dream that I'm taking a call,
> Catching the showers of flowers that fall,
> Or acting as Judge at a fancy-dress ball—
> But I wake and I'm still in the Chorus.

I said, with emotion, "You know just how I feel!"

Mr. Herbert, enjoying himself, recited the last stanza:

> They all like the third from the right,
> It's a pity my eyes are so bright,

> For nobody sees that I'm deep,
> A kind of volcano asleep.
> Don't praise my figure,
> I wish it was bigger,
> For I want to play in Grand Opera.

A few weeks later "The Third From the Right" appeared in *Punch*. *I* was immortalized by one of England's most distinguished writers in one of England's most distinguished magazines!

The call came at eleven A.M. Mimi Crawford was ill. I would go on in her stead!

My heart started pounding. I said to myself, don't get frightened. Or you won't be able to do it when the time comes. I rushed to the theater. There Mr. Ring, the stage manager, grabbed my hand. "Thank God, I thought you'd never get here!" He led me to Mimi Crawford's dressing room. Wardrobe women, pins in their mouths, swarmed about me, fitting Mimi's clothes to me. I tried not to think of the ordeal awaiting me—to go out on that stage alone, to stand alone in the brilliant spotlight, singing, dancing, acting, with every eye on me, alone. I dared not think about it: once I let my heart beat too fast, it would choke in my throat and not a word come out. And I thought, this is Johnny's triumph, because the stage had not been my idea, it was all Johnny's.

From the wings I heard the brief announcement: "Miss Mimi Crawford's part in this performance will be taken by Miss Sheilah Graham,"—and the audience's sigh of disappointment.

Then Mr. Ring's tense voice: "Sheilah, ready—two minutes . . . one minute . . . thirty seconds . . . on stage!"

There was an enormous fanfare of music as the overture

began, and I hurried out to stand, trembling, behind the closed curtains. I had to make a grand entrance—come from behind the curtains, part them, and stand there in the spotlight striking a pose, my arms outstretched, my head up—then go into my song. As I stood waiting for my cue I thought frantically, suppose my hands become paralyzed! But no. It was do or die, and I did it. At the right moment I parted the curtains and stood there, in a golden haze, my head up, smiling, knowing only, *don't be frightened, there is no failure, give it everything you have, don't tremble, give them everything—*

There was a wave of applause, a chord from the orchestra, and my voice rang out, clear as a bell:

> The voice of the desert is calling me,
> It constantly calls to me . . .

Then the applause came beating up from the stalls. I rushed back to change. "Jolly good!" from Mr. Ring. "Keep it up!" He hovered over me.

Nothing could go wrong that night. I had no clear idea of what I was doing. I was simply imitating Mimi Crawford down to the tiniest toss of a curl. I moved in that golden haze, I was bathed in applause, in the great wave of affection and admiration flowing to me from the audience.

Unbelievingly I read my first notice in the newspaper the next day: CHORUS GIRL LEAPS TO FAME—this, under my picture. And the story accompanying the photograph began: "Her fair beauty and dulcet voice enchanted a packed house at the Pavilion last evening. . . ."

For seven delirious performances, until Mimi Crawford returned, I played her role. In the midst of it a starry-eyed Johnny brought me the *Daily Express* for August 28, 1927. There was my picture again, and under it the words:

A BORN ACTRESS—

Miss Sheilah Graham is playing a great success in Miss Mimi Crawford's part in *One Dam Thing After Another.* That gifted young lady was not even a recognized understudy but stepped into Miss Crawford's part without even an hour's rehearsal. So successful has she been that she has been promised a speaking part in the next edition of the revue, although she is only a beginner. . . . Mr. Cochran is delighted with her aptitude and told me tonight that he considers her one of the most promising young actresses on the London stage.

It was incredible. I read it, Johnny read and re-read it. He said, "I knew it. Nothing can stop you now. Nothing!"

Mr. Cochran sent me a congratulatory note and enclosed a ten pound bonus. There was also an invitation to call at his office, high above the stage.

"You've done very well, my dear," he said. He was in high humor. I had heard that understudies were often offered leads in touring companies. I risked everything. "I've been offered a chance to go on tour, Mr. Cochran. But if there's any chance of getting out of the chorus for good, I'd like to stay with you."

He came from behind his desk and putting a hand under my chin, he tilted my face up to his, and said softly, "My dear, of course you're going to stay with me. I will make you a star."

I thought, despite my gratification, *Oh dear, how am I going to handle this?* Mr. Cochran was a kind man but he had a reputation with girls. *This man can make me a star. How far do I have to go for it?* I did not want Mr. Cochran to be more than an employer to me. I walked home with a cold weight in the pit of my stomach.

A week later he invited me to join him and a few friends—among them, Frederick Lonsdale, the prominent playwright, and Lady Diana Cooper—for lunch. I went, with Johnny's blessings. At last, I was moving in the right circles! "Watch and listen," he counseled me.

I was agonizingly self-conscious all through the meal. Oh, to be like these people! To speak easily, to be accepted—even more, to be famous! Yet, as I watched and listened, I was strangely disappointed. I sat silent, smiling politely, listening intently, and thinking, is this what they talk about? I had thought such distinguished personalities spoke in lofty, elegant language about matters of the highest importance. But Lady Diana at this moment was saying to another woman, "Did you see what Iris was wearing last night?" And another guest remarked, "God, if I ever hear Louise tell that tired story about the policeman and the American—" I listened to them and learned what small talk was. It was laughing gently and saying. "Well, *this* is a funny piece of cheese, isn't it?" And, "If I don't have my hair done after lunch, I'll be wretched all day—" They spoke about their latest marriages and divorces, about their diets and ailments. I thought, so this is what you talk about when you have nothing to say.

And it came to me, *I can do this*. Even if I stopped school at fourteen and can't open my mouth lest I show my ignorance, or get my *me-uens* wrong, I can do this. All you need to get by, even among the accomplished and the famous, is to speak casually about the trivial— or scornfully about anybody. That is all you need, once you are part of this charmed circle. I *can* become part of it, I thought.

I felt sure of it when, at the close of *One Dam Thing After Another,* Cochran signed me to a three-show contract with a speaking role in his next production, Noel Coward's *This Year of Grace*. I would appear with Jessie Matthews, Tilly Losch and other stars. My contract pro-

vided for ten pounds a week with an increase to twenty
by the third show.

I was able to help Johnny enormously with his mounting debts. I could only marvel that this good fortune had
come to me. I was nineteen, and making more than I had
ever dreamed of.

Johnny was very proud. "I told you," he said. "By Jove,
they're beginning to appreciate you. Now the world will
see in you what I've always seen. There's no limit to what
you can do!"

CHAPTER ELEVEN

M̲ R. NOEL COWARD snuffed his cigarette out. "No, no," he said, impatiently. "That's not the way to do it!" He hurried on stage. "Let me show you."

I had never expected to meet Mr. Coward. But the principals of *This Year of Grace* were rehearsing in a Soho hall when Cochran walked in with this slender, nervous, cigarette-smoking gentleman whom I instantly recognized from his photographs. I became flustered. He'll see right through my sham and *know* that I've had only a few months of dancing and singing lessons. But I had to go ahead, and while he and Cochran took seats in the empty stalls I went through my role with a male lead.

It was then that Mr. Coward bounded up on the stage.

"Here," he said. He took me in his arms. "Now, look at me as though you were disdainful of me—"

I was not sure what disdainful meant, so I promptly turned my most dazzling smile on him.

"No, no, no!" His voice became a thin quaver. I wanted to cry. He threw his hands up and looked at Cochran. I thought, in despair, *he knows I'm a fake.*

Cochran, from his seat, said quietly, "Sheilah, you can do better than that."

We tried again and this time, instead of casting a withering glance at him, I gazed at him soulfully. "Oh, my God," said Coward, and gave up. "Let's go on to the next scene."

Here I was to sing:

> I am just an ingénue,
> And shall be 'till I'm eighty-two,
> At any rude remark
> My spirit winces,
> I've a keen dramatic sense,
> But in girlish self-defense,
> I always put my trust in princes.

I was to have burlesqued the song, lisping the words in wide-eyed innocence. Instead, I sang it seriously. Years later, walking on Sunset Boulevard in Hollywood, I knew exactly how I should have sung it; and when Noel Coward came to Hollywood I sang it for him and he laughed, "Yes, just the way it should have been done." But now he sat glowering in the stalls; and when I glanced in his direction a few moments later both he and Cochran had gone.

We were to open in Manchester. I was tense and nervous. In one number I had to pirouette on my toes, but my insteps were too weak. I could not carry off what had taken others years of practice. Under the long ballet skirt which mercifully hid my bent knees, I staggered about like a drunken man.

Opening night my experience was almost a burlesque of every amateur's nightmare. I was to enter doing high kicks across the stage. The music swelled: I made my entrance: the audience gave me thunderous applause. I glowed with confidence. *I'll show them.* I kicked as high as I could—my left foot slid from under me and I sat down hard, on the stage.

The applause turned to laughter. My face burned as I scrambled to my feet. Now I couldn't get back into step with the music. The laughter turned to roars and shrieks—I staggered across the stage, making half-hearted attempts to kick, my smile frozen on my face, unbearably humiliated, saying to myself, *you can't cry, you can't cry, you have another number, you can't cry.*

Then I was off, rushing into the wings to change to my next costume. Suddenly, I saw stars: I had crashed into a huge, *papier-mâché* rock backstage, used for a Lorelei number. The noise echoed through the entire theater.

That did it. I lay there and cried and cried. Even Cochran, who put his arm comfortingly around me, could not persuade me to go back on stage until the grand finale.

But when we opened in London, three weeks later, luck was with me. *This Year of Grace* was a smash hit, and I with it. The reviews were flattering; my pictures appeared in all the newspapers: "Sheilah Graham Laughs" . . . "Winning Her Way" . . . "Little Sheilah Graham, the chorus girl who has had a romantic rise to fame." And after a few weeks, "Sheilah Graham, one of Mr. Cochran's most charming young ladies, who scores so brightly in *This Year of Grace.*"

And as my luck held, my quandary grew. I was married, my marriage was a secret, and I was going out with men. Sir John Carewe-Pole had been the first. Now Cochran, who exhibited me as his newest star, was taking me out to supper. And many of his friends were asking to meet me. Other invitations came. It was impossible to be starred at the Pavilion without finding yourself surrounded by gallant admirers. Night after night its front boxes, which extended onto the stage, were filled with men in blazing white shirt fronts and tails, who could reach out and touch you if they wished when a whirl or a step brought you next to them. Sometimes the Prince of Wales sat there; but always these boxes were occupied by the most glamorous, the most charming and elegant men in England.

One night two handsome men in the box kept their eyes on me. As I danced by I heard distinctly, "Hello, you pretty little ewe lamb." I smiled and danced on. A week later the box was taken by the same men. Again the odd salutation, "Hello, you pretty little ewe lamb."

That night, after the performance, three limousines waited to take the girls of the cast to a bachelor supper at the Savoy Hotel. Our table partners were officers of the Royal Guards. We sat at a long table with magnificent food and champagne, and gifts for each of us—compacts, lipsticks, silk stockings. Presently a young man wandered over and took the chair next to me. He was introduced: Captain Ogilvy. Later I learned he was the Honorable Bruce Ogilvy, equerry to the Prince of Wales. Then an older man, blue eyed—with a red mustache through which he hissed when he grew excited—came over and sat at my feet. He was Sir Richard North, in his fifties, and our host. Both occupied the front box at the Pavilion. It had been Sir Richard who called me the "ewe lamb." But I ignored him because I was fascinated by Bruce. He was about twenty-eight, strikingly handsome: blue eyes with long black lashes, a straight nose, a clipped Guard's mustache, sharp high cheekbones and a languid expression that seemed full of mischievous amusement. He snorted when he laughed—I found that irresistible.

Would I come to supper again the following Thursday night after the performance? And invite five of Cochran's Young Ladies? Sir Richard wanted to know, too, would

I honor him by taking tea in his town house the following Sunday?

I had discussed all this with Johnny. We reached an agreement. Going out would help my career: it would also be a means by which I would grow and develop and learn to hold my own with the upper classes. So I accepted the invitations of Sir Richard North and Captain the Honorable Bruce Ogilvy.

I was escorted home that first night by both Bruce and Richard, one holding my right hand as we sat in the cab, the other my left. They said good-by at the door. I floated in to tell Johnny my evening's triumph as a girl might tell her mother. I told him how they admired me, how beautiful and desirable they made me feel, how each wanted to see me again, how attractive Bruce was, that his mother, the Dowager Countess of Airlie, was a lady-in-waiting to the Queen. I told him Sir Richard was enormously wealthy, he had great stables in Ireland and loved to ride to hounds and said he had always wished he had a daughter like me. I told Johnny how respectful, how adoring, how charming these men had been. Johnny was more than pleased. His protégé was becoming appreciated in ever higher circles.

Each Thursday evening thereafter I was guest of honor at midnight suppers at the Savoy. I would open the menu to find that every dish had been named for me: *"Potâge à la Belle Sheilah;" "Poulet Polonaise à la Belle Sheilah;" "Bombe à la Belle Sheilah."* I was the ewe lamb, the sacrificial lamb, pursued by the wolves, and it was all done with such high spirits, such charm and insouciance, that it was like a fairy tale.

And I—I wanted to have everything this enchanting life could offer. I went out frequently with Captain the Honorable Bruce Ogilvy, with Sir Richard North. I

danced with their friends in the Irish and Welsh Cold-
stream Guards. And each time I was less gauche, my accent less noticeable. My voice, which had taken on something of Johnny's low, musical quality had now an added
touch of Bruce's quiet drawl—the hallmark of the upper
classes. Now I repeated the chitchat, the small talk I'd
heard when I had lunched with Lady Diana Cooper. It
was more than sufficient, for there were no intellectual
discussions at the Savoy suppers, nor at the other parties I
attended. It was considered bad taste to flaunt one's
knowledge. Just laughter and beautiful compliments and
admiring glances. Now *I* laughed gently and said, "This *is*
a funny piece of cheese, isn't it?" Sometimes I made a
humorous remark and they'd laugh and I'd think, pleased,
well, I can be amusing, too.

In this world nothing was taken seriously. One afternoon I accepted Bruce's invitation to have tea with him
in his mother's flat while she was away in the country.
It was a surreptitious visit. As we sat together, we heard
the front door open and close. We sat, hushed; a few
minutes later Bruce tiptoed to the door and tried it—
and turned to me. "Mother—she's locked it, and I don't
have a key! How are we going to get out?" And suddenly,
in a burst of mirth, "Good God, what will the Queen
say!"

It was an Alice-in-Wonderland world in which Bruce
could report that he had just come from the Guard's mess
hall where the Prince of Wales—he called him "Pragger-
Wagger"—and half a dozen other chaps had spent the
afternoon playing leapfrog over the tables. Or in which,
dancing with Bruce at the exclusive Embassy Club, we
passed His Royal Highness dancing with a lovely young
lady. "Oh Bruce," I whispered, "Dance me close to the
prince." He did. The two men nodded at each other and

H.R.H.'s eyes flickered over me. Later Bruce told me,
"Pragger-Wagger wanted to know who was the beautiful
blonde I was dancing with." "What did you say? I asked,
breathlessly. "I didn't give your name," he replied, with
a mischievous grin. "I don't want him to take you away
from me." Who would have thought it, the Prince of
Wales asking about *me*?

My past was as remote as a stranger's dream. Yet once
I had a narrow escape. One afternoon while waiting with
Elsa for a bus, I heard a voice shout, "Lily! Lily Sheil!"

I almost fainted. I managed to turn. There, hastening
toward me from across the street, held up momentarily
by traffic, was Leslie! Leslie, older, but still Leslie! He
waved excitedly.

For a moment I stood paralyzed. Then I grabbed Elsa's
hand and began running. "Quick—there's the bus coming—"

I was running, Leslie was running after me. It was like
a nightmare in which you are pursued by something un-
imaginably evil, and no matter how fast you run you
seem to be standing still. . . . But we were at the bus, we
clambered onto it, it pulled away. I clung, weakly, to a
support.

I said nothing when I came home to Johnny. He was
trying to forget his financial woes by writing an article on
Easter eggs, which he hoped to sell to a newspaper. He
had sent off many articles and had yet to sell one.

I said, perhaps a little sharply because I was still upset
by my experience, "Oh, Johnny, you're wasting your time.
People aren't interested in Easter eggs."

Annoyed, Johnny flung his pencil down. "Well, what
are they interested in, if you know?"

I thought. "Remember my first night in *Punchbowl*,

when I came out the stage door?" I had rushed down expecting to find the little alley crowded with stage-door Johnnies in evening dress and top hats, with a bouquet of flowers in one hand and diamonds in the other. Instead, there were only two bedraggled teen-age girls waiting for the star's autograph. "I think people would be interested in a chorus girl's experiences."

"By Jove!" He was enthusiastic now. "You have something there." He rubbed his nose. "Why don't *you* write it?"

I was taken aback. Yet, come to think of it, everyone liked my compositions at the orphanage. They had even been read aloud. I sat down with a pencil and a notebook of yellow paper and wrote, "The Stage-Door Johnny, by A Chorus Girl." After my husband corrected my elementary-school spelling and grammar, we sent it to the *Daily Express*. I had already learned to aim for the top and the *Express* was one of London's most widely-circulated newspapers.

Each morning I looked for my article to come back in the mail. Days passed. Finally I could not endure the suspense. At intermission one night I hurried to the backstage telephone and called the *Daily Express,* demanding to speak to the literary editor himself, Mr. Reginald Pound. Unbelievingly enough, he came on the line. "I sent you an article about four weeks ago and it hasn't come back. I want to know if you're going to print it." I gave him the name.

He said, "Odd that you should call tonight. We're using it tomorrow."

I had to sit down. Then I came to my senses. "Tomorrow!" I almost shrieked. "That's wonderful. Will I get anything for it?"

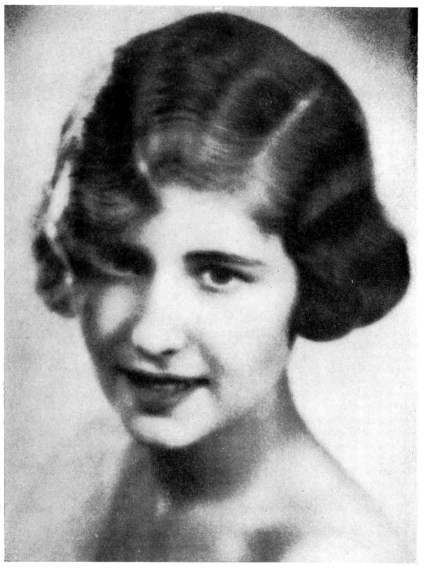

Lily Sheil's first appearance—at 19—as "Sheilah Graham." Ecstatic winner of a silver cup as London's most beautiful chorus girl, and soon to become the toast of London's musical-comedy stage, her true name and background were secrets shared only with her husband, Major John Gillam.

The photographs Sheilah used to document her elaborate myth of gentle birth and loving upbringing. *Left:* This elegant little boy, she told visitors, was her brother David, who died before she was born. Actually, it is a childhood photograph of Johnny

And this elegant little girl (*right*) was Sheilah, herself. Actually, it is a snapshot taken before her orphanage days and "renovated" so that it matched Johnny's: only the pout is real. Dress, curls, and flower were added later by a photographer.

By the time she was 21, Sheilah mixed with England's most exclusive society, attending grouse shoots in Northumberland, skiing with titled gentry in Switzerland. *Above:* At St. Moritz, her arm is about the young Duchess of Devonshire; Sir Samuel Hoare is second, the Honorable Jack Mitford, fourth to her left. *Left:* Sheilah in ski costume—snapshot by Jack Mitford.

On June 9, 1931, Lily Sheil, orphan and skivy, achieved the summit of her social dreams: she was presented at Buckingham Palace to King George V and Queen Mary. What had Johnny said? "There's no limit to the heights you can reach!"

Major John Gillam, winner of the D.S.O. at Gallipoli, resplendent in the court costume he wore the day he escorted Sheilah
to Buckingham Palace.

F. Scott Fitzgerald, as he looked shortly before Sheilah met him in Hollywood in 1937. "I found him most appealing: his hair pale blond, a wide, attractive forehead . . ." When they met, Sheilah was engaged to the Marquess of Donegall. She never married the Marquess.

BOOK MARK (Suggestions about Byron) BOOK MARK

The excerpt from long poems are short because of the fine print. I have never been able to admire but five or six of his short lyrics in comparison to his contemporaries

After chap 2 read The Isles of Greece   Ox. P. 565

After Chap 4   "   Childe Harold   Works
                        Canto III, stanzas 21-28

After Chap 5   "   Maid of Athens   Works P. 59

After Chap 7   "   So We'll go no more   Ox P. 569
                    She Walks in Beauty   Ox P. 569

After Chap 8   "   Don Juan, Canto One   Works
                        C XIII to C XVII

After Chap 10 "   Don Juan Canto Two   Works
                        C LXXII - C LXXVII
                        and Canto Eleven

At End " Once More: The First 3 Stanzas of "The Isles of Greece"
BOOK MARK   BOOK MARK

One of Scott's carefully worked out reading assignments for
Sheilah. The only student in the F. Scott Fitzgerald College
of One, she studied Literature, Politics, Modern and Ancient
History, Philosophy, Religion, Art, and Music. Scott planned
final examinations and graduation exercises for her.

Scott and Sheilah—taken by a sidewalk photographer on their visit to Tijuana, Mexico, early in 1940. "I sat beaming . . . and Scott, in a sombrero with a colorful serape . . . stood beside me, every inch the *caballero*." It was the only photograph they had taken together: he was to die before the year was over.

I heard him laugh. "I have requisitioned payment of two guineas."

In a daze I asked, "When do you print it?"

"Tonight."

"Could I possibly come down and see it printed?"

"Most certainly," he said.

The moment the performance ended, Johnny and I rushed to Fleet Street. Though Mr. Pound had left, there were instructions to take us to the composing room and show us my story in type. I breathed printer's ink for the first time.

That night I could hardly sleep. How magical this was! I had had a *thought*. I had put my thought on paper. They were paying me two guineas for it!

The next day, there was my article on the literary page, opposite the editorial page. I promptly telephoned Cochran and A. P. Herbert: "Don't forget to read the *Express* today. I have an article in it."

Everyone at the Pavilion congratulated me, particularly Mr. Cochran. "There's quite a lot going on behind that pretty face of yours, isn't there?" he said. Mr. Herbert came over to congratulate me and give me tips on the rules of composition. When I sat down again to write, my mind teemed with do's and don'ts. Self-consciously, I wrote four articles, one after another—none sold. I tried a fifth—and when that returned, I gave up. Too many problems were now harrassing me—and perhaps writing wasn't as easy as I thought.

This Year of Grace was the first—and last—of the three shows in my contract in which I appeared. For without knowing it, I was beginning to crumble under pressures growing too great for me.

Mr. Cochran was very attentive; still fatherly, still

jolly, he escorted me frequently to lunch. When we were in cabs, he kissed me. I was in a dilemma: how could I avoid what appeared inevitable? I was anxious, too, about my part in the show: my role had been whittled down, bit by bit, as my lack of experience showed itself. I was obviously inadequate in the more difficult routines. I struggled frantically to keep pace with girls who had been dancing since childhood.

At home Johnny's business problems, though he sought to hide them, weighed heavily. He could not hide the fact that my salary supported us. As it was, our bills were always overdue. I grew increasingly tense. I found myself on a furious merry-go-round, night and day. Morning lessons, afternoon rehearsals, evening performances, midnight suppers, a constant round of entertainment, dancing, food and champagne, and very little sleep. Exhaustion dogged me.

It was becoming harder to maintain my double life—as Sheilah Graham, escorted by Bruce Ogilvy, whom I liked more than I should, C. B. Cochran, who was most solicitous, Sir Richard North, who showed increasing affection toward me—and as Mrs. John Gillam, shopping on Wigmore Street and prevailing upon merchants to wait for their money. I began to suffer excruciating headaches and indigestion so agonizing that it bent me double. Small as my part had become in *This Year of Grace,* I found myself forgetting lines and bursting into fits of uncontrollable weeping.

A song in the show ran through my mind:

> Dance, dance, dance, little lady,
> Youth is fleeting to the rhythm beating in your mind.
> Dance, dance, dance, little lady,
> So obsessed with second best,
> No rest you'll ever find. . . .

I thought, yes, this is me—dancing and dancing, spinning and spinning faster and faster. . . .

At this point Cochran put me in a quandary.

I had prevailed on Johnny to take me to Torquay, a seaside resort, for a weekend of complete rest. "My dear," Cochran said, taking my chin between thumb and forefinger, "wire me where you are staying. I'll come and see you."

After a great deal of agitated thought, how to discourage him without angering him, I sent what I considered an ingenious telegram from Torquay: DELIGHTED SEE YOU OFFICE HOURS ARE NINE TO SIX.

He did not come to Torquay. Back in London I asked, a little apprehensively, "Why didn't you come up as you said?"

He replied curtly, "I didn't like your office hours."

I had lost Mr. Cochran as an admirer. It did not help my peace of mind.

It was Sir Richard, finally, who brought the merry-go-round to a halt. I had lunched frequently with him at his home, a narrow, elegant, gray-brick house in which my main impression was of shining mahogany and gleaming silver, with handsome paintings and hunting prints everywhere. After coffee, Sir Richard would sit on the floor at my feet, stroking my hand and looking up at me with his pale blue eyes. "My little ewe lamb," he would say, and kiss my hand. "I've never had anyone I wanted to take care of as much as you."

Sir Richard had never married. He had retired from the Indian Civil Service and he spoke often of the fact that he had no family, which helped explain the suppers and entertainments he gave so lavishly for young people. He had sent me gifts, enormous quantities of Fortnum and Mason's most expensive prepared foods—cooked salmon, smoked trout and ham, plover's eggs—and once a crate of grapefruit postmarked, "Florida, U.S.A." arrived for me backstage.

On one visit to his home he showed me his collection of prints. He paused in front of a beautifully intricate forest scene, all trees, branches, vines, and leaves. "This is a most unusual French print," he said. "How do you like it?"

Putting on my most intelligent expression, I examined it on the wall. "Oh, it's lovely."

"Look close—do you see anything interesting?"

I shook my head. "But look, my dear—" and there, amid the branches, faintly etched, were naked men and women making love.

I drew back, repelled, and stole a fearful glance at him, but he was smiling down quite pleasantly at me. I thought, isn't it strange when love can be so beautiful that this man should find enjoyment in something like this? Yet he was invariably kind to me, and remarked often on his loneliness. Once he said, smiling, "I'd like to adopt you," and I laughed. The afternoon came, however, when he said it most solemnly. "I mean it. I want to adopt you, legally. You will be my daughter, Sheilah."

I didn't want to be his daughter. When he pressed me at a moment when I was growing more and more distrait, I suddenly blurted out, "You can't, Sir Richard. You can't. I'm married."

There, I thought—it's out. The masquerade is over.

He blanched, then his face reddened. My words seemed to drive him into a strange excitement. He began to hiss through his mustache. "That doesn't matter. You must divorce at once."

"Oh, no no no," I cried. "I couldn't do that."

He went on eagerly as though he had not heard me. "I can arrange it easily. I will be the corespondent—"

I burst into tears and could not stop. He grew extremely distressed. "I'm sorry—I won't insist if you don't wish. Think it over—" He seemed so genuinely upset that I sobbed everything out to him—the weight of concealing my marriage, the struggle to keep up with the girls in the show, my headaches, my indigestion, my exhaustion. He said, "I will have my physician see you at once."

His physician was an associate of Sir Henry Simpson, physician to the Queen. I was examined; Sir Henry himself was called in consultation: I was suffering from extreme exhaustion and was on the verge of a complete nervous breakdown. My indigestion came from an inflamed appendix which must be removed at once. I must leave the show immediately and enter a nursing home. Sir Richard would take care of the expense.

The verdict came as a relief. At last I would be out of this spin. I would be cared for. I entered a fashionable nursing home off Harley Street and Sir Henry performed the operation. Later, Sir Richard said, "You must go to a warm climate to recuperate. I am going to send you to the South of France." When I protested I could not allow him to do so much for me, he brushed my protests aside. It was his pleasure to be able to help me. I could take my husband with me and remain until I felt strong again.

At the Hotel Eden, at Cap d'Ail, in the South of France, I marked my twenty-first birthday with Johnny. He was unhappy, humiliated, resentful—yet he knew we could not afford to foot the bill. "Business is going to get better," he said. "I'm sure of it." He calculated the cost of the doctors, the operation, the nursing home, the hotel, and entered the sum in a little book. "I'll pay him back very soon," he said.

Who could divorce Johnny?

Yet, Sir Richard had come close. My marriage to Johnny was slowly becoming a marriage in name only. I am sure that this contributed to a good deal of my emotional distress. For Johnny had virtually become the affectionate elder relative we pretended him to be: father, mother, brother, confidant. Despite myself, I had begun to long for a husband of my age who would be fiercely possessive, jealous of every man—the lover, not the patron.

The free, uninhibited life of the theater, too, underlined the lack in my marriage. Here love was an enormously exciting thing, a volcanic thing of impulse and emotions run riot. In this unrespectable, impulsive, impassioned world, people were always in love—they kissed and caressed openly; at any moment backstage, as you rushed down a stair or dashed to your dressing room, you came upon a couple in an embrace so close that it seemed nothing could tear them apart.

I had always thought kissing was secret, in the darkness of a garden arbor, in the back of a car, in the privacy of your apartment. In the theater, love was love in the great romantic tradition—you dared all, you gave all without thought of cost or consequences. It was unbearably exciting, a bright, glittering, overwhelming experience—and nobody said, "This is wrong." And when a love affair was over, when the man left as he must, the grief, though overwhelming, was exciting, too. This was the ecstasy of being young and unrestrained, of being gloriously responsive to the quickening of your pulse, to the inviting eyes and proffered hearts of the handsome men who courted you. From all this, to return to Johnny with his problems, to Johnny, who, however sweet, was more like a fatherly counselor than a husband. . . .

CHAPTER TWELVE

Sometimes, as I try to trace cause and effect, I marvel at how one's life is shaped by events. My illness and my recuperation in the South of France took Johnny away from the John Graham Company. His absence led, finally, to the company's bankruptcy when we returned to London in the spring of 1929. Forced to look elsewhere, Johnny was appointed as a national sales representative of a thriving brick-and-cement firm. Here, where personal charm rather than business acumen counted, Johnny did extremely well. For the first time since our marriage, we began to emerge from our financial quicksand.

It was just as well. Now that my marriage was known, it was time to turn a new chapter. In the South of France, Johnny and I had come to a decision. We must extricate ourselves from any further obligation to Sir Richard. I had had time to think about this man. Although Sir Richard had never overstepped the bounds of propriety with me, the curious prints on his walls, his yearning at my feet, his strange excitement at the idea of adopting me— all this disturbed me. I did not want to see him again. I wrote him a letter expressing our gratitude, promising to repay him when possible, but making clear my husband

and I felt it best not to be in his debt any more. We would manage, somehow. Sir Richard, obviously deeply hurt, never replied.

We had only been in London a few days when Cochran called to chide me for keeping my marriage a secret from him. If I wished, he said, there would be a part for me in *Bitter Sweet,* which he expected to produce next. But I was not ready to return to the stage. Perhaps I sensed, without knowing it, that my stage career was over. It had all been, I realized now, a tremendous ordeal.

For the next few months I rested, read, and sat in the sun in Hyde Park, practicing my French on the French nannies who came there every day with their charges. With the little I had learned at the Berlitz School, and the additional experience I'd had in France, I did not speak badly.

And then I met Judith Hurt, who opened a world to me that quite eclipsed everything the stage had to offer.

Miss Hurt and her mother came from Scotland. While we had been away they had moved into the third-floor flat directly above us at 128 Wigmore Street. I began meeting my new neighbor on the stairs—extraordinarily dainty and petite, her face piquant, with the blondest hair, and the pinkest skin and bluest eyes I had ever seen. About my age, she lived a gay social life: young men from Oxford and Cambridge were constantly stamping up and down the stairs and often I caught a glimpse of her, an exquisite figure of a girl, dashing down, her coat floating behind her. We came to know each other when she asked if she might keep her corsages in our refrigerator which stood on the stair landing. She was pretty, unassuming, and friendly, and I liked her immensely.

One afternoon I emerged to take my walk in Hyde

Park just as she and a tall, heavily bespectacled young
man, ice skates slung over their shoulders, came hurrying down the stairs. "Oh, Mrs. Gillam," Judith greeted
me cheerily, and introduced me to her escort, Jock West.
Behind his thick lenses Mr. West seemed to be examining
me from a great distance, but his smile was eager as he
took my hand. Judith said, "We're going to Grosvenor
House to skate—would you like to come?"

"Oh," I said, embarrassed. "I don't know how to skate."
Jock West spoke up. "I'll teach you. Love to. Please
come, Mrs. Gillam—we can get skates for you there."

I went with them to the most fashionable skating rink
in London. Jock taught me how to manage on ice. As
Judith and I sat on a bench watching him go through
a repertoire of graceful figure three's, she observed,
"Jock's a great friend of my cousin. You know, they were
both in Pop at Eton."

"Oh, yes," I said, having no idea what she meant. A
few minutes later, on the ice, sliding and slipping prettily
on Jock's arm, I said, "Judith told me you were in Pop."
He seemed pleased, so I added, "Tell me all about it."
He was delighted to do so. Pop, it developed, was the
most exclusive social club at Eton, whose members seemed
to spend most of their time carefully blackballing virtually everyone else. I learned from Jack that Judith's home
was near Aberdeen, that she and her mother took a flat
in London only for the season, and that she was engaged
to a Pop alumnus now in Scotland.

We got along famously. I learned to skate quickly:
sports had always come easily to me. I bought a red turtle-
neck sweater and a little black flared skirt that showed
off my legs. Skating at Grosvenor House as a guest of
Jock West or Judith Hurt, or learning to play squash
and tennis under Jock's tutelage, now took the place of

my afternoons in Hyde Park. Johnny, busy with his new job which often took him on selling tours through the country, watched my progress with satisfaction. Everyone at Grosvenor House knew everyone else; and to them I was the young, pretty Mrs. Gillam, whose husband never seemed too much in evidence and who was considered rather daring because she had once taken a fling at the musical-comedy stage.

One afternoon when I was practicing my figure three's, a tall man of military bearing, with blond hair graying at the temples, skated up to introduce himself. His name was Jack Mitford. He'd often seen me on the rink with Jock West. Would I like to waltz with him?

We waltzed together. He was a superb skater and taught me how to improve my figure skating. Later, he invited me to have a drink. At the bar a ruddy-faced man approached us and clapped him heartily on the shoulder. "May I present Captain Gill?" Jack said. He called him "Gillo." Gillo, I learned, was a ranking player on the All-England Polo Team. We sat at a little table while the two men discussed a new club they were forming, to be known as the International Sportsman's Club, of which Captain Gill would be secretary. It would be open to a limited international membership of both sexes; its quarters, at Grosvenor House, complete to skating rink, squash courts, swimming pool, and living accommodations, would serve as a town residence for members living outside London or in foreign countries. Already on the board of directors were the Aga Khan, Commodore Vanderbilt, the Duke of Westminster, the Duc de Alba, the Earl of Lonsdale, a number of French princes and Italian barons. . . . I swallowed as I listened. I told myself, this will be one of the most exclusive, blue-blooded clubs in the world!

When Johnny heard about it he was impressed. I had

skated with Jack Mitford? That could only be the Honorable Jack Mitford, brother of Lord Redesdale and uncle
of Nancy, Unity, and five other Mitford girls and one
Mitford son, Tom. The Mitfords, Johnny explained, were
one of the oldest families, older even than the royal family. Now I was meeting England's finest society—county
people—as differentiated from London, or town society.
County society was not as sophisticated, nor as rich—they
were true gentlefolk. "Wouldn't it be topping," Johnny
went on, carried away, "if you could join the new club?
The people you'd come to know—"

"Why Johnny," I protested. "That's ridiculous. I
couldn't possibly get into a club like that. Anyway, who
would propose me?"

"Jack Mitford," said Johnny. "There's one. Gill is
another. And if he's secretary he has a good deal to say."

It turned out to be far easier than I thought. The next
time I sat at the bar with Jack Mitford, I said, "I would
adore to join your club. Then I could skate all the time.
Do you think you and Captain Gill could propose me?"

He said, "Why, I think it could be arranged, Sheilah.
Let's go up and see Gillo." Gillo was in the club office
that had just been opened. I felt rather hopeful about
Gillo. He was a gallant army type who only a few days
before happened to follow me up a flight of stairs. "By
Jove, what ankles!" he had exclaimed. I had smiled sweetly
back at him. Now, presented with my request, he said, "Of
course."

I was proposed—Mrs. John Gillam, wife of Major John
Gillam, D.S.O.—and elected to membership.

Lily Sheil was a member of the International Sportsman's Club.

I presided at a salon in our flat. On the floor, chatting

gaily over a huge omelette I had prepared, were Judith
Hurt, her closest friend, Lady Joan Villiers, daughter of
the Earl of Clarendon, Jock West, Captain Gill, and Jack
Mitford. Jock was keeping my guests in roars of laughter
with a hilarious story of how he and his fellow members
of Pop "took turns kicking the bottom of the King of
Siam." I dashed in and out, with tea and jam, trying to
believe my eyes. These people, sitting on the floor in *my*
flat, eating *my* omelette. I thought, if only this were real:
if only I *were* the same as they!

Jack Mitford invited Johnny and me to dinner one
January night. The talk turned to Switzerland. The Mitfords were going to St. Moritz in a few days. I must come
along as a guest. Judith Hurt and her mother would be
in St. Moritz, too. So would many of their friends.

"Of course you must go," said Johnny later. "Think of
it—spending a fortnight in Switzerland with the Mitfords!" I outfitted myself with a skiing suit, heavy boots,
warm sweaters—and that winter of 1930 I accompanied
the Mitfords to St. Moritz. There I met Jack's brother,
Lord Redesdale, head of the clan, who looked like an
ancient Saxon king, a blond, blue-eyed giant of a man
with a striking head, great shoulders, and a hawklike look
to his finely chiseled face. I met Lord Redesdale's son,
Tom Mitford, a youthful edition of his father and, at
twenty-one, one of the handsomest young men I had ever
seen. I gazed at Tom Mitford curiously. How must it feel
to be the only son in a family of seven daughters? Outrageous fantasies danced through my mind. I had always
wanted children so I would have relations in the world,
but Johnny and I had not been successful. Perhaps I could
still found an aristocracy of my own. And I would choose
Tom Mitford to be the father, and my sons would look
like Saxon kings. . . .

St. Moritz was another fairy tale come true. I skiied. I
skated. I went skijoring. As the Mitford family protégé,
I dined at long tables with their friends, I listened to
them turn from French to German to Italian, speaking
each flawlessly, and I thought: *how little I know!* I was
introduced to Lord Grimthorpe, Lord Bradbourne, the
Duc de Yonne. I loved to hear them speak: such charming
voices, so modulated, so easy on the ear, such gentlefolk!
They treated me solicitously, graciously—they *cherished*
me—and again I lived on compliments. It was gratifying
to be told I was pretty, but when Jack Mitford remarked,
"Sheilah, you have such a lovely voice," I was beside myself with pride. It was as though I had won a diploma.

Back in London the fairy tale continued. Now I was
invited with Johnny to spend weekends at the houses of
county society, to ride, to play tennis, to swim, and lie
on the grass and, in the evening, dress for dinner and play
billiards. I thought little of world events. County society
made no pretense of keeping up with the times. These
were difficult days in England; the pound was about to
go off the gold standard, unemployment was rising and
there was great discontent—but all this seemed far, far
away to me.

One weekend I found myself a guest at Lord Brougham
and Vaux' shooting party, wearing tweeds, heavy brogues,
and thick gray woolen stockings, the very picture of a
county society woman. Lord Brougham and Vaux lived
in a castle with a moat: we dined in a great baronial hall;
ancestral portraits looked down on us, there were liveried
servants in attendance, and a giant fireplace emblazoned
with the family coat of arms over the mantel. I loved it.
I could not bring myself to shoot but I adored going along
with the guns, sitting on my shooting stick, watching the
beaters work their way through the underbrush and re-
spond, "Yes, m'lord," and "No, m'lord" to our host's in-

structions. In my room I would laugh with pleasure, and sigh, thinking: *how did I get here? but isn't it lovely!* When the shoot was over I was given six brace of pheasants and returned to London carrying the dead birds I did not know what to do with.

I felt my way carefully in this enchanted world. I had been taken up: I had been accepted. But there was danger of exposure at every turn. I never doubted that these people were better than I. They were better by right of birth, by right of environment, by right of education, by right of their calm acceptance of themselves as belonging. They had no secrets to hide, no pretenses to maintain— no ignoble impulses, stemming from fear or necessity, to crush. This, I believed, was why they were better human beings than I, and why, were they to know the truth about me, they would have been shocked, felt hoodwinked, and have no alternative but to cast me out.

It meant always being on guard. When other women spoke of their schools, their presentations at court, I trembled. I dreaded to hear talk of cousins and relatives. No one had ever met a cousin or uncle or aunt of Mrs. Gillam, or even a schoolmate. To all intents I might have grown on a tree.

I recalled a terrible moment at St. Moritz when I had gone skating with Lord Long of Wraxall and his mother. They introduced me to a lovely, dark-eyed woman. I had seen her at the bobsleigh runs, the fancy-dress parties at the Palace Hotel. "Let's skate together, shall we?" she suggested with a smile. Arm in arm we moved rhythmically across the ice. We were quite alone. Without slackening her pace she said, "You're an adventuress, aren't you?"

It was though the ice had suddenly yawned open before me. Skating along with her, arm in arm, I thought frantically, How shall I answer this? After a little pause I said, "Yes, I am." And having said "Yes, I am," I felt calm again. She knew the false from the real coin. She could expose me if she wished. Yet I knew she would not. When I saw her again she smiled courteously. She said nothing to anyone.

I *was* fortunate. For the people about me were gentlefolk, and the mark of gentlefolk was that they rarely embarrassed you. I could be sure that the Honorable Ursula Bowater, daughter of Lord Dawson of Penn, would never turn to me to ask: "Were you ever presented, Sheilah?" Or, "What school did you go to?" Nonetheless I was prepared for almost anything that might be asked— if anyone were so unbelievably rude as to ask me.

The story I allowed to get about was that I was the daughter of John Lawrence and Veronica Roslyn Graham —both solid-sounding names. We had lived in Chelsea, a fashionable yet Bohemian section of London. This slightly unconventional background could account for any oddness, any slips, in my social behavior. My father, who owned considerable property in the City, died on a business trip to Germany when I was little. I had had tutors, then gone to finishing school in Paris. My mother died when I was seventeen; I had married Major Gillam, D.S.O., almost immediately thereafter.

It was a good story. It lacked only one essential. I had not been presented at court. Every young woman in the circle in which I now moved so delightedly, yet fearfully, had made her curtsy, at eighteen, before Their Majesties.

"If only," I said to Johnny, "we could have managed that, too."

As I spoke, I could see another ingenious Gillam project in his eyes. "Do you know," he said thoughtfully, "you can be presented even now? Even though you're not a debutante?" He explained that debutantes were nearly always re-presented when they became married women. It was necessary only to be presented by someone who had, herself, made her debut at Buckingham Palace.

I had no such relative, to be sure, but Johnny recalled a most charming woman, the wife of Colonel Arthur Saxe, who had been at Gallipoli with him. Mrs. Saxe, a popular debutante in her day, now lived modestly outside London. She might welcome an opportunity to go to court again. . . .

He wrote to her. To my utter delight, Mrs. Saxe indicated that she would be happy to present Major Gillam's wife, if he could arrange for her to have a gown from Norman Hartnell (the queen's dressmaker) appropriate for such an occasion. And so it was done. My name was duly forwarded to the lord chamberlain. In return, when the time came, we received an imposing invitation, which read:

> The Lord Chamberlain is commanded by Their Majesties to summon Major and Mrs. John Gillam to a Court at Buckingham Palace on Tuesday the 9th June, 1931 at 9:30 o'clock p.m.
>
> Ladies: Court Dress *with* feathers and trains.
> Gentlemen: Full Court Dress.

As a major, Johnny was entitled to the rank of diplomat at court functions. From Moss Brothers, he rented a diplomat's court dress: knee breeches, black court stockings, a cutaway black velvet coat, silver buttons and white tie, shirt and waistcoat—and he wore the sword that I had always admired when I visited him in his bachelor flat.

On presentation night our hired Daimler with its chauffeur and footman slowly negotiated the turn into the Mall and joined the long queue of cars waiting for hours to be admitted within the Palace gates. The Palace was ablaze with lights. Everywhere crowds milled about—hundreds of home-bound clerks, office workers, men in bowler hats, stenographers, salesgirls—many dashing excitedly from car to car to peer inside and exclaim at what they saw. Dressed in an ivory court gown, with three white ostrich plumes in my hair, I sat regally between Mrs. Saxe, wearing a tiara and feathers, and Johnny, resplendent in his court dress and high plumed hat.

"Coo-er! Lookut those diamonds!" and "Lookut 'er! Wonder 'oo she is!" and "Lumm-ey! Ain't she beautiful!" The exclamations of the crowd, the rapturous look on their faces, the expressions of awe, envy, and excitement—

Was there a Mildred among them? And a Lily? Who can imagine how I felt?

Then our car rolled noiselessly forward and came to a halt before the Palace steps. Footmen in royal livery sprang to help us out: we mounted an enormous curved staircase and waited in double file outside the throne room with pale, nervous debutantes and those who were to present them. The procedure was to enter, have our names announced, proceed to a point in front of Their Majesties, curtsy, then slowly back out.

Now my stage experience came to my aid. I knew how to walk across a room, how to keep my head up, how to make an appearance before an audience. As I entered the throne room and the full scene burst upon my eyes, it was all I could do not to gasp. There, in magnificent royal robes of state, sat King George the Fifth and Queen Mary. Behind Their Majesties stood the Prince of Wales, and at his side the Duke of Gloucester, Prince George, Princess Mary, Princess Alice, the Dowager Marchioness of Milford Haven—I could not name them all. And behind the royal family, in banked rows of striking color, the

peers of the realm in their velvet and ermine. I thought
for a frantic moment, will I trip over my train? Will my
feathers tumble to the floor? Will I be sick? I heard the
lord chamberlain's voice boom out: "Mrs. Arthur Saxe
presenting Mrs. John Gillam."

Mrs. Saxe walked slowly forward and curtsied. Someone touched me on the arm and I followed her, at train's
length behind. I found myself directly in front of the
King and Queen and curtsied slowly and deeply. I raised
my eyes and dared look directly into the faces of Their
Majesties. Queen Mary appeared quite bored; the King
gave me, I thought, a piercing look; but behind them
Pragger-Wagger winked—or seemed to wink—at me! There
was an amused query in his eyes as if to say, "Haven't I
seen you before?"

Then I rose and, sweeping my train to one side, gracefully backed out to find myself with the others in an
enormous anteroom. There we waited until the King and
Queen and their entourage passed through. We formed a
corridor for them and, as they approached, the men
bowed, the women curtsied deeply. We remained in that
position while the royal procession moved by—first, the
lord chamberlain and his staff walking backward and
bowing then the King and Queen, their long trains behind
them held by two pages of honor, then the members of the
royal family. When the full court retinue had gone by,
we rose and proceeded from the room.

Later, downstairs, we ate little cakes and sandwiches
off plates of gold and drank champagne from priceless
crystal, and afterward Johnny took us to Quaglino's, London's most fashionable restaurant. I was flushed with
triumph as we danced. We had carried it off! I thought
exultantly, would one, meeting Judith Hurt and me,
note any difference, any difference at all, between us?

CHAPTER THIRTEEN

I SAID, remembering to choose my words very carefully, "How d'you do." Gracefully I gave my hand to the dazzlingly handsome young man who bowed over it.

Tom Mitford had introduced us. "Sheilah," he had said. "May I present my cousin, Randolph Churchill."

We were at Quaglino's, where Johnny had taken me months before on the night of my presentation. I had heard from Tom and Jock and other Etonians, a great deal about Winston Churchill's brilliant and arrogant son. Now in his early twenties, he was already a legend. His conceit, I had heard, had made him one of the most unpopular students at Eton and Oxford. But at this moment, as he joined us for a drink, I saw no arrogance, only charm in this extraordinarily attractive young man. He was tall, slim, with aristocratic features, a fresh, ruddy complexion, and soft brown hair. He and Tom had fun at my expense. Tom said, "Actually, I've always rather wondered about *Mr*. Gillam. He seems to be something of a mystery. I don't believe there *is* a Mr. Gillam—is there, Sheilah?" I smiled prettily and said nothing.

I watched Randolph with awe then and later when I grew to know him better. For all my admiration of the elite, I realized that those I had known were not intellectuals, nor had any desire to be. Randolph represented my first brush with brains among the upper classes—and it was disconcerting, for I discovered that he had nothing but contempt for most of the things I revered.

Randolph and Tom lunched together often; their table at Quaglino's was a rendezvous for politically conscious young men, and I was a frequent guest. I was introduced to a red-haired man with freckled skin and thick glasses, Brendan Bracken. They spoke eagerly of the time Winston Churchill, currently the unsuccessful M.P. for Epping, would return to power. The country needed him desperately, Randolph said.

Someone mentioned ex-premier, Stanley Baldwin. Randolph snorted. "An idiot—an imbecile!" He sneered at Ramsay MacDonald. He and the others spoke slightingly of several members of the House of Commons. Listening to Randolph's words of contempt for Ramsay MacDonald, I thought, it doesn't really matter what you achieve—it doesn't matter that you're clever and always at the head of your class. What matters is that you're not of gentle birth. That damns you forever, even if you become prime minister of England. It's marked on you like a tattoo. You can't erase it. You may try and some people may not see it, but others will—no matter how invisible it becomes. And you never know when you will meet those who can see it.

Tom Mitford went on holiday to Munich to spend a few days with his sister, Unity, attending finishing school there. Randolph began taking me to dinner at Quag's. One evening his guests included Charles Chaplin. My awe at meeting so great an artist was dispelled by Chaplin's astonishing obsequiousness to Randolph. "Of course, you've always had the advantages," Chaplin was saying. "I haven't. I've had to fight for everything I have." He told almost apologetically, of his childhood, his early poverty, his struggles as a music-hall entertainer. "How lucky you are to have been born with the name Churchill," he went on. "To be born to wealth and position." These were my sentiments, too, but to hear Chaplin express them shocked me.

Randolph was most condescending. "Oh, well, you've worked hard to get where you are—I wouldn't think my way of life is any better."

Chaplin shook his head. I grew furious. Why does he feel inferior to this patronizing young man? If I was awed by high society that was understandable, for I was an imposter in everything I did. But Chaplin was a genius! How dared he humble himself!

The conversation turned to Ramsay MacDonald's political party and Chaplin began a long analysis of Mr. MacDonald's problems. Randolph interrupted him. "Oh, Charlie, for Heaven's sake shut up! You don't know what you're talking about." He leaned insolently across Chaplin without so much as I-beg-your-pardon to stub out a cigarette in an ash tray. "Let's talk about things you know. Tell us about Hollywood, Charlie."

Chaplin took the rebuke without protest. Now he spoke brilliantly about the movie colony in America. I began to think, how wonderful it must be to live in America where people take you at face value. Americans don't think about your birth or upbringing. Indeed, they admire you if you dare climb upward, if you aspire to be rich, important, and successful.

Leaving the restaurant we waited in the foyer for Randolph's car. A crowd gathered to stare at Chaplin. He rewarded them with a bit from his famous tramp act—his little, splay-footed run, ending in an off-balance teetering on one foot. The crowd applauded.

I went back to Johnny. "You met Charles Chaplin!" he exclaimed. "Fancy that! You dining with Charles Chaplin!"

I thought, perhaps one should never come too close to a celebrity. It was a lesson I would learn far more effectively in Hollywood.

Tom Mitford, back from Munich, could talk of only one subject. "I've met the most fascinating man in my life!" he exclaimed. "Absolutely amazing. Sweeps you off your feet when he speaks! The most persuasive man I've ever met." It was Adolf Hitler. Randolph said scornfully, "That little man with a mustache—don't be ridiculous, Tom." But Tom spoke on. Unity, with fervent admiration, had introduced him to Hitler—all Germany would follow him, and very soon too, she insisted. They had both been invited to Hitler's home. It had been a remarkable experience. Of course, some of Hitler's ideas were shocking, yet— Tom and Randolph began a long debate about the historical role of democracy and fascism.

I had no idea what they were talking about, although I had read about Hitler, too. When they discussed such matters, or went on to argue about the Japanese march into Manchuria, or other affairs of which I was completely ignorant, I smiled and listened and smiled. No one deigned to ask my opinion, nor did I venture one. I was there to be decorative. I wore my smile like a mask to hide my inadequacy, and was grateful that they expected nothing from me.

Yet I returned from such luncheons fuming at myself. I would hurry to the International Sportsman's Club to take out my frustration on the squash court. I had become extremely adept, so that I was a member of the ladies' squash team. I played furiously, practiced furiously. Sometimes Jock or Judith would say, "Sheilah, why do you play so hard? It's only a game." But they could not understand that when I played squash, it was one of the few times I was not engaged in pretense. Smashing that little black ball I felt free, I felt co-ordinated and superior, I felt whole and honest.

Day after day, when I would practice, I would notice the captain of the men's team practicing with equal diligence. He was the Marquess of Donegall, who belonged to one of the most ancient peerages in the British Isles. Lord Donegall enjoyed trying his hand at journalism. His column on society appeared each week in the *Sunday Dispatch* and I followed it religiously to keep informed.

I admired his lordship from afar. He lived in a world of fun, titles, and money, traveling constantly, staying in France, Italy, and Spain with the Duc de this and the Earl of that. Now and then I saw him come into Quaglino's with a party of friends, the waiters bowing and scraping before him as he made his way to his table. He bore such exalted titles. He was Marquess and Earl of Donegall, Earl of Belfast, Viscount Chichester of Ireland, Baron Fisherwick of Fisherwick, Hereditary Lord High Admiral of Lough Neagh, and half a dozen others.

We both finished practice simultaneously one day, and met as we emerged. "Well," he said. "I've been watching you. You play a good game." He invited me for a cocktail. "How is it that I haven't met you before?"

"Oh, I travel quite a bit," I said vaguely. Donegall had reason to ask, for he knew everyone. He was about twenty-seven, a slender, attractive man, delicately turned out, with dark brown hair, impeccably groomed, large brown eyes—enormously sympathetic, and small, gentle hands. He was boyish, he laughed readily and I listened as he talked. "Tomorrow I've promised to go to the Plunketts and on Thursday, Westminster has asked me to Scotland—" He reeled off the enchantments I'd read in his column and which I had only begun to taste.

I set my cap for Lord Donegall. Following a squash tournament a week later, a small party was given for members of the ladies' and men's teams. I wore a pretty little skirt and red sweater. Lord Donegall entered the room and looked around. Our eyes met: I smiled at him. He made his way over to me and perched on the arm of my chair. How had I come out with my game?

"Oh, I won."

"Excellent!" he said. He had won his match, too. I said, "You know, you're a friend of a friend of mine—Tom Mitford." We talked about Tom. I went on, "Do you know Dennis Bradley?" naming another of Jock's Oxford friends. He nodded. "Are you going to Dennis' cocktail party next week?" I asked.

He looked down at me. "Are you?"

"Yes."

"Then I am," he said, with a smile.

I went to Dennis Bradley's party alone, and Lord Donegall accompanied me home. Johnny had gone that night to one of his regimental dinners; he would feel middle-aged, he complained, in a group of dashing young people. His lordship arranged to lunch with me on the following day.

That began our friendship. I told him enough about myself to make clear that I was a young society matron with time on my hands. Had I been Miss Graham and not Mrs. Gillam, Donegall would have wanted to know about my family, my schooling and other details. Now, instead, we talked about mutual friends and shooting in Northumberland and skiing in Switzerland. He was intrigued to learn that I had been on the musical-comedy stage, and impressed that I had sold an article to a newspaper.

We got along famously. In the months that followed, he escorted me to many social events. I was his guest at Ascot, and accompanied him to a fashionable boating party on the Thames. We spent hours driving through the countryside; and presently Donegall said, "I'm in love with you, Sheilah. I want to marry you." "Oh, Don!" I said. I took it as a joke. I was not in love with him. And who could conceive it—Lily Sheil, Her Grace, Marchioness of Donegall? My son would be the Earl of Belfast, my daughter, the Lady Wendy Chichester! No, I'd never be able to carry off anything like that. I said, "I already have a husband, you know." He said, "You have heard of divorce—" I laughed. "Don, you don't really mean it. Besides, your mother wouldn't approve." It was well known that the Marchioness of Donegall was most unapproachable where her son was concerned.

He said lugubriously, "You may be right." Then he smiled. "But don't forget I asked you."

Perhaps it was the stimulation of Randolph Churchill's table at Quag's which led me to try writing again, to reassure myself there was more to me than a smile. Or perhaps Lord Donegall's proposal, far-fetched as it was, had made me question again my marriage to Johnny. But one afternoon I sat down and without a thought for A. P. Herbert's rules of composition I dashed off an article entitled, " 'I Married a Man 25 Years Older,' by a Young Wife." I sent it to the *Sunday Pictorial*. They bought it. When they gave me my check, I saw with amazement that it was for eight guineas.

I walked slowly out of the *Pictorial* offices into Fleet

Street. The narrow, busy thorougfare was half-deserted now. It was twilight. I walked down Fleet Street in the twilight, repeating to myself, in wonder, "With this brain, from nothing I have made eight guineas!" I thought, this is my real career. A newspaper woman. This is how I shall become rich and famous.

On impulse I sent a letter to *The Saturday Evening Post,* which I'd heard was America's most popular magazine, asking if there were any articles I might send them from England. I enclosed tear sheets of my articles. While I waited, the *Daily Mail* bought a second piece of mine: " 'Baby or a Car,' by a New Bride." I said a car, knowing this would cause the greatest comment.

My inquiry to the *Post* brought a tentative assignment to interview Lord Beaverbrook. J. B. Priestley, the British author, had written a scathing attack on America as ignorant and boorish—this, after returning from a lucrative lecture tour of America. It had infuriated everyone in the United States. What was Beaverbrook's opinion of his fellow countryman who repaid American hospitality—and money—in such unsporting fashion?

I sent in my request for an interview with Lord Beaverbrook. Word came back. "Lord Beaverbrook is not available." He had gone to his country estate, Cherkley Court, about fifty miles from London. I set out in pursuit of him. At Cherkley Court, a butler barred my way. When I insisted that he must take in my message, he returned to say, icily, "His lordship will not see you." He closed the door in my face.

Next day I went again to Cherkley Court, and again the impassive butler barred the door. "He has to see me!" I almost wept. This time the message came back, "Lord Beaverbrook says that such persistence should be rewarded.

He will see you in town tomorrow afternoon at two o'clock."

When I presented myself at Beaverbrook's town house, I was ushered into a huge reception room dominated by the portrait of a strikingly beautiful woman. Suddenly a door opened and a little, gnomelike figure bounded into the room. I was conscious of a big head, sharp eyes, and an enormously wide, expressive mouth. It was Lord Beaverbrook. He saw me looking at the portrait. "That's my wife," he boomed. "Isn't she beautiful?"

I managed to nod. In the presence of that compressed, springlike energy, I felt drained of my own strength. His lordship appeared ready to explode any moment from sheer vitality. Without preface he said emphatically, "No, Miss Graham, I won't give you the interview you want. Priestley writes for me and I'll not speak against my own writers. If he doesn't like America, that's his business. But look here—I'll give you a better story." He led me to a sofa. "I'll tell you why the League of Nations should be abolished. I'll write it for you and you can say you wrote it. Take it to the Hearst papers here and they'll pay you twenty pounds for it."

I sank back into the cushions thinking, isn't this marvelous! What an auspicious way to begin my new career! The sun made bright patterns on the enormous Persian rug covering the floor. Beaverbrook gazed at me. Again, suddenly—he shot words at me like bullets from a gun, "Do you ride?"

A little taken aback I replied, "Yes, Lord Beaverbrook."

"Care to ride with me this afternoon at Cherkley?" he demanded.

I said, weakly, I'd be delighted. Yes, I had riding clothes at home, not too far away. I thought, this is simply fantastic. One moment I'm begging at his door, the next he's inviting me to ride with him. This is even better than getting the interview!

He leaped up, bounded to a desk and pressed a button. "My chauffeur will take you home to pick up your riding things. Don't be long now!"

An hour and a half later we were on two beautiful horses riding along a quiet lane in his forest at Cherkley. He said, as we chatted, "By the way, I want you to meet Mrs. Robert Carter." I looked at him, puzzled. We were alone. He chuckled. "You're riding her."

"You mean this horse?" I asked, uncertainly.

He nodded. "And this—" he patted the shoulder of his mare. "This is Lady Kitty Wallace."

I giggled. "What unusual names for horses!"

A puckish grin played over his face. "All my horses are named after my favorite ladies."

I considered this for a moment. It sounded outrageous but I wasn't sure. "Well," I remarked lightly, wondering whether I was saying more than I meant. "I hope you'll name a horse after me one day."

He rubbed his cheek with the butt of his riding crop. "Perhaps I shall," he said, with another grin. Then he began talking about himself. He talked incessantly, explosively, as we rode. He talked about his father, who had been a poor man in Canada. He told me about his wife's death, that but for his little granddaughter, Jean, he lived alone, and how ridiculous it was that he should have forty servants to wait upon him. Now and then he asked me questions but he rarely gave me time to reply. When we had finished our ride, he said, "Of course, you'll have dinner and stay over? We dine rather late."

I was in a dilemma. The best way out was to tell the truth. "I'd like to, Lord Beaverbrook, but I must call my husband and tell him."

A shade of irritation darkened his face. "Oh, you're married!" He said it sharply. "Of course, call him." He led the way to a telephone. But I felt him withdrawing. I got Johnny on the wire and for the first time Johnny, who I thought would delight in this coup, proved difficult.

"Are you sure it's all right for you to stay down there?" his voice came back. Beaverbrook stood nearby, tapping his finger impatiently. I looked at him as I spoke into the mouthpiece. "Of course it's all right, Johnny." But Johnny wasn't satisfied. "Is there someone there?" he demanded. "Can't you speak freely?" I was furious. I wanted a good interview. There were other guests at dinner. "Johnny, Lord Beaverbrook is right here. Everything is perfectly all right." So Johnny acquiesced. But when I put down the phone, Beaverbrook had withdrawn considerably.

After dinner we adjourned to a small auditorium where Beaverbrook prepared to show the latest American films to his guests. As we sat waiting, a footman entered and whispered in his ear. Lord Beaverbrook turned to me. "The car is ready for you," he said.

I was sent back to London. I rode back almost in tears, consoling myself with the interview he had promised to write for me. But when it came, I read the manuscript with growing consternation. Beaverbrook, writing as Sheilah Graham, described how I had waited for him to return from a ride in the forest. When he finally appeared, astride a horse, my first impression had been, this is Napoleon. For the man I gazed upon had the same air of conquering his destiny. This continued for three pages, closing with a demand that the League of Nations be abolished. He had printed the demand in his newspapers weeks before.

I thought, this is rubbish. Nobody will pay money for this. I was right. Nobody did. When I told Beaverbrook

I could not sell it to the Hearst editors, he sent me his own check for twenty pounds. "Tell them to forget it," he said.

A few days later, a hearty voice rumbled over my telephone. It was Lord Castlerosse, one of Beaverbrook's popular columnists. "I've heard about you bearding Max in his home. Very clever! I'd like to meet you." Would I have lunch with him?

Over lunch he said, "I know all about that League of Nations story—I have a far better idea for you." His suggestion was for me to do a story on the four "Paper Lords" of England: Lord Beaverbrook, Lord Rothermere, owner of the *Daily Mail;* Lord Riddell, owner of *News of the World;* and Lord Camrose, who owned the *Daily Telegraph.* "You can sell that to any American magazine and make a name for yourself," he assured me. "I'll help you." He would go so far as to write the section dealing with Beaverbrook and tell me where to obtain information on the others.

This was a major article compared to the flippant pieces I had written up to now. I jumped at the chance. Lord Castlerosse kept his promise. His section on Beaverbrook was witty and sardonic. One sentence read: "As a child I had a rubber doll, broad of face and mouth, and when I squeezed its middle, out went its tongue. That doll was like Lord Beaverbrook; and, as with rubber, you never quite know how far he will go." I toiled over the remainder of the piece. It sold to *Nash's* magazine for twenty-five guineas and created a considerable stir. I was a magazine writer!

In return, Lord Castlerosse required a favor of me. He had been left by his wife, whom he adored. I was to visit Lady Castlerosse and introduce myself as a reporter assigned to write about her friendship with a South African diamond millionaire. Lord Castlerosse counted on the threat of exposure to drive her back to his arms.

Hating myself, hoping that she would refuse to see me, I called on her. But when I was announced and the purpose of my visit made known, she came down so swiftly you could hear the swish of her gown. She said, aghast, "Oh, you can't write about that!"

I felt utterly ashamed. It was despicable to do this to another woman. But my visit achieved its purpose: she returned to her husband. I had made a friend of an important man but at a revolting cost. It taught me an old truth which I had long tried not to believe—you rarely get anything for nothing.

Now I, instead of Johnny, haunted the library researching material for articles. I studied American newspapers and to my astonishment often came upon the same article in a dozen different papers. I asked Lord Castlerosse how this was possible. "Syndication," he explained. America had hundreds of newspapers, each serving its own locality. Instead of selling your article to one newspaper, you sold it to fifty or a hundred—and your payment increased proportionally.

I thought, this is wonderful: this is the answer to everything. I *must* go to America. I won't have to carry the burden of my past so consciously there: I can support myself and stand on my own feet. At least, I could try.

The more I thought about it, the more attractive the idea seemed. I could go to the United States as an English authoress who had given up the boredom of high society for a career. I would sell a woman's column to American newspapers. Obviously, I had a flare for writing on subjects of interest to women—love, marriage, men. I knew a great deal about men. I had studied them almost to the exclusion of women. I believed I had gained a great knowledge of human motives—of Life.

When I broached it to Johnny, he took fire, too. "You go first and then I'll join you," he said. He had his job to keep. He knew I could do better alone, for I was young and pretty and there would be many helping hands. If my middle-aged husband came along, nobody would want to help me.

And so it was agreed.

But I realized that this marked the end of our marriage. If Johnny realized it, he said nothing. Though I knew I could never really give up Johnny, any more than one could give up one's parents—he would always be my family —I knew that I could not remain Mrs. John Gillam much longer. Somewhere I must find love again.

CHAPTER FOURTEEN

Armed with one hundred dollars, a return ticket, just in case, and a bagful of letters of introduction, I arrived in the United States in June, 1933. The most important American syndicate, I had been told, was the North American Newspaper Alliance, headed by John Wheeler in New York. When I walked into his office I could not know that I was meeting the man who was to be my employer through the years. I saw a pink-faced tough-looking man who swiveled around in his chair to look hard at me as I entered, an eager smile on my face. He had a half-smoked cigar in his mouth, he wore a green eyeshade and he spoke gruffly. His office, off Times Square, was spare, and simply furnished, with a few World War photographs in which I recognized him, much younger and even tougher-looking. Cigar, eyeshade, gruffness and all, he looked exactly as the American movies had led me to picture an important New York newspaper executive.

He read my letter of introduction, chewing his cigar from side to side. "Let's see what you've done," he said, abruptly. I opened a large envelope and drew out a clipping of my article on stage-door Johnnies. He read it swiftly. "Not what we want," he barked, handing it back.

Like a mother dispensing sweets to a child—one at a time, not to spoil him—I produced a second clipping. This was dismissed, too. When he handed back the third, I felt sick at heart. I gave him the entire envelope. He went through the rest of the material, stopping at my piece about young wives and middle-aged husbands. He read it through. "Pretty good," he said.

Since I could never stand suspense, I blurted, "Then will you give me a contract?"

He looked at me. "I don't know about that," he said, dryly. "Suppose you leave a set of clippings here and get in touch we me in a few days."

I dared to say, "I hope you'll give me the contract right away, Mr. Wheeler. You know, you're not the only syndicate I'm seeing."

He smiled for the first time. "You get in touch with me in a few days," he repeated. He rose and showed me to the door.

Mr. Wheeler liked my articles. I was obviously too much the beginner to write a syndicated column, but he referred me to Albert J. Kobler, publisher of the *New York Mirror*. On the strength of my English clippings, I was hired at forty dollars a week. Mr. Wheeler, whose advice I asked, suggested I might earn additional money by selling his NANA features to the newspapers, and so in my spare time I trotted about to the various editors. At the *Evening Journal,* Mary Dougherty, Woman's Editor, bought nothing but gave me an idea. "You ought to write your impressions of New York. Why don't you try it for us?"

I had already gained definite impressions of New York. I determined to write a shocking, attention-getting story for Miss Dougherty. Entitled, "Who Cheats the Most in

Marriage?" I examined the habits of the French, English, Germans, and Americans, and concluded that the English were the most guilty. I spoke of the *ménage à trois* as a common occurrence in England. "It is not unusual for all three—husband, wife, and lover—to live under one roof, the lover paying the bills while the husband looks the other way," I wrote. Among the French, I went on provocatively, the favorite phrase was, "Que-voulez-vous?"—"What do you expect?—if a man spent his afternoons with his mistress, his nights with his wife. The Germans, I declared were too stodgy to care. As for the Americans, I confessed that my first impression of New York had been twofold: first, men without wives, because the wives had all left the hot city for the country; and second, apartments without carpets, for the carpets like the wives had been sent away for the summer. These impressions belonged together, I declared, because invariably the men without wives entertained young ladies in the apartments without carpets. If it were not for the fact that gathering alimony is the main occupation of American women, I concluded, Americans would cheat the most.

I mailed it to the *Evening Journal* and went off to my job on the *Mirror,* where I was reporting events of no consequence.

Next morning the excitement broke. The *Evening Journal* wanted me in their offices, immediately. My article was terrific! The moment I arrived—on my lunch hour from the *Mirror*—a photographer was called and I was photographed in half a dozen poses—on the telephone, at the typewriter, smiling at the reader. They were going to publicize me as their find of the year—Sheilah Graham, the audacious, saucy lady journalist from England. How much did I want to work for them?

I said, "A hundred a week." I always liked big round numbers.

Even an audacious, saucy lady journalist from England wasn't worth one hundred dollars a week in 1933. Miss Dougherty countered, "We can pay you seventy-five dollars."

Seventy-five dollars from the *Evening Journal* added to forty dollars from the *Mirror* made one hundred fifteen dollars a week—"That will be acceptable," I said with dignity.

"Fine," said Miss Dougherty. I was hired.

The denouement came the following day when my story appeared in the *Journal*. The *Mirror* protested vehemently. How could I work for the *Journal* when I was on their payroll? And at the *Journal*, an icy Miss Dougherty called me in. It took some time to convince her that I was so new to journalism that I thought it proper to work for two newspapers at the same time in the same city. I was forced to give up the *Mirror*. But overnight I had become a full-fledged newspaper writer, my articles appearing three times a week under a headline that blazed: SHEILAH GRAHAM SAYS.

In the two years I spent in New York I became what I had pretended to be—a professional journalist. As on the stage, I was an amateur who learned how to keep up with professionals. I did so by combination of daring, brazenness, and desperation. I was the kind of reporter who climbed through the bedroom window to steal the photograph demanded by the city editor. I was terrified of small planes—yet I went up in a tiny, open, two-seater to cover Lindbergh's arrival from his top-of-the-world flight. I dreaded having anything to do with violence, yet I attended the Hauptmann murder trial, interviewed women moments after they learned their husbands had been slain in a gang war, and even surreptitiously entered Al Capone's home in Florida to describe its lavish interior for *Evening Journal* readers.

I stopped at nothing and everything had its value for me. When I was sent to interview Dorothy Parker, the distinguished writer for *The New Yorker* magazine, I asked her if it was true she had just been tattooed—and where? She laughed apologetically. "Yes, it is true—but only on my arm, I'm afraid," and invited me in for cocktails. I was dispatched to demand of George Jean Nathan, the drama critic, then seen everywhere with Lillian Gish: "When are you going to marry Miss Gish?" It was a brazen thing to ask. He smiled. "I can't tell you when I'm going to marry, but I'll tell you why I'm not going to marry her,"—and I obtained an even better story.

Through it all, John Wheeler was my friend and counselor. When I ran out of provocative ideas for SHEILAH GRAHAM SAYS, he suggested, "Write a piece saying that all dogs should be kicked out of New York. Tell them it's ridiculous to keep dogs in city apartments—unfair to dog and master." I did, and the *Evening Journal* was delighted to find itself deluged with angry letters demanding that Sheilah Graham go back where she came from. It was Wheeler who introduced me to the world of American publishing and advertising—Herbert Bayard Swope, the editor; Bruce Barton, head of his well-known advertising firm; Deak Aylesworth, president of NBC; Kent Cooper, general manager of the Associated Press. Through the people I met, and with my letters of introduction, I soon found myself part of New York sophisticated life.

Now instead of Quag's, it was the Stork Club, with Quentin Reynolds and Deems Taylor holding forth; instead of castles in Northumberland it was country homes in Connecticut where I sat on the floor listening to George Gershwin at the piano, and the voices I heard were those of Gene Tunney and Heywood Broun. Now I played tennis at the Piping Rock Club on Long Island and went riding on Vincent Astor's magnificent estate in Rhinebeck.

And all the time as the months passed, I sought to learn. Americans, I discovered, differed from the English. They were not ashamed of knowledge; indeed, they were eager for it; they did not think it bad taste to reveal what they knew, to check and challenge and throw themselves into exciting discourse. In polite English society one never showed off how much he knew. That was for Bloomsbury intellectuals and the odd types who climbed on soap boxes in Hyde Park. Now, at the parties I attended, I discovered a new facet of America—for the first time, I met women intellectuals of grace and charm. In England, the lady intellectuals I had brushed against were gaunt, dyspeptic women, forbidding and spartan, who gave erudition an unpleasant quality. They were women who never seemed to enjoy food: I hoped never to be so educated that I'd not care what I was eating.

Enviously I watched Dorothy Parker. Everything this warm, attractive woman said, seemed to get into print. Men flocked to her. I thought—you see, a woman need not be strikingly beautiful to draw admirers about her: she can do it, too, if she has high intelligence and flashing wit and knows a great deal about everything going on in the world. And it came to me that I would have a more difficult time getting by in America simply on a smile and a pretty face.

At one dinner party I met Clare Boothe, the playwright who as Clare Boothe Luce later became Ambassador to Italy. Here was cool beauty, brains, and talent. It proved an agonizing evening for me. About twenty guests, a cross-section of New York's literary and theatrical society, were present and the party crackled with epigrams and witty conversation. Someone suggested a game of hypothetical questions: suppose President Roosevelt, Pope Pius, and George Bernard Shaw died: which death would represent the greatest loss to the world? If Shakespeare and Plato met today, how might their conversation go? Everyone made a contribution but me. The evening was almost over and I had said nothing. I became desperate. Somehow I had to join in the conversation. I was wringing wet with the agony of feeling completely outside this scintillating group. Miss Boothe, who had been speaking brilliantly, paused for a moment to open a ruby-studded compact and powder her nose. I spoke up. In the dead silence I said, "That's a very pretty compact." No one said anything. Miss Boothe looked at me, finished powdering her nose, clicked her compact shut, put it back in her bag, and went on talking. That was the only thing I said all evening.

I went home and cried.

My ego was soothed when I received an affectionate letter from Lord Donegall. He thought constantly about me, he wrote. He was sorry he could not have seen me before I left. He was sending me under separate cover an important record which he wanted me to play as soon as possible.

When the record arrived a few days later, I placed it on my phonograph, settled comfortably with a bun and a glass of milk, and listened. His voice came: "My darling Sheilah. I have thought of so many ways to phrase this, and the simplest is the best. I want to marry you when you are free. I am hopeful that I can bring Mother on our side. Do think about this and consider it. And please don't send me an answer you don't mean."

I played the record several times and wrote to tell him how flattering his proposal was, and that I would think about it. I had no wish to marry Donegall and return to live in England, yet I could not bring myself to close the door completely. It reassured me to know that the Marquess of Donegall waited to marry me. It was pleasing to toy with the dream of myself as a marchioness.

My ego was further salved when John Wheeler invited me to have a drink at the Hotel Marguery and meet Lee Orwell—then publisher of the *Evening Journal*—and several of his friends. We were served and sat waiting when Mr. Orwell entered, accompanied by a fair, pretty woman of forty, who was introduced to me as Miss Margaret Brainard. Years later she told me she had thought I was an alcoholic when she met me that afternoon, for I had six old fashioneds lined up in front of me.

"Are you going to drink all of those, my dear?" she asked.

I shook my head. "I'm not drinking anything—I just eat the cherries."

Mr. Orwell broke into laughter and John Wheeler said dryly, "Don't you think it might be less expensive if I bought you the cherries without the drinks?"

That had never occurred to me.

Margaret thought this very amusing. She took a liking to me and became my closest woman friend in New York. I confided in her my hopes of becoming a successful, syndicated columnist, my distress at not knowing American customs. I told her about the marquess who waited for me—about everything save my true past.

I threw myself into work. I earned more money—sometimes as much as four hundred dollars a week—with radio interviews, magazine articles, and special assignments. In 1934, King Features sent me on a quick trip to London to cover the marriage of the Duke of Kent to Princess Marina of Greece. Johnny—as ever Johnny—met me at the dock waving a copy of the *Daily Express* with one of my New York stories. "You're a success," he shouted. "You're famous!"

On the visit Johnny and I finally agreed to a divorce. He was most reluctant, but he knew that the farce of our marriage could not continue indefinitely. "All right," he said sadly, at last. "But not right away, Sheilah. If you still want it after you've been in America for another year, I won't contest it."

I do not know how seriously I had Lord Donegall in the back of my mind when I talked about divorce to Johnny. When I saw Don, briefly, I said only that I was still thinking about his proposal. He must be patient. And Donegall, busy dashing about the country, seemed prepared to be patient.

Upon my return to the United States, an exciting new job appeared. Elsie Robinson, who wrote an advice-to-the-lovelorn column in more than one hundred newspapers, was about to retire. Eagerly I applied for her position. To my intense disappointment, I did not get it. Only later I learned why. When my name reached Joseph P. Connolly, head of King Features, which owned the column, he said, "Oh, no. That young lady is much too sophisticated." And he gave the column to some one else.

My fault had been that I had pretended too well. Mr. Connolly had seen me at publishers' dinners, laughing uproariously each time an off-color story was told. Actually, I hadn't understood them: but I wanted these brusque, successful, expansive Americans to think that I understood. I wanted to belong.

I brooded over it for weeks.

Then, quite unexpectedly, my New York interlude

ended. The North American Newspaper Alliance's Hollywood columnist, Molly Merrick, was due to renew her contract but wanted more money. Mr. Wheeler was not prepared to acquiesce, and it appeared that NANA would find itself without a Hollywood column. "I'll take the job at whatever she's making," I told Wheeler eagerly. "I know I can do it." I pleaded for the chance. Hollywood to me was sham and glitter and I thought myself qualified to understand sham and glitter.

Mr. Wheeler considered my request and finally yielded. Miss Merrick had been earning two hundred dollars a week: he slashed me to one hundred and twenty-five dollars a week, but he gave me the job. He was willing to let me prove myself. He knew that any girl who ordered old fashioneds for the cherries alone was not too sophisticated to write a gossip column from Hollywood.

On Christmas Eve, 1935, I flew to the West Coast. As the plane took off I suddenly felt blue and depressed. Was this a mistake? Should I have remained in New York where I earned three times as much? But it was not money I had come to the States for—or was it? What *did* I want?

I thought a great deal about this as I sat on the plane, listening to the steady roar of the motors. What was it I looked for? Love, security, a home—a family? I desperately wanted a child. I remembered a day at the orphanage when Miss Walton asked us, "What would you like to be when you grow up?" The other girls had said, nurses, cooks, teachers, nuns, typists, artists, dancers. I had replied, "a mother." It was true. Since I had no family, I yearned to create a family, out of myself. Oh, to have something that belonged to me, that was part of me—to be related to at least one living person in the world! That was part of it—to *belong* somewhere. That was why I loved to be with men: because they were warm and protective to me, because they made me feel beautiful and wanted and belonging.

But I had yet to find what I sought. The stage hadn't answered my need; nor the world of society. Whatever it was, I hadn't found it in London, and now in New York I hadn't found it either. True, I was learning about America, and having a good time in the process—good food, good clothes, gay companions—but I lived in a vacuum. I was still spinning about, looking—what was I looking for? Was it a man? Someone to care for me, someone who would love me body and soul and want me with him until the day he died? Someone whose love would rescue me from the fraudulence of my life? Was that it? Or was it success such as I had still not known, wealth that would allow me every luxury, the gratifying knowledge that I was climbing, climbing, gaining a higher rung each time. . . . Was it to be a marchioness? Even that seemed empty, now that it was within sight. . . .

My reverie was interrupted by the stewardess. She came down the aisle distributing pink paper hats and paper cups of champagne. "Just a little of the Christmas spirit," she said gaily.

I sipped the champagne and sat with my paper hat perched crazily on my head and looked out the window into the dark night.

Book III

CHAPTER FIFTEEN

From *Daily Variety*, Hollywood, August 6, 1936:

Studio publicity heads may take action to ban girl correspondent for big newspaper feature syndicate. Gal has been sniping at Hollywood pictures. . . . Has had several brushes with studios. . . . There is now talk of getting Hays to call in hatchet men.

Looking back on my first months as a syndicated movie columnist, there is no doubt in my mind that I landed in Hollywood on two left feet. The shock technique that had made SHEILAH GRAHAM SAYS so successful in New York was far less appreciated in the proud, tight little closed corporation that was Hollywood.

I had sensed at the beginning that I could reach the head of the class here in only one way—by having the sharpest, most startlingly candid column in Hollywood. Only in that way could I hope to compete with Louella Parsons, the most widely read Hollywood columnist in the country. I would write what I saw without fear or favor, as in New York I had begun by writing outspokenly of what others knew but dared not express.

The result was catastrophic. I knew no rules, recognized no sacred cows. In my brashness there was an element of desperation, too. I knew no one in the movie colony; in the first days I simply invited myself to parties. Time and again when I attached myself to a group at someone's home and hopefully ventured a few words, the group seemed to dissolve and I would be left standing alone. Again the horror of rejection, of feeling *outside,* of being *scorned*—as if these people knew instinctively that I was of commoner clay—came over me. I took it, perhaps unconsciously, as an attack on my very right to exist and as always, when attacked, I wanted to leap up and claw. Thus, in a movie colony where Clark Gable and Joan Crawford were major names, I wrote, "Clark Gable threw back his handsome head and exposed a chin line upon which a thin ridge of fat is beginning to collect." I wrote, "If they hadn't said to me, 'Miss Graham, we want you to meet Joan Crawford,' I would never have recognized her in this tired, sallow-faced woman." Kay Francis, I told my readers, painted on her famous widow's peak. I previewed Metro-Goldwyn-Mayer's new film, *Suzie,* starring Jean Harlow: "I can't understand why a company with the best producers, the best writers, the best actors, the best cameraman, should make a picture like *Suzie* which has the worst acting, the worst photography, the worst direction—"

It was this paragraph, appearing in my column before the picture's release—just as M-G-M was enthusiastically advertising it throughout the country—that led to reports that Will Hays, Hollywood czar, might be asked to take action against me.

John Wheeler sent me an anguished telegram. "You are *not* Walter Winchell." Why must I strike so hard? I could not explain. To everything I saw and heard, my reaction was immediate: this is the way I feel, right or wrong. Perhaps because so much of my life had been pretense I now had to be absolutely, compulsively honest, at whatever cost. Perhaps I merely feared exposure and thought the best way to establish a defense was to write as truthfully as I knew how. That, at least, would be added to the scales if and when the awful moment of exposure came.

Some of my difficulties also rose from ignorance. Marion Davies invited me to her magnificent beach house. I reported that it was a beautiful mansion, the drawing room filled with priceless paintings. "But I cannot understand why Miss Davies allows her hall to be cluttered up with such horrible caricatures." No one informed me that these were paintings of Miss Davies in her various screen roles.

I was dined at the Trocadero Restaurant, then the most fashionable in Hollywood. I wrote: "Not even the doubtful pleasure of rubbing elbows with Louis B. Mayer can compensate for the high prices charged for rather inferior food." No one told me that the Trocadero's owner, Billy Wilkerson, also owned *The Hollywood Reporter,* a most influential trade paper. With one sentence I had made an enemy of the powerful Louis B. Mayer and had invited Mr. Wilkerson and his *Reporter* to declare open season on Sheilah Graham.

But Sheilah Graham's column *was* read.

"Robert Benchley will show you around," John Wheeler had told me. "I'll write him."

Now I sat at the Brown Derby restaurant with Robert Benchley, the celebrated wit and writer for *The New Yorker* magazine. He was round-faced, quizzical, with a little mustache and cornflower-blue eyes creased in a constant smile of good humor. He was given to sudden, booming laughter which made me congratulate myself on my own wit. He could not get over the fact that an English girl of my social background—tutors, French finishing school, presentation at court—should have become a Hollywood columnist embroiled in altercation with some of the biggest names in the movie colony. "Well," he said, chuckling, "Little Sheilah, the Giant-Killer." I should be playing croquet on some English greensward instead of frantically dashing about from studio to studio picking up gossip.

We had discovered that we were neighbors. I had taken a small apartment on Sunset Boulevard; Benchley lived across the street in a hotel romantically named, "The Garden of Allah," a favorite residence of screen writers. Once owned by Alla Nazimova, the great silent screen star, it consisted of tiny two-story Spanish stucco bungalows, quite charming, each with two apartments. They surrounded a main house with pool and patio where pretty starlets promenaded in their brief swim suits. Benchley and I spoke of people we knew—Deems Taylor and Dorothy Parker were his close friends—and when I finished the glass of sherry in front of me, he said, "Let me order something else for you." Before I could stop him, I was served a gin drink.

I looked at it doubtfully. "Are you sure these mix? I've heard you can get deathly ill—"

Benchley grinned. "Take my word for it," he said. "Best mixture you could possibly have." I drank it down and before I reached my apartment a few minutes later, I was deathly ill.

Next day Mr. Benchley was on the phone. How did I feel? he asked solicitously. I was furious. If this was Benchley humor, he could save it for *The New Yorker*!

"Yes," he said, sadly, in a most apologetic voice. "I was

afraid of that." I heard his self-deprecating chuckle. "After you left I began to think perhaps I might have given you very bad advice." As a peace offering, he invited me to dinner. I accepted and all was forgiven. Through Benchley, in the weeks that followed, I came to know his fellow screen writers at the Garden of Allah—Edwin Justus Mayer, author of *Children of Darkness*, John O'Hara, who had just written *Butterfield 8*, Marc Connolly, author of *Green Pastures*. I was delighted to be greeted again by Dorothy Parker, who had come to Hollywood with Alan Campbell, a playwright she had just married. I began to know Hollywood.

It was, I discovered, a frantic city and a slumbrous village, in which great wisdom and great absurdity, enormous talent and enormous mediocrity, existed side by side. The Hollywood I came to was the Hollywood of Norma Shearer and Shirley Temple, Jean Harlow and Constance Bennett; where friends at a dinner hid a tape recorder under the chair of John Barrymore as he whispered romantically to Elaine Barrie, and everyone wagered huge sums on Jock Whitney's ponies at the newly opened Santa Anita track. It was the Hollywood of the President's Birthday Ball, of Nelson Eddy and Jeanette MacDonald, Mary Pickford and Buddy Rogers, Ernst Lubitsch and Irving Thalberg—a city of dreams and dream makers where the sun shone brightly and only when you thought about it did you realize that you were chilled. . . .

That first year and a half, until the summer of 1937, I was a girl on the town and enjoyed it. By now Johnny was resigned to our divorce: in early 1937 I instituted proceedings. My papers would be ready in June. After the first outcry over my column, the protests had died down and I discovered how pleasant Hollywood could be for an unattached girl who earned her own living, was beholden to no man, and whose social and professional life so neatly complemented each other that it was difficult to know where duty ended and pleasure began. The items for my column came not only from my conscientious daily visits to the studios but from my friends—and that circle grew.

Through Bob Benchley and Eddie Mayer, a big, thoughtful, extremely good-hearted friend, I came to know many eligible men in Hollywood. I was always on tap for tennis or dancing, or to be taken to dinner, or to a party at the David Selznicks, or the Basil Rathbones, or the Frank Morgans. It was preferable to go escorted than to go alone. And in the midst of my busy days, running through them like a leitmotiv to dull the sense that time was fleeing, were the affectionate letters from Lord Donegall reminding me that if and when I made up my mind in far-off Hollywood, his lordship would be on hand.

In June I made a quick trip to London for my divorce, and once again saw Johnny: the meeting was sad, but we parted friends. On my last day I lunched with Donegall.

I remember I had just finished my steak-and-kidney pie when an elderly man at another table waved to me. I waved back. Donegall asked curiously, "Who is that?" I wiped my mouth with my napkin. "My lawyer, Mr. T. Cannon Brooks, a most respectable gentleman." And, I added, "It may interest you to know that I got my divorce this morning."

Don nearly dropped his knife and fork. "What!" he exclaimed, delightedly. "How could you have sat through the whole meal without telling me?" For a moment he was overcome. "Sheilah, darling," he said. "Now the way is clear!" He took my hand and pressed it fervently, his large brown eyes brimming with emotion. I was touched. I thought, I *am* fond of this man. I *could* learn to love him. I had not told him about the divorce because I feared he would hunt through the vital statistics and come upon the notice and so learn my real name. But Donegall did not press me. He was too busy with plans. "Well! Now that you're free I'm coming to Hollywood myself to make up your mind for you. You'll see I mean this. I'll be there in two weeks."

Two weeks later Donegall turned up in Hollywood to urge his suit. He took me to a fashionable jewelers and bought me an engagement ring. As he slipped it gently on my finger he said, "This will do until I have one made up in London for you." He met Bob Benchley and liked him instantly. "Bob will be our best man," said his lordship masterfully. We would be married on New Year's Eve—under British law I could not remarry until six months had elapsed. Our honeymoon would be spent on a cruise around the world. Now he had to return to London—there was Mother to persuade, he was sure he would succeed, but if she proved difficult, we'd go forward with the marriage anyway. He kissed me long and ardently. Was my mind made up?

Only now, as Donegall's plans took such confident shape, did it occur to me that this *could* come true. Perhaps, I thought, this isn't a top-of-the-bus dream. He means it. He followed me to Hollywood to ask me. He has given me the ring. I dared believe it, and I found myself trembling. It could happen. I saw the headlines: "Cochran Young Lady Marries Marquess." I thought, this will be the most fantastic climax of all to this fantastic journey I have taken through life.

I saw the proud coronet on my stationery, my lingerie, my linen, the centuries-old coat of arms. I saw myself at Buckingham Palace, sitting as a marchioness, a lady, a viscountess and a baroness, above all other peers of the realm, below only the dukes and princes of the blood royal. I saw my name and the name of my issue in *Burke's Peerage*, and in *Debrett*. The gentle birth I had been denied and had envied every waking moment since I first knew who I was, I would now bestow upon my children. . . .

I thought, almost fearfully, am I strong enough to see this through? Can I get away with it? Must I tell everything to Donegall? Perhaps I don't have to tell Donegall everything.

I accepted the hand of my suitor, the Marquess and Earl of Donegall, the Viscount of Chichester, the Earl of Belfast, the Baron Fisherwick of Fisherwick, the Hereditary Lord High Admiral of Lough Neagh.

Benchley was among the first to congratulate us. He would be honored and delighted to be the best man at our wedding. When was Donegall returning to London? Tomorrow, said my fiancé. "Then we'll celebrate tonight," said Benchley. He was all enthusiasm. "Let's have a party." He thought for a moment, and added, with a grin, "It's July Fourteenth—Bastille Day in France. We'll celebrate the Fall of the Bastille, too!"

And at the party Robert Benchley gave to celebrate my engagement to Lord Donegall on the night of July 14, 1937, I saw F. Scott Fitzgerald for the first time.

CHAPTER SIXTEEN

IT BEGAN at my house high in the Hollywood hills, which I'd rented a few weeks before. Benchley lent me his German boy to serve. Donegall and I were toasted in champagne, and I wandered happily among my guests—Eddie Mayer, Frank Morgan, Lew Ayres, Charlie Butterworth, writers and actors and their wives and girls. From my little terrace the lights of Hollywood far below gleamed and flickered like tiny paper lanterns strung through the streets of some distant, festive city floating in the sky. It was a night for dreams.

I clung to Donegall's arm. What more lovely dream of splendor could I wish for? The toasts and good healths came fast. Benchley's boy served industriously, we all drank, and amid the laughter and gaiety I heard Bob shout, "Let's all go to my place! Remember the Bastille!"

Noisily we piled into half a dozen cars parked outside and drove down the hill to the Garden of Allah. We trooped into Bob's small drawing room and there was more champagne, and more guests—Dorothy Parker, Alan Campbell, a European actress named Tala Birrell—and the party went on even more merrily. Donegall's arm was around me, Frank Morgan was telling a hilarious story, and almost casually I became aware of blue smoke curling lazily upward in the bright radiance of a lamp. Then I saw a man I had not seen before. He sat quietly in an easy chair under the lamp, and from a cigarette motionless in his hand the blue smoke wafted slowly upward. I stared at him, not sure whether I saw him or not: he seemed unreal, sitting there so quietly, so silently, in this noisy room, watching everything yet talking to no one, no one talking to him—a slight, pale man who appeared to be all shades of the palest, most delicate blue: his hair was pale, his face was pale, like a Marie Laurencin pastel, his suit was blue, his eyes, his lips were blue, behind the veil of blue smoke he seemed an apparition that might vanish at any moment. I turned to laugh with Frank Morgan; Bob spoke to me; when I looked again, the chair was empty. Only the blue smoke remained in the heavy air, curling upon itself as it slowly flowed into the updraft of the lamp. I thought, someone *was* there.

I turned to Bob. "Who was that man sitting under the lamp? He was so quiet."

Bob looked. "That was F. Scott Fitzgerald—the writer. I asked him to drop in." He peered owlishly about the room. "I guess he's left—he hates parties."

"Oh," I said. "I wish I'd known before. I would have liked to talk to him." I thought, he's the writer of the gay twenties, of flaming youth, of bobbed hair and short skirts and crazy drinking—the jazz age. I had even made use of his name: in SHEILAH GRAHAM SAYS, when I wanted to chide women for silly behavior, I described them as passé, as old-fashioned F. Scott Fitzgerald types, though I had never read anything he wrote. It might have been interesting to talk to him.

Then Benchley was launched on a long, brilliant speech in which every sentence, Eddie Mayer told me later, was the tagline of a dirty story, and I quite forgot the man under the lamp.

Next morning I drove Donegall to the airport and saw him off to New York, London—and his mother. "She'll weaken, I know she will," he assured me. He was most tender, most affectionate, on the ride out. "Good-by, your ladyship," he said, and kissed me. I drove back lost in lovely dreams. *Your ladyship!*

A few days later Marc Connolly asked me to a Writers' Guild dinner dance at the Coconut Grove in downtown Los Angeles. He had taken a table for ten; so had Dorothy Parker, chairman of the evening. I don't know how it happened but a moment came when I found myself sitting all alone at our long table, and at Dorothy's table, parallel to ours, sat a man I recognized as Scott Fitzgerald, all alone at his table. We were facing each other. He looked at me almost inquiringly as if to say, I have seen you somewhere, haven't I? and smiled. I smiled back. Seeing him clearly now, I saw that he looked tired, his face was pale, pale as it had been behind the veil of blue smoke that night at Benchley's, but I found him most appealing: his hair pale blond, a wide, attractive forehead, gray-blue eyes set far apart, set beautifully in his head, a straight, sharply chiseled nose and an expressive mouth that seemed to sag a little at the corners, giving the face a gently melancholy expression. He appeared to be in his forties but it was difficult to know; he looked half-young, half-old: the thought flashed through my mind, he should get out into the sun, he needs light and air and warmth. Then he leaned forward and said, smiling across the two tables, "I like you."

I was pleased. Smiling, I said to him, "I like you, too."

There was silence for a moment. This was my first evening out since my engagement and, in a magnificent evening gown of gray with a crimson velvet sash, I felt exquisitely beautiful, as befitted a girl who was to become a marchioness. I felt myself radiant, caught in the golden haze as when I parted the curtains and stood before the audience in Mimi Crawford's place on the stage of the London Pavilion. . . . To be sitting now, alone, while everyone was dancing, seemed such a waste. I said to Mr. Fitzgerald, "Why don't we dance?"

He smiled again, a quick smile that suddenly transfigured his face: it was eager and youthful now, with all trace of melancholy gone. "I'm afraid I promised to dance the next one with Dorothy Parker. But after that—"

But when everyone returned to their tables the band stopped playing; there were many speeches and when they were over everyone scrambled to go home and I did not see him again. Marc Connolly took me home and once more I had brushed against this quiet, attractive man and we had careened off in opposite directions.

Yet something was at work.

At seven o'clock the following Saturday evening Eddie Mayer telephoned just as I was closing the door to go out. "What are you doing tonight?" I was bound for a concert at the Hollywood Bowl with Jonah Ruddy, resident correspondent for several British newspapers, who had helped me on a number of stories. I told Eddie.

"A pity," he said. "Scott Fitzgerald is with me and I wanted you to join us for dinner."

I said, unhappily, "I'd love to, Eddie, but it's really too late to cancel Mr. Ruddy—"

"Why don't you bring him along?" suggested Eddie.

We met at the Garden of Allah and went to the Clover Club, a gambling place with dining and dancing upstairs. Scott said little on the way out—there was a reticence about him that made me feel he belonged to an earlier, quieter world. His clothes, too, spoke of another time: he wore a pepper-and-salt suit and a bow tie, and though this was July, a wrinkled charcoal raincoat with a scarf about his neck and a battered hat. It was hard to believe that this was the glamor boy of the twenties. At the bar we were introduced to Humphrey Bogart and his wife, Mayo Methot. "Won't you have a drink with us?" Bogart asked Scott.

He shook his head and said, pleasantly, no. Bogart seemed surprised. We sat with them for a few minutes and Scott made some light jokes about a picture he was writing for M-G-M. The Bogarts laughed and I caught respect and deference. Jonah Ruddy, who seemed to know something about everyone in Hollywood and so was not easily awed, seemed most impressed, too.

Now, finally, I danced with Scott, and as we danced, the room and everyone in it—Eddie, Jonah, the others dancing and chattering about us—faded away. It is hard to put into words how Scott Fitzgerald worked this magic, but he made me feel that to dance with me was the most extraordinary privilege for him. He did it by his words, which seemed directed to me alone; he did it by the way he tilted his head back, a little to one side, as though he were mentally measuring, and then took complete possession of my eyes, my hair, my lips, all with a kind of delighted amazement at his good fortune to be dancing with me. He gave me the delightful feeling that hundreds of attractive men were just waiting for the chance to cut in on him and to snatch me away because I was so irresistible—and the feeling, too, that he would not let me out of his arms if he had to fight every one of them. He did it, too, by the rapt attention he gave to what I said, as though I was never to be dismissed as shallow or unimportant, that my opinions were of value and were to be respected. Once, to something I said, he exclaimed, "Oh, that's very witty. I want to remember to write it down when we get back to the table." I was immensely flattered. *This man appreciates my mind as well as my face.*

We danced; we never sat down. The room went round and round. Now, though the courtliness, the exquisite manners were there, on the floor he was like an American college boy. He was only a few inches taller than I but he was sinewy, strong, and firm, his step gay and youthful and sometimes we danced cheek to cheek. I thought, now I know what it must have been like to dance at a college prom. I said, "I *love* dancing!" He said, "I do, too." I went on, "When I was a girl in England, I lived to dance—it gave me such a feeling of freedom—" He nodded, his blue eyes still wonderingly on my face as if there were nowhere else to look. He was so easy to talk to, so understanding. In London I had met Evelyn Waugh, the writer, who wrote about the twenties too, but Waugh had been so bored with me that I had been struck dumb. I could talk to this man. He asked me endless questions. How old was I? "Twenty-seven," I said, lying by a year. How old was he? Forty, he said, with a little grimace. "How did a girl as beautiful as you come to be a columnist?" he asked. I preened myself and smiled. I had been on the stage, I had been a dancer, I tried to become a Shakespearean actress, but that had been dreadful. I told him of the note from Kenneth Barnes, Director of the Royal Academy of Dramatic Art: "It is imperative that you improve." He put his head back and laughed. He thought it very funny.

We danced the tango; we took over a corner of the floor as our own and danced separately, experimenting with the most amazing steps; we laughed together, struck at the same moment by the same absurdity; we were completely impervious to our surroundings. I thought, *this man is not forty, he is a young man, he is a college boy, he is utterly delightful*. When, finally, we returned to our table where Eddie and Jonah sat with admirable patience, we looked at them as though they were strangers who had usurped our seats. Scott took out a notebook and to my intense pleasure wrote down my bon mot. Then he sipped a Coca-Cola and took me on the floor again while Eddie and Jonah grinned at each other. Would I have dinner with him? I said, yes. When? I said, Tuesday. Good, he said. Finally our little party broke up and I was taken home. And I thought about Scott.

He had spoken hardly at all about himself, deliberately, it seemed, focusing the attention on me. "Eddie told me that you're engaged to the Marquess of Donegall," he said. I nodded. "And you're to be married in December?" I said yes, but I could not help smiling up at him. If I flirted, it was because it was my nature to flirt; but far more than that, it was because I liked him enormously, I liked the way he made me feel about myself. I wanted to please him because he admired me and from what little I had seen and heard, to be admired by Scott was a great compliment.

Eddie told me later that Scott had arrived in Hollywood only a few days before my party and had moved into the apartment directly above him in one of the Garden of Allah's charming little bungalows. He had come west on a six-month contract to write the screen play for *A Yank at Oxford*. Eddie smiled a little sadly as he told me this. They had hired Scott Fitzgerald, he went on, because Scott's first novel, *This Side of Paradise,* a remarkable first novel which made him famous as a young man just out of Princeton, dealt with college youth. But from *This*

Side of Paradise to *A Yank at Oxford*—Eddie shook his head. It was obvious that he thought it a great waste of this man's time to write for pictures.

On Saturday night Scott had wandered downstairs and dropped in on Eddie. Because he seemed lonely, a little lost, Eddie suggested they dine together. Scott said, "You know, I saw a girl here I like." He described her. "You must mean Sheilah Graham," Eddie said, and when Scott remarked, almost casually, "I'd like to meet her," Eddie telephoned me.

By Tuesday I had learned a little more about Scott Fitzgerald. He was married but his wife Zelda, a great beauty with whom he was very much in love, was in a mental institution and had been for some time. It was a tragic story. So that, I thought, lies behind the sad line of his mouth, explains the hint of melancholy lurking behind his reserve. From scraps of conversation between Eddie and Bob Benchley, I gathered that Scott and Zelda had lived a rather daring, unconventional life, full of outrageous pranks and escapades. Once they had jumped fully dressed into the fountain in front of the Plaza Hotel in New York. They would hire taxicabs and ride on the hood. I thought to myself, that isn't screamingly funny. I gathered, too, that though Eddie and his friends looked on Scott as a great American writer, nobody paid much attention to him now. People were reading his contemporaries—Ernest Hemingway, Thomas Wolfe, John Steinbeck—while Scott was appearing only now and then in magazines such as *Esquire*.

Tuesday afternoon a telegram arrived from Scott. He could not keep our engagement that evening. His daughter had just arrived from the East and he was taking her to dinner. I recalled that he had spoken of his fifteen-year-old daughter, Scottie, who attended boarding school in

Connecticut. Helen Hayes, a friend of the Fitzgeralds,
was bringing her to California on a brief visit. I stared at
the telegram, astonished at the intensity of my disappointment. For a moment I was dismayed: how could I be so
shaken by this? I was to marry Donegall in six months:
how could I be so affected by a broken date with a man—
and a married man—whom I had seen for the first time
less than ten days ago? Yet suddenly I knew I must see
Scott again. Nothing else mattered. I telephoned him.
"Scott," I said, "it makes no difference, your daughter
being here. I'd like to meet her. Can't we all go to
dinner?"

There was a pause. Then, reluctantly, "All right. I'll
pick you up at seven."

Scottie was a pretty, vivacious girl with her father's
eyes and forehead, which made me like her instantly.
Two boys she had known in the East had called and Scott
had invited them, too. At dinner, however, Scott was an
altogether different man from the charming cavalier who
had danced with me. He was tense and on edge: he was
continually correcting his daughter unfairly and embar-
rassingly. "Scottie, finish your meat," and "Scottie, don't
touch your hair," and "Scottie, sit up straight." She en-
dured it patiently but now and then she turned on him
with a despairing, "Oh, Daddy, please—" As the evening
progressed Scott grew increasingly nervous, drumming on
the table, lighting one cigarette from another, and drinking endless Coca-Colas. It was obvious that he loved his
daughter but he fussed about her unbearably. My heart
went out to Scottie who would sit there, silently, and
sigh as if to say, why doesn't he stop it? Then she and the
boys would fall to giggling, only to have Scott interrupt
with a heavily jovial story which they apparently found
not funny at all. Scott and I danced a few times but he

was distracted and worried. The evening was a strain for everyone. I thought, is this the man I found so fascinating? This anxious, middle-aged father? It was a relief when he said to his daughter, "Scottie, don't you think it's time for you to be in bed? I ought to take you back to the hotel." We dropped the boys off, then dropped Scottie at the hotel where she was staying with Miss Hayes, and Scott took me to my home on the hill.

He stood at the door, saying good-by. I felt utterly lonely and on the point of tears. There had been such a magical quality about him the other night and now he was only a faded little man who was a father. He said good night. I did not want him to go; I felt inexpressibly sad that something that had been so enormously exciting and warming had gone. I thought, oh, what a pity to lose this. In the half light, as he stood there, his face was beautiful. You could not see the tiredness, the grayness, you saw only his eyes, set so beautifully in his head, and the marvelous line from cheekbone to chin. I wanted desperately to recapture the enchantment that had been and I heard myself whisper, "Please don't go, come in," and I drew him in and he came in and as he came in he kissed me and suddenly he was not a father anymore and it was as though this was as it should be, must be, inevitable and foreordained.

CHAPTER SEVENTEEN

IN LATE AUGUST there came a cablegram from London:

BEST NEWS ON EARTH DARLING STOP MOTHER
IS ON OUR SIDE STOP THIS MAKES THINGS SO
MUCH EASIER STOP WIRE ME SWEETHEART MY
LOVE

DON

I sat at my desk before a window that looked out on the green mountainside. I could not write my column: that *The Good Earth* was setting new attendance records, that John Barrymore had unaccountably vanished from the set of *Romeo and Juliet*, that Louella Parsons printed items before I had them—my mind refused to deal with these. I wanted to see Scott. I wanted to see the quick, warm smile that lingered in his eyes long after his mouth reverted to its secret melancholy. I wanted to see the look on his face when he saw me, the look that said, What a precious treasure you are and how lucky I am to have found you! I wanted to be with him, to talk to him, to hear his voice. In the most compelling way he had become my entire world—as though I had been caught up in a huge, overwhelming event that had no past, no future, but simply *was*.

Almost absentmindedly I reread Donegall's cable. Poor Don! He had won her over—and I did not really care. For a moment the words struck me as almost ludicrous. *Mother is on our side.* Instead of wiring I wrote a pleasant letter to him that I was delighted his mother approved of me, I was very busy, I would write again soon. If an earldom was slipping through my fingers, I felt curiously untouched by it. There was little room for Donegall in my world—now.

In those first weeks Scott and I talked incessantly. We saw each other almost every evening. He wrote at the Metro studio during the day and I used those hours to gather items so that I would be free for him at night. He had bought a second-hand Ford coupé and each day about six o'clock I'd hear his rattlesome little car come chattering up my hill, and then the cheerful "Toot! Toot!" of his horn as he rounded a bend in the road just before my house. With his battered collegiate hat and raincoat, his pullover sweaters and jaunty bow ties, he reminded me more and more of all I had read about American college boys of the twenties. Enroute to dinner sometimes we stopped off at the Garden of Allah for a highball with Eddie, or John O'Hara, or Albert and Frances Hackett, writers who belonged in his world. Scott invariably took Coca-Cola and I a little sherry. Then we would go on to a little restaurant.

We talked. What sorcery had brought me from London and him from St. Paul, Minnesota, and thrown us together here in Hollywood? He had wanted to see me again after his first glimpse of me at Benchley's party.

Later that night Bob called Scott to say he was sorry Scott had left so early and wouldn't he like to come down now for a midnight snack? Scott, never at his best with strangers, had asked anxiously, "Who's still there?" Bob had said, "Frank Morgan, Mrs. Morgan and Tala Birrell. Everyone else has left."

Thinking I was the European actress Tala Birrell, Scott had gone back to Benchley's, only to discover his mistake. Then, at the Writers Guild dance—he hadn't wanted to go there, but Dorothy Parker prevailed upon him—he had seen me again: we had exchanged two sentences and I had vanished. And when he had concluded that I was too elusive ever to be captured, Eddie Mayer, like a smiling Aladdin brandishing a telephone instead of a lamp, had produced me. . . . Listening to Scott, I had had no idea how much all this had meant to him—that some day he would make use of it in his own book.

Scott wanted to know everything about me. He probed like a reporter after a story. Instinctively I knew he would scorn the shoddy. I was prepared to suffer any ordeal rather than reveal the truth about myself. I thought, he has chosen me. I want him to be proud of the woman he has chosen. He must never feel that his girl is in reality a grubby little waif who has gotten to him by a series of deceptions. I wanted him to have the best because he deserved the best. So I related my well-rehearsed story. My mother died when I was seventeen; my rich aunt presented me at court; I found society boring, so I had tried the stage, which led to an article on stage-door Johnnies and that to New York and Hollywood.

I squirmed when Scott gazed at my "family" photographs: my brother David who died before I was born, my sister Alicia, my grandfather (this was Sir Richard resplendent in hunting kit with top hat and pink coat astride a magnificent horse from his stables in Ireland). I felt trapped. To the one man I longed to unburden myself completely, who treated me with such respect, I had to tell and even authenticate my spurious story. When he pressed me too hard, I managed to shift the conversation to him.

I was learning to know his boyishness and yet his dignity, which allowed one to go so far, and no further. We had been invited to a party given by Gladys Swarthout and her husband, Frank Chapman. I knew everyone now, Scott knew no one. At one point I saw him wandering about nervously, looking lost. I was on a settee chatting with friends; I gestured to him and patted the seat beside me. "Scott, come and sit here next to me." His face tightened and he turned away. Later he said, "Don't ever do that." I protested, a little hurt. "But Scott, you looked so uncomfortable—" He said, "I can perfectly well take care of myself." Those were his sharpest words to me until now. I said to myself, you cannot take liberties with this man. You cannot patronize—or pity him.

I felt this even more strongly when we attended a movie *première*. "Let's not go in the front, Sheilo," he said. Although it was important for me to interview the stars who thronged the lobby, I slipped into a side entrance with him and we took unobtrusive seats in the back. Was he protecting his fallen estate? Until the house lights dimmed he fidgeted nervously, his head down, his eyes on his program. He wanted not to be seen—as though he feared people would recognize him and be sorry for him as a writer whose works weren't being read.

I tried to bolster him in my own way. "Scott," I said one evening, "I feel badly. Here you are, a famous writer, and I've not read a thing you've written. I want to read every one of your books."

"Do you really?" he asked, pleased. I discovered that when he spoke of his work he never disparaged it: he spoke of it with great seriousness. It was not a subject for self-deprecation or witticisms. "All right, Sheilo. I'll get you my books. Let's get them tonight." After dinner, we strolled into Hollywood's biggest book store. Scott asked, "Have you books by F. Scott Fitzgerald?"

The clerk, a young man, said, "Sorry—none in stock." He turned inquiringly to another customer.

"Do you have any calls for them?" Scott pursued.

"Oh—once in a while," said the clerk. "But not for some time, now."

I did not look at Scott as we walked out but I said hurriedly, "Let's try another place." It was the same story there. At the third bookstore, a small shop, the owner, a gray-haired man, was on a ladder placing a book on a high shelf. He came down slowly. At Scott's question he shook his head but said, "I believe I can get hold of a title or two. Which ones are you interested in?"

"I'd appreciate that," Scott said, carefully. He gave him the names of three: *This Side of Paradise, The Great Gatsby, Tender Is The Night*. The gray-haired man said, "I'll do my best to find these for you."

Scott said, almost diffidently, "I'm Mr. Fitzgerald."

The other's eyes widened. He put out his hand and shook Scott's warmly. "I'm happy to meet you, Mr. Fitzgerald," he said. "I've enjoyed your books very much." He was quite impressed. He took Scott's address. "I'll really get these for you, and if there aren't any about, I'll order them from the publishers."

Scott thanked him and we left the store. I wondered,

how must he feel to have been so famous once and almost unknown now—the courteous, self-effacing man who escorted Sheilah Graham to dinners and *premières,* but always slipped in the side entrance with her, and always, when introduced to her friends, had to face the same reaction: a widening of the eyes, a smile of surprise as though they were astonished to find that F. Scott Fitzgerald was still alive.

There was so much I did not know about Scott. Salaries in Hollywood are no secret: I learned that he was being paid a thousand dollars a week for the period of his six months' contract. Compared to the hundred and sixty a week John Wheeler was now paying me, this was a fortune. I thought only eccentricity led Scott to ride about in his little second-hand car, and to wear nondescript clothes. Only later was I to learn that he was in debt more than forty thousand dollars, that the cost of Zelda's sanitarium and keeping Scottie in boarding school were tremendous burdens; that more than a year before he had suffered a terrifying breakdown, a period of utter panic in which he thought he would never write again, that drinking had been his demon and his despair; that he had come to Hollywood in a desperate attempt to re-establish himself, hoping to earn enough money to pay his debts and perhaps be enabled to return to serious writing again.

I knew none of this because Scott told me none of it. I knew him only as a charming courtier who sent me flowers several times a week, always with an amusing little note, who thought up new surprises for me, with whom no hour was mundane. The day after our first dinner, a lovely bouquet had arrived with a card, "Welcome To The New Arrival." It showed a stork carrying a baby. Scott, with a pen, had embellished the drawing until the baby had become a delightful caricature of himself, complete to battered hat. To one side he had sketched a little suitcase on which he had printed his name. Sometimes the notes accompanying the flowers were signed, "F. Scott Fitzdillinger," if we had been discussing gangsters the night before, or "From Dmitri to Gruschenko" if—at his suggestion—I had begun to read *The Brothers Karamazov*. He loved to clown—when we played Ping-pong, a favorite game, he'd cross his eyes ferociously and gaze off to the left while smacking the ball to the right. When he lunched daily at the Metro commissary, he was able to maintain the pretense for nearly a week that he had a twin brother, Irish Fitzgerald, who also ate there. Each time our waiter sought to resume a conversation of the day before, Scott would say, perplexed. "You must have been talking to my twin brother, Irish." The waiter would protest: "But didn't you tell me yesterday the reason the planets moved around the sun—?" "No, no," Scott would interrupt, straight-faced. "That was my brother, Irish." The next day Scott became Irish Fitzgerald: "Are you sure you're not confusing me with my twin brother Scott?" The waiter would reel away completely bewildered, leaving Scott as delighted as a little boy with the success of his game.

I knew him as a man who, for all his gaiety, his antic humor, his private sorrows—which only later I came to share—could envelop me in infinite tenderness, who seemed to know, almost as with a sixth sense, that behind my banalities and frivolities I was engaged in a desperate struggle the nature of which I was not even sure; and that he would never judge, never censure, but understand and, understanding, cherish and protect me.

There was no way for me to know about his earlier life, the deep emotional relationship he had had with another woman before he met me. I knew only the Scott I knew and he began to exist for me only on the day I met him. All that had happened before was unreal and had never happened.

Yet he continued to probe into my own life. It was not a one-time interrogation: it came at intervals, now in my home, now at his apartment, or as we drove or dined. What of the men I had known before him? How many times had I been in love?

I said, yes, I had been in love before. There was my former husband, Johnny. Scott was enchanted by Major John Gillam, D.S.O., and his endless troubles with the John Graham Company, the reluctant sister from whom he borrowed, his confidence until the very day of his bankruptcy that a fortune would fall into his hands tomorrow. Yes, I had been very much in love with Johnny. "And any others?" Scott asked, half-teasing. The way he asked the question seemed to make it a challenge and I responded to it. I wanted to shock him. "Oh, I've had romances," I said. "You know, I'm an English girl and we're quite straightforward about such things. If we love a man, we love him."

"Yes?" said Scott, still half-teasing. "I know all about love among the British upper classes. And as one of Cochran's Young Ladies I imagine you must have been quite popular. More than one romance?"

We were driving at this moment to lunch at Malibu Beach, perhaps twenty miles from Hollywood. I was at the wheel and so I did not see his face as I replied, rather flippantly, "Why, of course. Eight, if I remember." I thought eight an interesting number. "There was a titled gentleman, there was a captain of industry, there was—"

I chattered on and then, hearing nothing from Scott, I

stole a glance at him. He sat looking straight ahead, a set smile on his face, and it came to me that he was not enjoying this. He was shocked. I said, a little unhappily, "Scott, I'm sorry we got on this. You're angry."

"Oh, no, no, no," he said. And then, almost with asperity, "Tell me, who were they?"

I tried to dismiss the subject. "Oh, this was ages before I met you, Scott, and you know how I exaggerate and anyway it doesn't have anything to do with you—"

Now he looked at me. "When a man falls in love it is a completely new experience," he said. "But for a woman it is an additional experience to those she has already had." I wasn't sure I knew what he meant. Did this mean that he could not compare me to Zelda but that I would compare him with others?

He was quite silent, then, and as I drove I tried to undo the damage. I had been provoking him, I said, I wanted to see how he would react, I was being silly and coquettish, I was teasing him—

Gradually he came back to his original mood. He smiled at me. "It's all right, Sheilo," he said, and changed the subject. For a little while we discussed an offer I had received to appear on a half-hour weekly radio show emanating from Chicago which would cut to Hollywood for a five-minute summary of movie news by me. It was a marvellous opportunity. I had been offered a hundred dollars a week; Scott, who was beginning to involve himself in all my activities, advised me to ask for two hundred dollars. I had done so, and the Chicago advertising agency in charge of the account was to make a decision soon.

It was on the way back from Malibu that Scott said, "Tell me about yourself before the stage, Sheilo. What kind of a girl were you when you were growing up?"

"Oh, Scott, I've told you—" I began. But it was difficult to evade him. When Scott was after facts, he was relentless. What I had said about the other men apparently had set him off. Where had my people come from? Was Graham a Scotch name? German? Had my father been in business, the professions? What was his full name? "John Lawrence Graham," I said. I was wretched. "And your mother's?" "Veronica Roslyn Graham," I said, feeling even worse. He kept on probing. What sort of woman was my mother? Where was my sister Alicia now? What part of London had I grown up in? What was I like as a child? What school had I gone to—

No sooner had I answered one question than the next one came. I kept up with him as best I could, but suddenly the burden of it all became too much and I burst into tears. I had to bring the car to a halt on the side of the road and I wept. Scott was utterly dismayed. He put his arm around me and exclaimed in alarm, "What is it, what is it? What have I said to hurt you?" He held me close. "I'm sorry, Sheilo, I had no idea—is there something you don't want to tell me? You needn't—"

And I blurted it out. I was sobbing almost hysterically. "If you must know, I never went to a real school—I was brought up in an orphanage. I left school when I was fourteen. I come from the slums of London, from the poorest, shabbiest people—I've lied and pretended. I'm phony. Oh, Scott, you'll hate me—my name's not real, even the pictures you saw aren't real. I'm not what you think at all—"

The tears came uncontrollably. I thought, *he'll never want to see me again. I'm drab, drab, all the glamor is vanishing, I'm turning into clay before his eyes.* But he held me close to him and rocked me in his arms like a child, back and forth, saying, "There, there, don't talk any more. I'm sorry. I'm always so curious about everything. Don't cry." He took out his handkerchief and dried my tears and made me blow my nose. "It isn't that bad, really it isn't," he said, tenderly. "Please believe me." And we sat there, parked at the side of the road for a long time, his arm around me, while I told him, trying to catch my breath, unburdening myself of all the guilt, telling the story I had never told anyone. His reaction was not shock or distaste, but one of tremendous pity for my childhood. I told him everything: the orphanage and our clipped heads, my experience as a skivy, at Gamage's, my yearning to better myself, my top-of-the-bus dreams. I told him about my marriage and our desperate finances, the masquerade Johnny and I maintained, my frantic shuttling back and forth between showgirl and housewife, my turmoil over Cochran, Sir Richard, and the men pursuing me, my endless search for I knew not what—love, security, identity. . . . "I wish I could have known you then," he said, again and again. "I would have taken care of you, you could have come to me." He spoke with such tenderness that I broke down again. "Yes," I sobbed, "where were you then? Why weren't you there? I had no guideposts, I had no one to tell me right and wrong—"

We talked together for a long time. The burden that had been unbearably heavy was lifted at last from my shoulders. There are no words to express the relief I felt now that I need no longer lie to him.

After a little while, he took the wheel and I snuggled next to him and we drove slowly back to Hollywood.

Lost in a dream, I sat on my terrace, looking down on the garlanded lights of distant Hollywood. Mr. James

Wharton, of the Chicago advertising agency, had written me. Two hundred dollars a week was satisfactory: they were signing a six-month contract, my broadcasts to begin the first Monday in October. But it was not this I thought about now. In my hand I held a poem Scott had written and sent to me. It was a poem for me and about me. I had never read anything so beautiful. I read it again and again, now to myself, now aloud, lingering on the words. He had misspelled my name but he misspelled many words and would continue to do so to the end of his days, and it did not matter. The poem read:

FOR SHIELAH: A BELOVED INFIDEL

That sudden smile across a room,
 Was certainly not learned from me
That first faint quiver of a bloom
 The eyes initial extacy,
Whoever taught you how to page
 Your loves so sweetly—now as then
I thank him for my heritage
 The eyes made bright by other men.

No slumbrous pearl is valued less
 For years spent in a rajah's crown
And I should rather rise and bless
 Your earliest love than cry him down
Whoever wound your heart up knew
 His job. How can I hate him when
He did his share to fashion you?
 A heart made warm by other men.

Some kisses nature doesn't plan
 She works in such a sketchy way
The child, tho father to the man
 Must be instructed how to play
What traffic your lips had with mine
 Don't lie in any virgin's ken

I found the oldest, richest wine
  On lips made soft by other men.

The lies you tell are epic things
  No amateur would every try,
Soft little parables with wings,
  I know not even God would cry.
Let every lover be the last
  And whisper, "This is *now*—not **then**"
The sweet denial of the past
  The tale you told to other men.

I'm even glad someone and you
  Found it was joyous to rehearse,
Made it an art to fade into
  The passion of the universe.
The world all crowded in an hour,
  Textbooks in minutes—that has been
Your fate, your wealth, your curious dower,
  The things you learned from other men.

The little time you opened up
  A window, let me look inside,
Gave me the plate, the spoon, the cup,
  The very coat of love that died
Or seemed to die—for as your hand
  Held mine it was alive again
And we were in a lovely land
  The world you had from other men.

But when I join the other ghosts
  Who lay beside your flashing fire
I must believe I'll drink their toasts
  To one who was a sweet desire.
And sweet fulfillment—all they found
  Was worth remembering. And then
He'll hear us as the wine goes around
  A greeting from us other men.

                              —S.

That night I wrote Lord Donegall that I could not marry him. For a moment I had tears in my eyes for my lost dream of being a marchioness. But how could I marry Donegall, being so much in love with Scott?

CHAPTER EIGHTEEN

In mid-september, Scott flew East to visit Zelda. She was in a sanitarium in Asheville, North Carolina. Now and then, I had learned from Eddie Mayer, he took his wife out of the sanitarium for a few days. Her doctors believed these brief visits back into the world might help her. Scott and I had yet to speak of her. Once I had ventured to broach the subject of his wife: he had pushed it aside. I did not press him. In everything I took my cue from Scott: whatever he wished was how it must be. Now he had said, "I'll be out of town for a week or so—I'm going to visit Zelda." I had said, "All right, Scott. Let me know when you get back." I knew he loved her; I had been told he loved her. I accepted the fact that there was a Zelda but she had no reality for me, for I had never seen nor met her. When Scott returned, he was subdued but threw himself into his work at Metro.

In his absence I had written my five-minute radio script. I showed it to Scott the night before my first broadcast. He read it carefully. "You don't mind if I reword it here and there?" he asked. And though tired from his own writing at the studio, he sat down with a stubby pencil and a pack of cigarettes and painstakingly—and completely—rewrote my copy. He worked with the utmost concentration and as he worked he twisted the hair above his forehead so that a tuft stood up, as on a kewpie doll. It gave him a strangely boyish appearance. "Cut out all these exclamation points," he said. "An exclamation point is like laughing at your own joke." He underlined words I should emphasize, corrected my grammar. "When you tell an anecdote, tell it so your listeners can actually *see* the people you are talking about." When he was finished, I was confronted with five minutes of beautiful, flowing prose. I was immensely grateful but asked, rather timidly, "This won't be over the heads of my audience, will it? People who listen to movie gossip aren't usually intellectuals, Scott." He laughed. "It will be good for them."

The show was at seven P.M. in Chicago, which meant five P.M. on the West Coast. Since Scott was still at work at that hour, he could not be with me for my broadcast in the CBS studio in Hollywood. But he left a conference at Metro to hurry across the street to a garage and listen to me over their radio.

My debut was not auspicious. After the Chicago announcer said, "And now we take you to the well-known columnist, Sheilah Graham, in Hollywood," there was a forty-second pause while seventy-five engineers across the country pulled connecting switches. At the first words from Chicago, my director in Hollywood raised his arm and held it there: I was to begin the moment he dropped it. I watched him with the terror I might have felt waiting for a cobra to strike. Finally, after what seemed an interminable time, his arm came down sharply. What with the suspense and my pounding heart, my voice climbed to a high register and in a thin shriek I panted, "Hello, everyone (gulp) this is (gulp) Sheilah Graham in Hollywood."

I had difficulty swallowing and breathing but I managed to read my script to the end.

Scott called immediately. "You were quite good," he said. "Oh, Scott, I was terrible and you know it," I said. "No, no," he insisted. "You sounded a little breathless, but that was all."

The sponsor agreed with me. Would I mind, they asked by telephone the next day, if a professional radio actress in Chicago spoke for me on the succeeding programs? She would be announced as Sheilah Graham. In the future I need only provide the script.

Scott was outraged. "Absolutely not. There's nothing wrong with your voice. You have a contract, they must use *you*. You'll get over your nervousness if they'll give you a chance."

I believed him. Obviously, it was the tense, silent waiting, the poised arm of the director that unnerved me. But Mr. Wharton, on the telephone from Chicago, was adamant. His sponsor insisted upon another voice. I grew angry, then furious. I would *not* be relegated to second-best! "I'll fly to Chicago at my own expense and do next week's show from there," I told him. "I'll prove to you that I'm fine if I don't have to worry about engineers throwing switches from here to New York."

Mr. Wharton doubted that my presence would influence the sponsor, but he could not prevent me from going to Chicago. If I insisted, very well. He'd talk to me there. I told Scott. And Scott said, quite suddenly, "You need someone to help you in this fight. I'll go with you." I was tremendously relieved. With Scott to handle Mr. Wharton he would certainly win our point, and the prospect of our first trip together excited me. "Are you sure you can leave?" I asked. It was an overnight flight to Chicago. "Can you leave your work? You know we can't get back before Tuesday."

"Don't worry about that," said Scott, almost impatiently. "I'll arrange it."

He called for me in a cab Sunday afternoon and we went on to the airport. He seemed tense as he sat beside me, smoking one cigarette after another. I knew that he had been taken off *A Yank At Oxford* after a few weeks' work and was now writing *Three Comrades,* a film to be made from Eric Maria Remarque's famous war novel. In recent days Scott had appeared harassed. I was aware that he disliked clocking in each morning at the studio, that he found the interminable story conferences an ordeal, and was unhappy when he had to fight for a line or a scene in his script. His six months' contract was coming up for renewal and he was not sure that Metro would renew it.

We arrived early at the airport. There a press agent, Mary Crowell, asked me if I'd come with her briefly to meet a young actress. As she took my arm Mary said to Scott, "We'll meet you in the bar, Mr. Fitzgerald. I'll keep Miss Graham only a few minutes."

Five minutes later we sought out Scott, to find him seated at a little table in the bar with a glass of water in front of him. Mary asked me, "What will you have?" I said a brandy, because brandy settled one's stomach and I felt apprehensive about Chicago. Scott said cheerfully, "Bring me a double gin." I looked at him with surprise. His face was flushed. *He's drinking,* went through my mind. *That isn't water. It's gin.* And then, *I never saw him drink before.* Our order had no sooner arrived than Scott tossed his down and before the waiter could leave, he said, "I'll have another double gin."

I felt a twinge of concern. His eyes were bright, he ran his hand repeatedly through his hair, disheveling it, and

he was talking nonsense, a kind of complimentary nonsense, to Mary and me: she looked adorable, I had a skin
like peach note paper. Now the waiter was back with his
drink. Before he could lift it from the tray, Scott said,
"And when you come back, bring another one." As the
drink was set before him, I half-playfully, half-anxiously
pushed it aside. Scott, with sudden vehemence, grabbed
my arm and thrust it away.

Well, I thought, indignantly. He's being most childish.
Here I am, going to Chicago to do battle, and he's come
along to help me, and look at him. He's *tiddly*—Bruce
Ogilvy's word for his fellow officers when they had a few
drinks and began playing leapfrog over the mess-hall
tables. But at this moment Scott winked at me—a slow,
outrageous wink—and my anger filtered away.

When our plane was called, he got into his raincoat
with some difficulty but refused to button it, so that he
literally flapped his way to the plane, his coat flying behind
him, his hat perched precariously on the back of his head.
As we settled down in our seats I saw a bottle in his coat
pocket.

The plane took off. "Scott—" I began. "Shh—" he said,
with exaggerated caution. He tugged the bottle free and
took a long drink. I began again "Scott, please—"

He looked at me, his head to one side. "Do you know
who I am?" he asked. "I'm F. Scott Fitzgerald, the writer."
He slapped my knee. I held his hand, thinking, *I hope he
doesn't make a scene.*

The stewardess came by with an armful of magazines.
Scott smiled up at her. "Do *you* know who I am?" he
asked. She was a pleasant, dark-haired girl of about twenty-
one. "No, sir," she said. "I don't have my passenger list
with me."

He said, expansively, "I'm F. Scott Fitzgerald, the very well-known writer."

I blushed. The girl smiled politely and moved on.

Scott turned to the man across the aisle, and stared at him challengingly. "Do you know me?" he demanded.

The man threw him a tolerant glance. "Nope. Who are you?"

"I'm F. Scott Fitzgerald. You've read my books. You've read *The Great Gatsby*, haven't you? Remember?"

The other looked surprised. "I've heard of you," he said, grinning, but there was a note of respect in his voice.

Scott turned to me. I was so embarrassed I could not determine whether he was being triumphant or sardonic. "See? *He's* heard of me." He turned back to the man and engaged him in a long, confused conversation.

I sat there, heartsick. Scott had finished his bottle by now; his words ran together and the man listened to him with a kind of amused disdain. How could my gentle, well-bred, impeccably mannered Scott, who possessed such great personal dignity, change so completely? He could not go on to Chicago in this state. There was only one thing to do. Our plane stopped en route at Alberquerque. I got Scott's attention. "Scott, I think you'd better get off the plane at Alberquerque and go back to Hollywood. It was a mistake for you to come. You're in no condition to help me—you'd be a hindrance. I don't like you this way at all."

Scott, in his seat, bowed elaborately. "I'll get off," he said, his words running together. He thought heavily for a moment. "Yes, go fight your own battle. You'll always be alone. So will I. We're both lone wolves."

He fell into silence and I sat next to him, utterly miserable. I had thought, at last I have found someone to look out for me, to protect me, someone I love and respect . . . I had counted on his help, and he had failed me.

When the plane taxied to a halt at Alberquerque, Scott tipped his hat. " 'By." I said, "Good-by, Scott, I'll see you when I get back."

I got into my berth and lay there, the light on, and I began to cry. He was right. He is a lone wolf because of his great talent, and I because I have so many secrets and am never satisfied. All my life the moment I am about to become part of a group, I must move one rung higher, and then I am alone again. I'll never belong anywhere. I felt lonely and abandoned as I lay there. *I wish I hadn't told him to get off. What's wrong with a man having a drink, even if he does overdo it once in a while?*

The plane took to the air again. I reached up to turn out my light, when the curtains parted and Scott's head popped in. He was pixie-faced. "Hello!" he said.

"Oh Scott, I thought you'd gotten off!" I said it with tremendous relief. I sat up and pulled him to me. "I'm glad you didn't get off and I love you." "Sure I got off," he said carefully. "Needed another bottle."And presently he went to his berth and fell asleep.

In Chicago, in the morning, en route to the Drake Hotel, he looked gray as chalk. He said little as we went to our adjoining rooms and unpacked. I telephoned Mr. Wharton, who came over promptly. He turned out to be a slender pleasant man in his thirties. Scott came into my room to meet him. In the twenty minutes that had elapsed, his face had become flushed again. Mr. Wharton was honored to meet Mr. Fitzgerald. "This is an unexpected pleasure," he said cordially. Scott sank into an armchair and we got down to business.

"Now, I've brought my script with me, Mr. Wharton," I began. "I know I can do the show to your satisfaction if

I don't have that appalling forty-second wait. That throws me off completely."

Mr. Wharton was noncommittal. I smiled at him. "You are going to let me on tonight, aren't you? I've come all this way—" We discussed the subject for some minutes, Scott taking no part. "Well," said Mr. Wharton, finally, as he rose. "I can't promise anything, Miss Graham. I'll have to talk it over and I'll let you know this afternoon."

I said, taking him to the door, being my most gracious, "I know you're going to let me on that program tonight. You simply must, Mr. Wharton."

Suddenly Scott leaped from his armchair and with a tremendous bound confronted Mr. Wharton. "Does she go on or doesn't she go on tonight?" he demanded pugnaciously.

I stood dismayed. Mr. Wharton, astounded, his hand on the doorknob, backed away. His face paled. "Well, I don't know, Mr. Fitzgerald—I can't give you a decision—I have to check with—"

Scott took a step nearer and put his face inches from Mr. Wharton's. "Take your hands out of your pockets," he said in low, melodramatic voice, and suddenly his fists were up, in the posture of a fighter, and he swung wildly at Mr. Wharton. The latter ducked the blow and fell back. I became hysterical. I threw myself between them and pushed Mr. Wharton out the door. "Go, please go, I'll call you later." I slammed the door and turned to face Scott. I was shaking, my legs trembled. "How dare you!" I screamed. "Are you crazy?"

Scott turned away. He spoke almost to himself. "That s.o.b." he said. "He'll see. You're going on and he's not stopping you. Just let him try."

I threw myself on the bed and lay there, moaning. "Oh, this is the most horrible thing that ever happened in my

whole life! How could you do this to me! It's so terrible!"
I cried. "Go away! Go away, I hate you!"

Scott ran his hand through his hair, grumbled to himself, and lurched into his own room, slamming the door.

When I had calmed down so that I could function, I
telephoned Mr. Wharton and apologized. "These things
happen," he said, tactfully. "Let's just forget it." He was
happy to inform me they had agreed to let me do the show
myself. I was to come to the CBS studio at five P.M. for
rehearsal before going on the air.

We had won! Suddenly my anger at Scott began to vanish. He *had* tried to be my champion. He was not in his
room: perhaps he was out walking it off, I thought. I
lunched by myself and at five P.M. I was on the stage of a
small studio theater at CBS. Standing before the micro-
phone studying my script, I looked up—and there was
Scott seated in the front row of empty seats, smiling impishly at me. I put my finger warningly to my lips. Scott
nodded and made an elaborate show of putting his own
finger to his lips.

But as I was about to go into my speech, he came to his
feet. "Now Sheilah," he said in a loud voice. "Don't you
be afraid of them. Nothing to be afraid of. Speak slowly
and distinctly—" He began to beat time to my words with
an invisible baton.

I was crimson with shame. "Scott," I pleaded in an
agonized whisper. "Please sit down and be quiet."

But Scott continued to conduct me until two stagehands
appeared and escorted him out.

Since I was completely unnerved now, it took several
rehearsals before I satisfied the director. Then, at seven
o'clock, I went on the air. I felt I had done well as I took
a cab back to the Drake Hotel. My only concern now was
Scott.

As I entered my room I heard muffled voices from Scott's. The door between was closed. I pushed it open and stood, dumfounded. A tray of food was on a serving table; Scott sat in a chair beside it, a napkin around his neck like a bib—and sitting facing him, knee to knee, was a younger man carefully feeding him. Each time Scott opened his mouth, the stranger deftly thrust in a forkful of food. As I stood there, speechless, there was a brief struggle. Scott had suddenly tried to bite the stranger's hand. "Oh, stop it, Scott!" the other said, more in annoyance than anger. I noticed that Scott's bib—and his friend's shirtfront—were splattered with coffee. "How am I going to get this down if you're going to play games?"

They became aware of me. "Hi, Sheilo," said Scott, genially. The stranger rose, brushing pieces of cut-up steak and breadcrumbs from his trousers. "Sorry you had to walk in on this Mack Sennett comedy," he said, with amazing aplomb. "You're Miss Graham, of course." He introduced himself. He was Arnold Gingrich, Editor of *Esquire* magazine.

I stammered, "Oh, this is awful, just awful! Have you ever seen him like this before?"

Scott spoke up. "Show her those articles, Arnold!" His language became abusive. Arnold gently persuaded him to lie down on the bed and presently Scott dozed off.

Yes, Arnold said, he had seen Scott like this before, but this was the worst he could recall. We could only try to sober him up in the three hours remaining until plane time. The airport limousine made a regular stop at the Drake: once we got Scott into the car, perhaps the fresh air would bring him around and I would be able to get him on the plane.

While Scott dozed fitfully, Arnold told me what had happened. Scott had telephoned him an hour ago to say he was at the Drake Hotel, and Arnold must come over at once. He came, to find Scott surrounded by water tumblers of gin and a sly look on his face as if to say, "Ha, ha, everyone thinks I'm drinking water but these are gin." Scott told Arnold about me: he had come along to Chicago to help me iron out my difficulties at CBS and was waiting for me to return now. We were flying back to Hollywood on the midnight plane. "Well," Arnold said to him, "we'd better start sobering you up right now. I'm going to order you a steak sandwich and a quart of black coffee. You can't let her see you in this condition when she gets back. Besides, they'll never allow you on the plane." Scott became perverse. He would eat only if Arnold would feed him. Arnold humored him. When the steak arrived he cut it into small pieces and began to feed Scott. Every now and then Scott tried to bite him. When Arnold attempted to pour black coffee into his mouth, Scott promptly spouted it back, like a small boy. It was in the midst of these incredible proceedings that I had walked in.

The articles Scott had demanded, Arnold explained, were a series of three pieces he had written for *Esquire,* "The Crack-up," "Handle With Care," and "Pasting It Together," in which Scott described a nervous breakdown he had suffered two years before. Scott wanted me to read them in the hotel room. Arnold went on to explain that Scott had been a frequent contributor to the magazine in 1934 and 1935; that he was drawing money in advance for articles yet to be written; and for some time had sent nothing to the magazine. Arnold said, "I visited Scott in Baltimore in late 1935 to see why he'd stopped sending us articles." He had found Scott wretched, drinking, and at his wits' end. "I just can't write any more," he told Arnold. "Everybody wants me to write about young love and I can't write about young love." He had dried up as a writer;

he had tried desperately but couldn't prime the pump; his tremendous expenses had used up every penny of the moneys advanced by *Esquire* as well as by *The Saturday Evening Post;* he wanted to write, he wanted to make up the advances, but he couldn't write. He might never write again. He had reached a terrifying blank wall.

Arnold told him, "Scott, I must have a manuscript from you because our auditors are on my neck wanting to know what we're paying you for. Even if you do a Gertrude Stein, even if you just fill a dozen pages saying, 'I can't write, I can't write, I can't write,' five hundred times over, at least I will be able to report that on such and such a date a manuscript arrived from F. Scott Fitzgerald. I will have something in my files to prove you're doing work for us. Otherwise, I've got to stop sending you money."

Scott promised he would try. "All right," he said. "I'll write whatever I can write about why I can't write." The results were the "Crack-up" sketches and, later, a series, "The Afternoon of an Author," which Arnold published in *Esquire* as fiction. Apparently writing the first sketch helped Scott conquer his writing block, for he began to contribute regularly again to *Esquire* and continued after he came to Hollywood.

I listened as Arnold swiftly outlined this background. My heart went out to Scott. How little I knew about this man who spoke never of his troubles but was so sympathetic and understanding about mine.

Arnold said, looking at me, "You know, of course, that Scott with liquor is as different from Scott without liquor as night is from day?"

I said, "I know it now. This trip is the first time I have seen Scott drink. And if there's anything I can do, he won't drink again."

When the airport car came we managed to help Scott into it. Before he left, Arnold gave me his telephone number. "Just in case," he said. "Don't be afraid to call me at any hour."

The limousine was empty save for one other couple. We took seats behind them. Scott had bid an extravagant good-by to Arnold: he must send those "Crack-up" sketches to Hollywood so I could read them. Now he sat, half-dozing. We had almost reached the airport when he roused himself. He looked around at the empty seats, then focused on the back of the young woman in front of us. He turned to me and said audibly, "Doesn't she have lovely hair?" The girl shifted self-consciously in her seat and glanced at her escort with a smile. Scott went on, almost musingly: "Isn't she pretty? Such lovely hair, such poise—a very lovely young woman."

At this the girl half-turned to flash Scott a pleased smile. Scott said to her, "You silly bitch."

I could not believe my ears. The girl turned, startled, and stared at him, with fright in her eyes. The man turned to face Scott, white with anger: what might have happened I do not know because we had come to a stop at the airport and the driver waited for us to get out. "Scott, be quiet!" I implored him. "They won't let you on the plane if they see you've had too much to drink." I still could not use the word *drunk: drunk* sent me back to my childhood horror of the man crawling in the street. Scott was not drunk: he had had too much to drink.

Nor did they let him on the plane. Getting out of the limousine he tripped and fell. He fought with the driver who raised him to his feet. I took his arm and we managed to get to the counter. The clerk looked at Scott and said politely, "I'm sorry, sir, but I can't permit you on the plane."

My heart sank. The next plane for Hollywood would not leave until five A.M. Five hours! And I had Scott on my hands, belligerent and quarrelsome and, at this moment, steadying himself at the counter as he demanded to know where he could buy a plane.

In desperation I rang Arnold Gingrich. I had to get Scott back to Hollywood. Arnold's advice was to get Scott into a taxicab and ride about for the next five hours. By then Scott would be sober. But I must keep him away from a bar. Meanwhile, Arnold promised that he would telephone every bar in the vicinity of the airport so that if Scott did get into one, they would serve him only beer.

I followed Arnold's advice. Most of the time Scott slept on my shoulder in the back of the cab. Now and then he woke to demand, "Driver, stop at the first bar." I had warned the driver. Every few minutes Scott would rouse himself and exclaim, "You s.o.b., I told you to stop at the first bar!" then look up at me, "Hello, baby," and then tell the driver off again. I would soothe him and he would fall asleep. And so it went until nearly five A.M. when we drove back to the airport and Scott, though drowsy, was permitted aboard. We were asleep on each other's shoulders when our plane landed in Los Angeles.

A week later I flew to Chicago, alone, to do my show. Scott had awakened once on our trip back to Hollywood. In what appeared to be a moment of absolute sobriety, he had apologized. He had said, "Don't worry. I can stop this whenever I want, but I must get out of it in my own way. I'll report sick to the studio and tell them I won't come in for several days. Then I will get a doctor and nurses. It will take at least three days." He did not say so but I gath-there these would be three days of hell. "I won't call or see you during that time," he said. "Don't call or try to see me." He had smiled wanly. "I'll telephone you when I'm all right again."

I had said, a little coldly, "As you wish, Scott."

Now, in Chicago, with my broadcast over, I thought, I'm halfway to New York. Why not go on and see the new Broadway shows?

I was packing when Scott called from Hollywood. He had heard me and I had done well. He would meet my plane in the morning. "I'm not returning to Hollywood until the end of the week," I said. "I'm going to New York."

Scott said, in a voice suddenly flat, "You have someone in New York."

"Oh, Scott, I have no one. I'm just going to see some shows and catch up with what's happening there."

There was a brief silence. He said, quietly, "Sheilah, if you go to New York I will not be here when you come back. I'll give up my job and leave Hollywood and never return."

I gasped, "You can't do a thing like that, Scott!" "I will," he said evenly. He meant it. I was overwhelmed by the enormity of that decision. I said, "Let me think about it and I'll call you back." But as I spoke the words I knew I would not go on to New York. I did not know that Scott, when he had come with me to Chicago, had left his studio in the middle of a picture, without a word to anyone. I did not know that his drink at the airport, which led—which had to lead—to all the others, had been his first in months: that he had taken it to bolster his courage, knowing that his unauthorized departure gave Metro just cause not to renew his contract. Yet he had risked that to help me. As I spoke to him on the telephone I knew only that if I was important to him, he was everything to me; that I did not care if he drank, though I prayed he would not drink; that nothing mattered save that Scott and I were together. I had had my first anguish with him, but that, too, was part of love; whatever he did, however he acted, I was in love with him and all else in my life faded into the background.

I returned to Hollywood that day.

CHAPTER NINETEEN

SCOTT BURST IN, his eyes dancing with excitement. He had seen a notice in the *Los Angeles Times* that the Pasadena Playhouse was to present the play version of his short story, "A Diamond As Big As The Ritz." We were going to the opening—we'd make a festive occasion of it. Dress in evening clothes, dine at the Trocadero, and go on to Pasadena—not in his bouncy little Ford but in a sleek, chauffeur-driven limousine he'd hire for the night. I was as enthusiastic as Scott. A play based on one of his short stories! And at the Playhouse, which was sometimes a prelude to Broadway!

At the Trocadero, Scott was in excellent humor. He looked dapper in his best white dinner shirt and tuxedo. I wore my gray and crimson evening gown decorated with a lovely corsage he had sent me in honor of the occasion and, very proudly, a silver-fox jacket he had bought for my birthday. This was the first genuine fur piece I had ever possessed. Scott laughed as I sat forward in my seat lest I wear down the fur.

It had been weeks since Chicago. Metro had picked up

his option, assuring him an additional twelve months of employment, and he was once more on his Coca-Cola and coffee regimen. We had spent much of our time going to the movies, Scott watching the screen with the rapt attention of a student. He considered motion pictures a powerful medium for the writer: he was determined to master the technique of screen writing. Twice before he had tried his hand at it in Hollywood, in 1927 and 1931, but only briefly.

This time he would really devote himself to the task. He had once studied short stories in the same fashion, he told me, analyzing the plots of a hundred *Saturday Evening Post* stories. Now, at Metro, he had pictures run off daily in order to study them. Hollywood itself—its people and its habits—he found fascinating. The studio had talked to him about writing a new Joan Crawford picture. He told me about it gleefully. "Their first title was 'Infidelity'; now they've changed it to 'Fidelity.'" This amused him. He had been amused, too, by his first meeting with Miss Crawford. Quite humbly he had told her, "I'm going to write your next picture." She had smiled at him. "Good," she had said, fixing him with her burning eyes. "Write hard, Mr. Fitzgerald, write hard!" Scott, telling it, threw back his head and laughed.

He was very interested, he said, as our limousine took us to Pasadena, in the struggle going on between the forces of Irving Thalberg, who died at the age of thirty-seven a year before, and those of Louis B. Mayer. He saw this as a war between art and money, between the unselfish boy genius, represented by Thalberg, and the ruthless industrialist, represented by Mayer. The idea of a novel had been simmering in Scott's mind, he told me, ever since he met Thalberg, on a previous visit to Hollywood. "No one's yet written *the* novel on Hollywood," Scott went on. Until now, most writers had approached Hollywood almost sneeringly, treating it as though it were a cartoon strip peopled by one-dimensional comic-book characters—every producer gross and illiterate, every writer charmingly unstable, every star an overgrown child. Scott would write a serious novel about Hollywood: he would build it around Thalberg, and the struggle for power—the creative versus the commercial, would be its basic theme.

It occurred to me that I was of some value to Scott, for I could never tell him too much about Hollywood. He was fascinated when I told him a classic story. Upon Thalberg's death, an invitation to be a pallbearer at the funeral had been sent by mistake to Harry Carey, a one-time Western silent screen star who was no longer busy in films. The invitation had actually been meant for Carey Wilson, a well-known producer. But Harry Carey had received it: when all Hollywood turned out for Thalberg's funeral, there was Harry Carey among the pallbearers carrying the body of Thalberg. The next day Harry Carey's phone never stopped ringing. He was offered one job after another. From that day he began a new, successful career. "A perfect story," said Scott. He was not interested in gossip as gossip, but only as it illuminated the character of those in power. It was all material for the book yet to be done. He repeatedly whipped out his notebook to jot down an observation, dialogue he had overheard, a phrase or sentence that had come to him. "A writer wastes nothing," he once told me.

He talked about "A Diamond As Big As The Ritz." He knew that someone had turned it into a play but nothing had come of it. Now that it was being put on by the Playhouse, he began to have hope again. He had telephoned the Playhouse, telling them he was the author of the story, and asked them to reserve two seats for him "somewhere near the back."

Our car drew up before the theater and the chauffeur helped us out. It was strange to see no cars discharging other first nighters, no activity at the box office. "Could I have gotten the date wrong?" Scott asked me, perplexed. With a sinking feeling I waited in the deserted lobby while he went off to find someone. When he returned, his walk wasn't quite as jaunty. "It's the students—they're giving the play in the upstairs hall," he said, trying to be casual. I said nothing as we climbed the stairs and found ourselves in a small hall with a little stage and perhaps fifteen rows of wooden benches. No one else had arrived.

We sat on a bench in the back, waiting, and I tried to chat animatedly of what I had done during the day, to ask countless questions about *Three Comrades*, about the disagreements over the script he had been having with Joe Mankewicz, its producer, about his plans for "Fidelity" or "Infidelity" or whatever its final title would be.

About ten minutes before curtain time a few students arrived, women and girls wearing mostly slacks and skirts—perhaps a dozen in all. They looked curiously at us sitting alone on a bench in full evening clothes. The lights finally went down, the curtain parted, and the play began. It was an amateur performance but Scott laughed while the students giggled and in the end his applause outlasted theirs. They wandered off and we were left alone again. Scott rose. "I'm going backstage," he said. "It might encourage them to know the author came to see them."

He returned a few moments later and we went down the stairs to our waiting limousine. We drove back to Hollywood and did not talk much. At first Scott said, almost cheerfully, "They were all nice kids—they seemed a little awkward when I introduced myself. I told them they'd done a good job." As we rode on, however, despite what chatter I could manage, Scott grew more and more glum, and finally sat silent and depressed next to me. Of course they were awkward, ran through my mind. They were embarrassed to meet a man they had thought dead.

Bob Benchley had told me, "Scott doesn't like parties." It was true. The only ones he cared to attend were those given by his friends, the writers. Even then, when too many strangers were present, a curious lackluster settled over him. His eyes grew dull, he seemed to shrink into invisibility so that he became unnoticeable in a room. At a party given by Alan Campbell, Somerset Maugham was the guest of honor. Before he left he said to Alan, "I'm told F. Scott Fitzgerald is in Hollywood. I should like to meet him." "You did, tonight—here," said Alan. Maugham had no memory of him. Scott had been introduced to him with the usual mumbling of names and then, in his characteristic self-effacing manner, had retreated to join me in the corner of the room. We had sat there very quietly for a while, and then as quietly we had left.

Sitting in the corner of the room at parties became a habit with us. Some of this was due to Scott's natural reserve; some to his awareness of my fear that I might embarrass myself and, therefore, him. Scott's friends were addicted to the kind of witty parlor games I'd suffered through in New York. They enjoyed charades, or contests involving intricate puns and plays on words, literary characters and historical events—in all of which I was beyond my depth.

Among these people, America's top writers, composers,

and playwrights, I knew I could not get by with a smile and small talk about a piece of cheese, or what a ridiculous hat Paulette Goddard wore the other night. Even Benchley, who took little seriously, made me feel he was enormously learned; I often found him, between scenes in his pictures, sitting in a corner of his set immersed in a book. Once, at a gathering, I had tried to poke fun, Benchley fashion. A young woman was speaking eloquently about Willa Cather. I asked gaily, "And who is Willa Cather?" She looked at me. "Doesn't Willa Cather's name mean anything to you?" I said airily, "Oh, well, we never heard of her in England." Someone chuckled and suddenly I realized with acute embarrassment that I must have made an inexcusably stupid remark. Thereafter, I tried to hide behind a façade of vivacity. I would burst into a party to relate an incident at the studio, or a choice bit of gossip. Finally, Scott rebuked me. "Sit back," he said. "Let them come to you. Don't be too eager—it makes you unattractive."

"I can't help it," I said. "I don't mind parties at the homes of the stars, but I dread the ones given by your friends. I can't keep up with them." At the Ira Gershwins', the Donald Ogden Stewarts', the Nunnally Johnsons', I would sit at the dinner table with my hands clenched and damp in my lap.

"I'll give you something to hang on to," Scott said one evening as we set off for the home of Albert and Frances Hackett, two of Hollywood's most distinguished playwrights. "When we get there, pretend that everyone there bores you. That will give you just the right distance and you'll lose that overeagerness."

I tried it. All evening I sat there saying to myself, "George F. Kaufman bores me. Oscar Levant bores me.

Ogden Nash bores me." It worked, after a fashion: I felt
more relaxed, I knew that my mouth was not turned up in
the strained smile of one too anxious to please. When Mr.
Kaufman or Mr. Levant or Mr. Nash wandered by, I
looked up, calmly and sweetly, and let it go at that. "You
don't have to *prove* anything," Scott had said. I was beginning to realize that I could be accepted at a gathering
without making a contribution—literally, that it was not
necessary for me to perform as my price of admission.

But generally Scott protected me. He mingled briefly
with his friends and then found his place beside me in a
corner of the room, and there we remained, quite content,
while the wit and repartee flowed about us. Once Alan
Campbell came up to us to say, almost enviously, "You
two always look as though you had a secret you were going
to talk about later." He was right. Our secret was us.

I remembered how apprehensive I felt after telling Scott
the truth about myself. I had watched for any betrayal, any
lessening of his chivalry, his thoughtfulness, the gaiety of
his little notes. *Now that he knows I'm only Lily Sheil, will
he still respect me? Will he love me as much?* Two or three
night afterward we were in my living room, I working
on my column, Scott immersed in a book of Tennyson's
poems. Without preface he began to read aloud. I stopped
my work and listened:

> Now sleeps the crimson petal, now the white,
> Nor waves the cypress in the palace walk;
> Nor winks the gold fin in the porphyry font.
> The firefly wakens: waken thou with me.

He paused, to look at me for a moment and then go on,
in a voice of infinite tenderness:

> Now folds the lily all her sweetness up
> And slips into the bosom of the lake.

So fold thyself, my dearest, thou, and slip
Into my bosom and be lost in me.

"Oh, Scott—" Tears sprang to my eyes. He took me in his arms and I rested there. I looked into his face, searching it, trying to find its mystery, its wonder for me, and I said, almost prayerfully, "If only I could walk into your eyes and close the lids behind me, and leave all the world outside—"

He held me close and I clung to him. . . .

Our secret was ourselves. At night, when we did not go out, we put on records and danced as we had done at the Clover Club: wheeling and pirouetting, or tap dancing together or separately, brushing past each other and bowing with an elaborate, "Pardon me," if we touched. Or as I watched choking with laughter, Scott performed his own little stiff-legged dance while reciting Swinburne's "When the Hounds of Spring." Or we'd box together, Scott bouncing about me on his toes, making ferocious faces as he sparred with me: "Sheilo, keep your chin in or I'll slug you!" Or, while I prepared coffee, he whipped together a batch of fudge in my kitchen and we gorged ourselves, as happy, as uncomplicated, as two children together.

By early 1938 we were virtual recluses in Hollywood. I attended few evening events or industry parties. So that I could be with Scott, Jonah Ruddy for a weekly fee covered these occasions for me. We rarely went out: it was enough for us to be together, and when we were not together hardly an hour went by that Scott did not make me aware of his presence. He telephoned me five and six times during the day. "What are you wearing?" he would ask. "How do you look?" I almost blushed, thinking, this is like my magic mirror at the orphanage. At this moment, as though he *could* see me, he would ask, "What are you thinking of?" And, "When will I see you?" Always a gentle question, always his constant, reassuring attention. Each evening, when he came in the door, I would run to him eagerly. I wanted him to know how much he was wanted. My living began when he arrived.

If his telephone calls slackened, there were always his notes of endearment, which like a treasure hunt he left about my house for me to find. Or a little card accompanying a bouquet of violets, "For Sheilah—from her chattel, Scott." Or a message when we were separated for twenty-four hours: "Missing you is a luxury like everything about knowing you, lovely, lovely, Sheilah." Or a note an hour after we quarreled over I know not what: "Darling, I am sorry I was difficult tonight. You are dear Sheilah and nothing can change that. Please feel better dear sweet Sheilah. Dear face, dear heart, dear, dear, dear Sheilah." I felt bathed and laved in an endlessly flowing devotion.

Sometimes I might say, a little wistfully, "Scott, I'd like to go on a visit to New York." Then Scott would sit down and lead me through a gentle catechism.

"Why do you want to go to New York, Sheilah?"

"I'm not really sure why. To go to the Stork Club and '21' and places like that."

"Why do you want to go to the Stork Club and '21' and places like that?"

I thought. "To see the people, I guess."

"But who are the people you see at such places? They're not real. I have been there. I have given all that up. What can you get from such people? What can you get from New York?"

"Oh . . ." I could not find the words. "New York excites me. It thrills me."

He shook his head. "Sheilah, what you are looking for, you have found. You are looking for love, for someone to understand you. You have me. I love you and understand you. There's no need for you to go to New York."

And I thought: of course, he is right. All my life I have been seeking excitement. Now I have the excitement engendered by Scott. I have him. It is enough, and I am content. There is no need to go in search.

Yet I did not realize how carefully Scott guarded what was between us until a letter came one Monday morning from Margaret Brainard. She was coming West. She had taken a position with the newly opened Saks Fifth Avenue store in Beverly Hills. She would arrive at the end of the week. I told Scott about her, how warm and understanding she had been when I first came to America, how close we had been, what confidences we exchanged. "I'm so happy she's coming, Scott. I've already written her that she must stay with me for the first few weeks—I want to show her a wonderful time, introduce her to people—"

Scott listened, strangely subdued. "When will she be here?" he asked. "She arrives Saturday," I said. He changed the subject. On Wednesday he chose a moment to say, "I've been thinking about Margaret staying with you, Sheilo. Are you sure that's a good idea?"

"Oh, of course," I said. But his tone led me to wonder, is it really a good idea?

On Thursday he said, "Dear, let's go away this week end. Let's go to Santa Barbara."

I stared at him. "Scott, we can't. You know Margaret is coming on Saturday. I'm going down to meet her and bring her here."

He went on doggedly. "But I would like to go away. I'm tired—I must get away. I could use a week end out of town—"

"But Margaret—" I began again.

He said, "Well, you know, I think Margaret would be happier in her own apartment. These last few days I've been looking for one for her."

"You have?" I said, nonplused.

He nodded. "I'm sure she'll be happier in an apartment."

"I think that would hurt her feelings terribly, Scott."

"No," he said firmly. "I don't think so. As a matter of fact, she can move in the moment she arrives. It's all set." He produced a key. He had rented an apartment for Margaret and paid a deposit. It was very convenient, he said, a block from Saks Fifth Avenue. "Just what she'd want." I stared at the key. "If she were with you all the time, Sheilah," Scott was saying, "perhaps I couldn't see you as much. And I do want to get away this week end. Now that she has an apartment, we can go. You leave this key for her with a note."

I went to Santa Barbara with Scott that week end. I left a note for Margaret saying that I would return Monday, that an apartment waited for her, and here was the key. I wrote that I was sorry I could not meet her as I had promised.

This Scott made me do to my best friend. He was jealous of her. He was so obviously unhappy, I could not refuse him. Had he feared she might say: *Sheilah, this isn't the man for you. He is married, with a wife in an institution. He can never marry you. Is this what you want, Sheilah? What of your dream, your longing for a husband and children, for the family you never had?*

On one occasion his distress at the thought of anyone coming between us led me to take utterly ridiculous measures. I had received a wire from John Wheeler that he was on a tour of newspaper publishers taking the NANA service and would be in Los Angeles for two days.

Scott at once became nervous and apprehensive. "You're not going to see him, are you?" he asked. I said, "Of course I am, Scott. I have to see him. He's my boss."

As the day of Wheeler's arrival approached, Scott grew more and more glum. He would not be reassured. And as had happened many times before when I found myself in difficulty, inspiration came. The night before Wheeler arrived, I went into the Good Samaritan Hospital for a minor operation, something my doctor had said could be done "any time—no hurry about it." I chose this time so that I would be too ill to see John Wheeler. Scott took me to the hospital, reassured at last.

When I came out of the ether I found he had written on a memo pad next to my bed. "So glad it went well, my blessed. Will be back when you wake up in the late afternoon." And below it: "Second note. I am here—it is 5:30—and you are getting rapidly out of the ether and very sick. You asked me several questions and said you couldn't believe they did it while you were asleep. I love you and I am coming back in the morning quite early and sit with you. It has been a day for all of us and I must go eat and get a bit of sleep. Thank God it is over and you're well again."

In the morning when I was still asleep he sat at my bedside for a while, and when I awoke I found still another note: "Rest well, darling." Three days later I was out of the hospital. John Wheeler had come and gone.

It was in the midst of Scott's unceasing tenderness that he came one evening to say, "Zelda wants to see me. I must go and visit her again." He added, "You don't mind, do you?"

I was touched that he should ask me, but the truth was that I minded terribly. He was going to his wife, I had no call upon him, yet I dared say, more in complaint than demand, "Scott, must you go?"

He did not grow angry. "I must take out my poor Zelda —I cannot abandon her there." It was the most he had said about her until now. He added, "I won't write you while I'm away." And he was gone.

Suddenly the devotion that had enveloped and sustained me was no more. I had no idea how long he would be away. Six days passed, eight days, ten days. I woke with a leaden heart each morning. The fact that Margaret was in town meant nothing. For ten days I had no lunch or dinner with Scott, no word from him, no telephone calls, no messages, no evidence that he was in the very air about me waiting only the invoking of his name to materialize and be at my side. I knew what desolation was.

On the eleventh morning a telephone call. "Sheilo!" It was Scott, at the airport. He sounded gay, excited, happy. "We're going to be married!"

I could not catch my breath. When I found my voice I echoed him mechanically: "We're going to be married?"

He said, "I'm getting a divorce. I'll tell you all about it when I see you." He went on eagerly, "Wait for me—I'll be right over."

I hung up in a dream. Something must have happened. I remembered the strange stories I had heard about Zelda. Someone, having known her a few years before, described her as an Ophelia, wandering about in the shapeless, waistless dresses she had worn fifteen years before, a thin, silent woman of unpredictable moods, now lost and withdrawn, now shaken by sudden violence and despair. What could have happened? I sat down at my desk and slowly began writing my name: "Mrs. F. Scott Fitzgerald." I will be Mrs. F. Scott Fitzgerald.

Then Scott arrived. His face was flushed, his hair dissheveled, his shirt untidy. "Baby!" he cried, gaily, and clasped me in a bear hug. *He has been drinking,* went through my mind, and my heart was leaden again. "Are you getting a divorce?" I asked. "Have you told her?"

"Yes, I am, I am!" He was emphatic. "I haven't told her yet but I will!" He released me and began pacing back and forth, growing more angry as he did so. "I'm through. I've tried to do my best. Why should I have all this responsibility?" He lit a cigarette with a trembling hand and inhaled deeply. "Do you know what she did this time?" he demanded. "Tried to get me committed. Called a doctor and said I was insane and should be put away."

I had to sit down, suddenly weak. I was appalled at this sudden, overwhelming glimpse of human suffering. "Oh, Scott—" I said helplessly.

He sat down, agitated. "I'm sick of this situation. I should have ended it long ago." He jumped up. "Back in a minute," he said. He dashed out to his car, to return more flushed than before. He had taken another drink.

I said, heartsick, "They'll find out at the studio you're drinking and you'll lose your job."

He became dramatic. "Don't tell anyone!"

I persuaded him to go back to the Garden of Allah and sleep it off. He left, unsteadily.

At two A.M. that morning my doorbell rang. It rang continuously. Someone's finger was on the button and was not being taken off. I hurried down and opened the door. Scott stood there, swaying, holding his shoulder. Behind him a cab waited, its motor running. "I think I've broken my shoulder," he said thickly.

I threw on a coat and helped Scott into the cab and took him to the Queen of Angels Hospital. He protested. Why was I taking him to a hospital? "Stop babying me!" In his time he'd broken nearly every bone in his body. He would not go to a hospital. I said, "If you want me to talk to you ever again, you be good and let me get this shoulder set for you."

As we waited in the reception room, he suddenly bolted for the door. I raced after him and held him back with all my strength. "Scott, you can't go, you've got to have this set. Stop behaving so stupidly!"

The superintendent, a tall, serene nun, broad and beautiful, approached us. "Sister, he wants to go, he won't stay," I almost wept. "He has to have his shoulder set."

She said, "Come," and Scott followed her like a lamb.

I sat, waiting, thinking, why could I not have her calmness, her sureness? Why must I become emotional? I cannot help him if I am always emotional when he is in trouble.

Fortunately, Scott had only sprained his shoulder. When he left me earlier that night, he had returned to the Garden of Allah as he had promised. But someone had invited him to the bar; he had been drinking there for some time. Then, trying to park his car, in some fashion he had wrenched his shoulder. Then he had come to me.

I took him back to the Garden of Allah. I pleaded with him. He must do whatever was necessary to stop his drinking, as he had done before. He looked up, unexpectedly contrite. "All right," he said. "I'll get the doctor. I can quit whenever I want. You know that, don't you?" I nodded. "I know it, Scott." "All right," he said. "Now, don't come to see me—I don't like anybody around when— I'll telephone you—"

I helped him to his room and left him there.

For three nights I could not sleep. What am I to do? About him? About myself? He was not *tiddly*—he was *drunk*. He was not *tiddly* in Chicago—he was *drunk*. *Face the awful word!* When will he drink again? How many times before had he been drinking and I had not known? The horror I had fled—the floundering man in the gutter, the East End with its sickening odor of beer, its reeling men, its cursing and brawling and violence through the night—was this to be mine again? I thought, I can't bear it. I can't bear this irrationality, this insecurity. I must make things normal and right.

But I cannot give him up, I realized desperately. And then, with a great sense of release, the idea came to me. I will cure him. I will take him away from the Garden of Allah, away from his drinking friends and the temptation of the bar; I will take him to the sea. I will find him a home by the sea where he will get all the fresh air and sunlight he needs, where he can swim and walk and relax and regain his health. As far back as I could remember the sea had had the power to make me whole. It will make Scott whole, too.

On the third day, I drove to Malibu and looked for a beach house. I found a charming white clapboard cottage with green shutters and a captain's walk. To its side was a little garden, entered through a latticed white archway from which hung a tiny seafarer's lantern. There was a sunroom, dining room, four bedrooms, and vases of fresh flowers everywhere. There would be a place for me to work and sleep on week ends. As I entered the spotless kitchen, a motherly looking colored woman was baking cookies: the air was fragrant with their aroma. Outside, the waves broke gently on a sun-drenched beach. I fell in love with the place. It could be had on six-months' lease for two hundred dollars a month, and Flora, the cook-housekeeper, would remain for another fifty dollars a month. Scott would actually save money, for his rent was three hundred dollars monthly at the Garden of Allah. I said to Flora, "If Mr. Fitzgerald takes this place will you promise to keep the cookie jars filled?" She smiled. "Oh, yes, ma'am!"

The owner turned out to be Frank Case, who managed the Hotel Algonquin in New York and knew Scott. He'd be happy to rent to him. Enormously pleased, I drove back to Hollywood.

On the afternoon of the next day, flowers arrived from Scott. That evening he telephoned. "Sheilo, when can I see you?" His voice was weak and far away. "Can you come and see me now? I want to see you now, Sheilo."

I found him sitting up, his face pale. He was dressed neatly, with a perky polka-dot tie and a pink shirt. "That's a daring tie, Scott," I said. He smiled at me. "I hope you weren't too lonely," he said. It was as if nothing had happened. I said, because I still did not know what alcohol was, "Scott, please don't drink any more. I don't like you when you drink. It frightens me."

He said, gently, don't let's talk about it.

I told him about the house at Malibu. He would be able to work there in peace. At the Garden of Allah, guests came in at all hours of the night. It would be healthful. He'd not have to go out for meals. It would be only a forty-five-minute drive to Metro. I could come down evenings and week ends. If he had to remain in town he could always stay at my house.

He wanted to please me. "If you think so, Sheilah," he said.

On a spring afternoon in 1938, I helped him move out of the Garden of Allah to the beach house at Malibu. He had little luggage and many books and papers. On the way we stopped at a florist and I piled the back of the car high with flowers. I would keep the beach house gay for Scott. Malibu would mark the beginning of a new life for both of us.

CHAPTER TWENTY

Scott, at Malibu. He is in an ancient gray flannel bathrobe, torn at the elbows so that it shows the gray slipover sweater he wears underneath. He has the stub of a pencil over each ear, the stubs of half a dozen others—like so many cigars—peeping from the breast pocket of his robe. One side pocket bulges with two packs of cigarettes, from the other the top of his notebook can be seen. He has been working this week end on a script: his forelock sticks up, kewpie-doll fashion, and he paces back and forth, now and then pausing to kick away an imaginary pebble from in front of him.

In his room, off the captain's walk, the floor is littered with sheets of yellow paper covered with a large flowing hand. He uses his stubby pencils—he sharpens them carefully with a penknife but never to a fine point because he bears down heavily—and writes at furious speed. As soon as one page is finished he shoves it off the desk to the floor and starts the next. Now he has come to a halt, hunting an elusive word. He may wait for twenty minutes, stubbornly, until it comes to him. He refuses to consult the dictionary or thesaurus. "No, it's in my mind. I'll think it out," he says impatiently. "Anyway, if I go to the dictionary I get so fascinated I'm good for an hour there."

I am learning more and more about Scott. He does not sleep well. At night I hear him pacing the floor, and in his medicine cabinet are sleeping pills and, to wake him in the morning, benzedrine. I shop and plan the meals but he eats less than he should, and often bizarre combinations that put Flora almost in tears: turtle soup and chocolate soufflé can make a dinner for him. He lives through the day on Coca-Colas and highly sweetened black coffee, sometimes topped off with fudge, as though he cannot get enough sugar.

He follows world events avidly. I marvel how, for him, what happens today falls into place with what happened fifty years ago, a century ago. History lives for him. In contrast, to me it is as if it had never happened. How do we *know* there was a French Revolution? Or that Julius Caesar ever lived? Who cares? I can't relate them to me, so why should they be so important? I know that Scott isn't getting along well at Metro, that he worries about Zelda and Scottie and himself—yet he is concerned with everything about him. Is it that I am not noble enough to be genuinely interested in anything except my own needs? Or is it that I'm not well-enough educated to put together this jigsaw puzzle of past and present?

On Sunday mornings we sit before the Cases' enormous console radio, listening to Hitler's speeches. They infuriate Scott. He jumps up and pads restlessly about the room. "They're going to do it again. They're going to have another war—and we'll be in it, too." He sits down, lights a cigarette, listens again to the ranting, hysterical voice, the thunderous *"Sig Heil! Sig Heil! Sig Heil!"* It echoes through our little beach house. He turns to me.

"I'd like to fly over there and assassinate Hitler before he starts another war. I'd do it, too, by God!" He tells me, with a sudden, disarming smile, "You know, Sheilo, I wanted to fight in the last war. They pulled the rug from under me. The Armistice came and I never got across."

We switch off the radio and Scott talks about the studio. He is working with collaborators, and unhappy. "They see it one way, I see it another. I've got to get them off the script," he says. He cannot tolerate the endless story conferences. "All the brains come in," he says. "They sit around a table. They talk about everything except the subject in hand—and when they do talk about that, they don't know what they want, they don't know where they're going, they repeatedly change their minds—it's disgraceful." After six months of strenuous work he had completed the screenplay of *Three Comrades*, only to discover that Mankiewicz, his producer, had rewritten it. Infuriated, Scott dashed off a bitter, profane letter to him. I prevailed upon Scott to tone it down. "You'll only antagonize him and he'll never restore your script," I said. Even in its restrained form, Scott's letter reflected his intense hurt. "To say I'm disillusioned is putting it mildly. . . . You *had* something and you have arbitrarily and carelessly torn it to pieces. . . . I am utterly miserable at seeing months of work and thought negated in one hasty week. Oh, Joe, can't producers ever be wrong? I'm a good writer—honest I am. . . ."

When *Three Comrades* opened, Scott and I drove into Hollywood to see it. "At least they've kept my beginning," he said on the way. But as the picture unfolded, Scott slumped deeper and deeper in his seat. At the end he said, "They changed even that." He took it badly. "That s.o.b.," he growled when he came home, and furiously, helplessly, as though he had to lash out at something, he punched the wall, hard. "My God, doesn't he know what he's done?" Scott had now been on four pictures and his one screen credit—the all-important requirement for future work in Hollywood—was on a picture he was ashamed of.

There had been no drinking. Nor did he allow me to refer to the subject. From his nurse at the Garden of Allah I had learned the nature of his three-day cures. They were periods of intense bodily torture in which he had to be fed intravenously, he retched day and night, tossed and turned sleeplessly, and emerged wan, shaken, bathed in sweat, utterly exhausted. I knew now why he had refused to let me see him at such times. But I had said once, at Malibu, "Now, don't you think it was silly to have gone through all that agony for the stuff in a bottle?"

He had become angry, an anger of great reserve and great dignity. His face paled, his eyes seemed to grow closer together, his nose became long and thin with annoyance, his face dropped but with his head up he said sharply, almost arrogantly, flinging the words at me, "It's none of your business. I don't care to discuss it." Then, abruptly, "About dinner—will you ask Flora to make me a lettuce salad and oyster broth?"

I came to know other aspects of Scott. I had counted on getting him bronzed and healthy in the sun and fresh air, but he avoided the sun. When we strolled on a Saturday afternoon to the Malibu Inn to spend an hour at the football slot machine, Scott insisted on walking on the shady side of the road. He never swam or even waded in the inviting surf, although I took a dip every day. "I'm too busy—I have work to do," he would say. Then, one morning, by mistake I lifted his cup of coffee to my lips. He dashed it out of my hand. "Don't ever use my cups or spoons or towels or anything else of mine," he said sharply. "I have tuberculosis." A surge of terror swept through me: my father had died of tuberculosis. "Scott, are you sure? How do you know?" He looked at me. "I've had it on and off since college. It's not bad now but it flares up if I don't watch myself." That explained his raincoat and scarf in July, his avoidance of the sun and the water. I thought, perhaps he does have T.B. Or is this one of his pranks? Or is he a hypochondriac? I recalled that if I drove over twenty miles an hour he would gasp, "My God, slow down, you're killing me." Does he imagine things? At newsreels we moved two and three times during the evening because he insisted the people seated behind him were kicking the back of his chair. Each time we moved I wondered why this never happened to me.

Though Scott involved himself in everything I did, checking over my contracts and even my business letters, he remained curiously aloof toward my column. He was not interested in reading it. He accepted it as the way I earned my living but he gave it no further attention. Once however—as my champion—he helped me with it. This came after an upsetting encounter with Constance Bennett. One day I visited her set, picked up a few items and prepared to leave, just as happy that I hadn't come upon Miss Bennett, about whom I had written rather unflatteringly. At this moment her producer, Milton Bren, accosted me. "Have you met Connie Bennett yet?" "No," I said, "but I must rush away." "Oh, come on, she's on the set, I'll introduce you," he said. He took me to a sound stage and there was Miss Bennett holding court with a group of friends. "Connie," he said innocently, "I want you to meet Sheilah Graham."

Miss Bennett measured me with a slow, insolent glance, then drawled in a voice that carried to every corner of the huge set, "It's hard to believe that a girl as pretty as you can be the biggest bitch in Hollywood."

There was a hush. For a moment I was a drowning woman. To lose face, to be publicly insulted and humiliated. . . . Without thinking, fighting for my life, I heard myself say clearly, "Not the biggest, Connie. The second biggest."

Miss Bennett was so taken aback she couldn't think of a retort. To bridge the moment she offered me a cigarette. I said coolly, "I don't smoke, thank you," and pressing my advantage, I said, "Sit down, Connie, and tell me what's bothering you."

"Nothing's bothering me," said Miss Bennett, but she sat down on a bench. I sat down next to her. "Now, what did I write that you object to?"

Suddenly she regained her poise. She rose. "I never read your column," she said icily. She turned to Milton Bren, and flung her arms gaily around him. "Oh, Milt, why do you let these strays clutter up the set?" She maneuvered him away so that I was left sitting alone. I knew I was defeated. There was nothing I could say—and even had there been, she was no longer there to hear it. I smiled a ghastly smile. I was chained to the bench: I could not leave. I felt I had to go of my own volition and in my own time. When an unhappy Milton Bren returned, I said to him, half-crying, "Do you think if I go now it will still look as if she threw me off the set?"

He said, embarrassed, "Oh, Sheilah, of course you can go. I'm so sorry—"

All the way to Malibu as I drove I repeated over and over, *Not the biggest, Connie. The second biggest. Not the biggest, Connie. The second biggest.* When I saw

Scott I burst into tears. "This must be avenged," he said, darkly. All evening we discussed how to get back at Miss Bennett. "What part is she playing now?" he asked. I told him she played a ghost in the latest of her *Topper* series. Scott recalled that Connie had attended several dances at Princeton shortly after he had left there. Together we composed a paragraph which appeared in my column the following day. I wrote, "It's lucky no children happened to be on Constance Bennett's set yesterday. Her language was absolutely shocking." The next words were Scott's: "Poor Connie. Faded flapper of 1919 and now, symbolically, cast as a ghost in her latest production." It was F. Scott Fitzgerald's only contribution to Sheilah Graham's HOLLYWOOD TODAY.

Now, finally, at Malibu, Scott let me read his three "Crack-up" articles, giving me the tear sheets from *Esquire* with the observation, "I shouldn't have written these. I don't know if I ought to let you read them, but go ahead. Tell me what you think." He left the room.

Reading the pages I found it impossible to recognize Scott in the man who wrote so bitterly, so despairingly. This was the Scott who existed before I knew him. Writing eloquently, beautifully, he compared himself to an old plate that had cracked—one that could "never again be warmed in the stove or shuffled with the other plates in the dishpan; it will not be brought out for company but it will do to hold crackers late at night or go into the ice box under leftovers." He spoke of the "real dark night of the soul [where] it is always three o'clock in the morning, day after day"; of a "call on physical resources that I did not command, like a man overdrawing at his bank."

The three articles, which had appeared in *Esquire* in February, March, and April of 1936—only a year before we met—breathed despair and hopelessness and a kind of helpless gallantry. They spoke of "the world of bitterness, where I was making a home," and then ended on a note of proud yet absolute wretchedness: "I will try to be a correct animal though, and if you throw me a bone with enough meat on it, I may even lick your hand."

I walked into his room with the tear sheets. "I don't see why you wouldn't want me to read these, Scott. What really is wrong with them? You're a writer. You've told me a writer must write the truth. This is how you felt then. But this is not you now." They reminded me, I said, of the melancholy writing of Edgar Allan Poe. "I don't see this as an admission of defeat but as a stage through which you passed—and one you're not in now."

He rubbed thoughtfully at his cheek as if to rub away an invisible spot. Edmund Wilson the critic, who had been at Princeton with Scott and whom he admired enormously, said he should not have written them. Ernest Hemingway, whom Scott had enthusiastically recommended to Scribner's, his own publishers, had been furious with him. Both thought he had revealed too much about himself. "I don't know if I'll ever speak to Ernest again," Scott said somberly. In "The Snows of Kilimanjaro," a short story which appeared in *Esquire* not long after Scott's series, Hemingway had written about one of his characters: "He remembered poor Scott Fitzgerald and his romantic awe of . . . [the rich] and how he had started a story once that began, 'The very rich are different from you and me.' And how someone had said to Scott, 'Yes, they have more money.' But that was not humorous to Scott. He thought they were a special glamorous race and when he found they weren't it wrecked him just as much as any other thing that wrecked him." Recalling it now, Scott grew angry. "Ernest claimed he was free to write that way about me because of what I'd written about myself. I don't think I can ever forgive him." He added, "That was hitting me when I was down."

I was indignant. How callous, how patronizing Hemingway had been! Scott, a "wrecked" man? I could not think of him like that. It was utterly absurd. And in any event, Scott was right about the rich and Hemingway was wrong. This was a subject I felt qualified to speak about. I told Scott so.

"The rich *are* different from us, Scott. I saw it. Monte Collins was different because he was rich. So was Sir Richard. All my life I've seen the allowances made for the cruelties and peculiarities of a rich man. Don't you think Monte thought himself special and glamorous? And Sir Richard? They were different because everyone agreed they were—and because they accepted it as their right to be considered different."

Scott laughed at that. He seemed pleased that I did not condemn him for writing as he had; and I was flattered that he valued my opinion.

Now I read his books. First, *This Side of Paradise*. I was disappointed. I thought its characters were young and immature. I finished it only because I knew Scott had patterned the hero upon himself. He asked, "What do you think?"

"Well," I said judiciously, "it's not as good as Dickens."

"Of course it's not as good as Dickens," he said irritably.

I loved his short stories, and I could not say enough about his novel, *Tender Is The Night*. I had never read such hauntingly beautiful prose. Scott said he liked it better than anything he had written, but most people preferred his novel, *The Great Gatsby*. I read it and agreed with them. "I think it's just perfect," I said. "Everything—just the way it is."

"You do?" he asked, pleased. "They read things into it I never knew myself." He talked about the critics. He could not forgive them for their treatment of *Tender Is The Night*. Someday he hoped to rewrite it, for it should have been two books. We talked about my reaction to his work. I had judged it intellectually, not emotionally, he said. At one point he observed, "Basically you are led by your mind."

I treasured his words.

Slowly, now, he began to tell me about Zelda. He spoke sadly, with great compassion. His confidences might be set off by a letter from her. These came on occasion, marked by brilliant, arresting language, but often little more than beautiful words strung together without meaning. Sometimes, by a letter from a member of her family reporting her progress or lack of progress. Sometimes it could be one of his letters to Scottie. He wrote his daughter frequently—after a trip abroad she was to enter Vassar in the fall—and he read them to me. They were a father's letters full of advice and concern. He tried to control her every thought, her every act, from a distance of three thousand miles. He wanted to know her grades—only A's would do; her friends—"I don't think so-and-so is good for you"; even the particulars of her diet—"Are you eating enough ripe fruit?" I tried to advise him, thinking, what would I have wished to hear from my father if he were alive. Zelda and Scottie were always on Scott's mind. When he spoke of one he found himself speaking of the other.

He had met Zelda during the war in Montgomery, Alabama, when she was seventeen, a Southern belle with red-gold hair who had every man at her feet. He was twenty-two, a lieutenant stationed at a nearby camp. He fell deeply in love with her but her family, he said, disapproved of him. He had no money and little prospects, and after the Armistice he seemed no better off, writing slogans for a New York advertising agency. "All I lived for was to save up enough money to visit her—" When he did so he found much of her time taken up by another suitor, a personable young golfer named Bobby Jones. For a time he feared that she would marry Jones. Not until Scribners accepted *This Side of Paradise* and he began selling to the magazines, could he win Zelda.

He brought her to New York on their honeymoon. As he spoke, I began to gain an inkling of the excitement and happiness that must have been theirs, this extraordinarily attractive young couple, she so beautiful, he so famous so young, both so much in love, both living as gaily and irresponsibly as the times themselves. She, too, was talented. She wrote beautifully, painted well, had aspirations to be a dancer, was an accomplished sportswoman, and in a drawing room could be as magnetic as Scott. They were the fabulous Fitzgeralds, living in a whirl of liquor, parties and gaiety—Paris, the Riviera, New York—and at the height of their popularity it was fashionable to quote everything they wrote, said, and did.

But the shadow of the future appeared early in their marriage. He began missing shirts, handkerchiefs, underwear. What had happened to his linen? Zelda would tell him nothing. One day he opened a closet to find it piled to the ceiling with weeks of soiled laundry. She had never sent it out: she had simply tossed everything into the closet.

When Scottie was born, it was Scott who interviewed the nurses and housekeepers and handled everything concerning their home. Though both were living bizarre lives, trying to "outdo, outdrink, and outwrite" each other, there came new evidences of the illness that was ultimately to crush her. One night in New York she said unexpectedly, "I want to see a dead man." Scott, who indulged her as he indulged himself, took her to the county morgue and they spent the night going from corpse to corpse. Again, in Baltimore, Zelda announced after one of their innumerable parties, "I hate people. Dogs are better. I'm going to sleep in the dog kennel tonight." She was as good as her word.

When they were living in Paris, in the late twenties, she suddenly took up ballet dancing. She was determined to become a member of the Russian Ballet. She studied and danced without halt. After a while it became a compulsive, terrifying thing. She danced before a mirror for nine and ten hours at a time, until she fell unconscious. "I thought I would go out of my mind," Scott said. This phase passed. Finally, he came home one day to find her sitting on the floor, playing with a pile of sand. When he questioned her she only gave him a mysterious smile. He took her to a doctor and heard the dread words, *"Votre femme est folle." Your wife is mad.*

They returned to the United States, and now came the long ordeal of physicians and treatment. In a desperate attempt to keep her out of an institution, Scott hired nurses and attendants and sought to care for her in their home. It grew impossible. Though there were periods of sanity when she would be merely eccentric, he never knew when she might slip over the border and become dangerous to herself and others. Once, hearing a train, she ran toward it. Scott reached her just in time to stop her from throwing herself in front of it. On another occasion, when he invited a young writer to their home, Zelda came into his study as the two men stood together, Scott with his arm around the other's shoulder, reading a manuscript. Scott was pointing to a sentence. "Bill, I'd change this to read—" Zelda came up silently behind them, put her hands to Bill's face and raked his cheeks with her nails. He broke away, bleeding, to stare at her in horror. Scott led her into another room. She had always been jealous of his friends, particularly if they were writers.

Ultimately, because there was no other way, he sent Scottie to a boarding school and placed his poor Zelda in a sanitarium in Asheville, North Carolina. Here he came on his visits from Hollywood, taking her out for a few days each time. Once, feeling she was better, he planned a perfect afternoon for her—a pleasant drive and a quiet lunch at the home of old friends. To make certain that nothing would upset her, he asked that no one else be invited. He hired an open car and drove Zelda, wearing a bright red trailing dress of the twenties—she seemed to prefer such clothes, apparently associating them with her happy years—down the mountains from Asheville to their host's home in nearby Tyron. At the beginning of the meal Zelda was herself—alert, warm, charming. But half way through, a change came over her. Before their eyes she began to withdraw, to fade, to vanish from their midst though she still sat there; and by the time coffee was served, she was in a world of her own, remote and unreachable. Miserably, Scott drove her back to the sanitarium. On the way she wrenched open the door and tried to leap from the moving car. For some time after that he made no attempt to take her from the institution. Instead, when he visited, they played tennis, which was believed good therapy, or he watched from the sidelines while she tried a set or two with one of the doctors. On one occasion, losing a match, she suddenly turned on her partner and belabored him over the head with her racket.

Then came the time Scott took her to New York for a week end. It was here she tried to have him committed. The morning after their arrival he woke in their hotel room to find Zelda gone and his pants missing. He tried to ring the desk clerk: the switchboard was dead. He went to the door; it was locked. After a few minutes of almost nightmare horror he got through to the clerk. "Now, take it easy, Mr. Fitzgerald," the latter said soothingly. "A doctor is on his way." When the physician arrived with two cautious bellboys as reinforcement, Scott discovered that Zelda had told everyone her husband was insane, that she was permitted to take him out of the sanitarium only at intervals, but now he had suddenly become violent and must be taken back at once. After Scott managed to convince the doctor that it was Zelda who was ill, the two men set out in search of her. They found her in Central Park digging a grave in which to bury Scott's pants.

This, in essence, is what Scott told me, little by little, reluctantly, as though compelled to do so, as though in the telling the intolerable weight on him was somehow lessened. I tried to be of comfort. At one point he said, "She would never bend. That is why she broke. You know how to bend." And then, dispassionately, "We would have been better off had we married somebody else. We were bad for each other."

My reaction was strange. I began to brood. For hours

I would sit in a chair, facing a window looking out on the sea, motionless, saying nothing; thinking, what am I doing here? I had gotten a divorce from Johnny so that I could be free to marry; I could have been a marchioness; my child might have been on its way even now. But, no. I had fallen in love with a man I could not marry. He was married to a woman he could not divorce. Now, in truth, knowing this much about Zelda, knowing his pity and compassion for her, I knew he could never, he would never, divorce her. We were both helpless, Scott and I.

Scott, working in his room, would wander downstairs to see what I was doing. It must have frightened him to find me sitting there, without moving a muscle, staring straight ahead. It must have reminded him of Zelda's brooding. Suddenly I was far away and he could not reach me, he could not follow me.

"Dear—" he would begin.

I made no reply.

Then, "Dear, is there anything the matter?"

"No." I stared straight ahead.

"There must be—you look so sad."

"No. There's nothing the matter."

Silence.

"Perhaps—" He was very gentle. "Perhaps if you took a walk along the beach you'd feel better."

"No." I still did not turn my head.

"Well . . ." His voice died away. Then, almost apologetically, "I'll go up and finish some work."

I would hear him mount the stairs and still not look in his direction. I was held in a strange spell, a coma, an almost physical paralysis. I was punishing him for not being able to marry me. Yet there was nothing he could do about it. Nor I. I could leave him—but it was impossible for me to imagine life without him. There was nothing to protest; there was nothing to be done; this was the normal injustice of life. We were two helpless people who happened to meet each other.

And hearing Scott pace, back and forth, knowing he was not working, I wept. For him. For me. For his poor Zelda.

CHAPTER TWENTY-ONE

A LETTER to me from Scottie:

> . . . waited until we were safely on the Atlantic to tell
> you how much I love the sweater. It's so marvelously soft
> and really I just adore it because I love nice sweaters
> more than anything in the world. . . .

I thought, she is only sixteen but already she has her
father's gift of making you believe you are the most
thoughtful, perceptive person.

> . . . Let me congratulate you on doing such a good job
> on Daddy—you are *definitely* a good influence. I hope he
> isn't going to get so upset every time I do anything
> wrong. . . . Anyhow thank you so much for all your trouble.
>
> Love,
> Scottie.

Scottie had come on her second visit to Hollywood to
stay briefly with her father before going on a conducted
tour of Europe this summer of 1938. The tour had been
Scott's idea. "War is coming—I'm sure of it," Scott had
told me. "I want her to see Europe as it is, and while she
can."

His daughter's arrival with Peaches, a schoolmate, posed

a problem. Scott, a little unhappily, broached the subject to me a few days before they came. "I hope you won't feel hurt, Sheilo, but I don't think it would be good for Scottie to know that you're staying here." Would I remove my clothes and my belongings from the beach house for the duration of his daughter's visit?

It was as though he had shut a door in my face, but I complied, thinking, he's like a little boy who believes that if he pretends he doesn't see a thing, no one else sees it. Yet I had noticed a straitlaced, almost puritanical streak in Scott which surprised me because it was so contrary to the picture I had gotten of him as daring, noncon- forming, and unconventional. He *had* been shocked when I spoke so casually to him of other men I had known. At parties he was acutely uncomfortable if anyone told a suggestive story: his face froze and he invariably walked away. He winced each time I forgot myself and used any of the colorful language I had picked up from my friends in the British aristocracy, or from the chorus girls back- stage at the Pavilion. I finally eliminated even "damn" from my vocabulary. Sometimes he sounded like a dis- approving schoolmaster. Once, we were watching a film. One of the characters said, "That stinks!" Scott moved in his seat. When he heard the word a second time, he all but got up and walked out. He hated the word. "It's offensive," he would say. The word "lousy" also made him uncomfortable.

Now, when Scottie arrived, although my week-end clothes, my make-up case, my possessions, were nowhere in evidence, she knew. She had only to see us together. I would catch her watching me with those clear blue eyes, Scott's eyes, trying to make up her mind whether she liked the situation. When I realized, after the second or third day, that she had decided, and in my favor, I was enormously relieved. I liked her and wanted her to like me.

Scott, as usual, was difficult and short-tempered with her. He was annoyed because for a lark one week end she and another girl had thumbed a ride to a Yale dance in New Haven instead of taking the train. He referred to it again and again until I interceded for her, even daring to tell him, "Now, Scott, you stop picking on her. What she did was perfectly harmless. Let her alone." He took it from me, grumpily, but he took it.

Still, if he harassed her, there were times when he was the ideal father. One evening she came to him with a problem. Two boys from the East who bored her almost to tears were calling on Peaches and her the next night. She had no idea how to entertain them. Scott used this as a springboard for a little lecture. "Scottie," he said, "You must have a plan. I'll give you one. Go out and buy half a dozen of the latest dance records. When dancing wears off, remember—action creates conversation. Take them into the kitchen and make fudge. You'll be so busy mixing, buttering pans, talking about what you're doing, that no one will be bored. If you're still stuck after that"—Scott was all but rubbing his hands in delight at his own resourcefulness—"bring them to me. I'll show them my pictorial history of the war. It fascinates everyone." There was a gleam in his eye and I knew what it meant. Scott's book contained gruesome photographs of soldiers with half their faces shot away. He delighted in shocking visitors with it.

Scottie listened attentively to his advice. Then her face clouded. "My God!" she exclaimed, at that moment sounding exactly like her father. "If they have a good time they'll want to come again." Scott threw up his hands.

The sweater I had bought for her trip was the first

present I gave Scottie. I enjoyed doing this. Had I a family I would have showered them with gifts. Scott refused to accept anything from me except on Christmas or his birthday, so I bought presents for his daughter on the flimsiest excuse. Scott and Scottie—and in far-off London, Johnny—were as much of a family as I would ever have, I thought.

Scottie had no sooner left than we entertained other guests. All during that summer of 1938 Scott's friends were in and out. They included Harold Ober, his New York literary agent, to whom Scott, as I learned later, owed considerable money; Cameron Rogers, a screenwriter, and his wife, Buff Cobb, daughter of Irvin S. Cobb, the humorist—both friends of long standing; and Charles Marquis Warren, a brilliant young writer from Baltimore whom Scott considered his protégé. Charlie, who was 22, worshipped Scott and invariably addressed him—to Scott's annoyance—as "sir." He came often to lunch and later the two men would talk shop while I put on my bathing suit and prepared for a dip. Each time I passed by, Charlie followed me with his eyes. And each time Scott would say irritably, "Charlie, look at me when you talk to me, dammit!" Once Charlie sighed: "God, sir, isn't she beautiful!" Scott stopped in the middle of a sentence and glowered at him. "Look, you're bigger than I am, but I can take you—"

Later, after Charlie left, Scott turned to me. "Why does he 'sir' me? How old does he think I am?"

Cameron Rogers, his wife Buff, and Scott were engaged in animated conversation. Scott, leaning forward eagerly, was expounding on the Thirty Years' War. Buff was saying, "I don't think you can understand Wallenstein unless you consider Richelieu who helped mold him."

Cameron nodded. I had never heard of Wallenstein, Richelieu, or the Thirty Years' War. Now Scott was deep in the subject, occasionally turning to smile at me to show me that I was included.

I thought, suddenly, I will not be in this position again. They discuss Franz Kafka and T. S. Eliot and Wallenstein and Richelieu and the Thirty Years' War and I sit out the outside, looking in. If I want to stay in the same world as these people I must do something about it. Eddie Mayer had once told me that Proust's *Remembrance of Things Past* was one of the most fascinating and instructive books he had ever read, giving a vivid picture of turn-of-the-century European society. I had bought the book only to find it too difficult. Now I brought it to Malibu and forced myself to read it. Scott was surprised and amused to find me poring over Proust while my trade publications lay untouched. "How do you like it?" he asked. "It's so hard to grasp," I admitted. "My mind seems all thumbs when I try to get into it." I had not really studied a book since I was fourteen.

"Don't read more than ten pages a day," Scott suggested. "Read slowly and carefully and assimilate what you've read before going on." I stuck doggedly to his schedule until half way through Volume One the horizons suddenly widened: I began to see everything bigger than life. When I read of the cup of tea that brought back the past so sharply to Proust, I smelled again the potato soup and soapsuds of my childhood. I grew excited. His characters became alive for me, especially Madame Verdurin, who at every crisis buried her face in her hands. I became so fascinated with Madame Verdurin that I began imitating her. If Flora burned the soup, if I forgot a telephone call, if Saturday dawned wet and raining, I clapped my hands to my face. Scott would roar.

I talked about Proust all summer. He was *my* Thirty Years' War.

Meanwhile at Metro Scott's unhappiness mounted. After three months of labor on *Fidelity,* he greeted me one evening with, "I've been taken off the story." The studio found the subject too daring. The change in title had not helped. He had been shunted to a new story, Clare Boothe's *The Women*. He was very depressed. He had never gotten over the fact that *Three Comrades* had been rewritten—that Scott Fitzgerald had to be rewritten was galling to him—and now it appeared that he had fallen down on still another assignment. I said, because I thought it might cheer him, "Let's have some people over. Why don't you invite a lot of your friends?"

"That's it," said Scott. His face lit up. "We'll have a party."

It was quite a party.

As always, Scott had a plan. High point of the day would be a Ping-pong tournament. Scott carefully prepared a list of players, complete to handicaps. Eddie Mayer, the first guest on that Sunday afternoon, arrived with his seven-year-old son, Paul, while Scott and I were playing a practice game. The boy watched us critically for a few moments, then piped up challengingly, "I'll take on the winner." This amused Scott. He made short shrift of me and then played Paul in great style—crossing his eyes, slamming the ball with his back to the table or over his shoulder, so that he managed to lose. Then he brought out boxing gloves and he and Paul sparred, Scott ferociously flicking his thumb against his nose and daring Paul to give him one "right on the button."

The other guests arrived, among them Nunnally Johnson, the writer, and his wife, Marion, Cameron and Buff Rogers, and Charlie Warren with a lovely starlet, Alice Hyde. Charlie was recovering from a back injury and wore a brace, but insisted on coming when he heard that Scott had invited Miss Hyde to be his date. I hurried about dispensing Flora's hors d'oeuvres, sandwiches, and coffee, while Scott became busy serving drinks to everyone. He insisted on drinking only water himself.

The party was in full swing when Scott noticed two small faces peering wistfully through the white picket fence that separated our house from our neighbor, Joe Swerling, the screen writer. The youngsters were his sons, Joe, Jr., six, and Peter, eight. "Come on over and join the party," Scott called to them. He lifted them over the fence and introduced them to Paul, then went on to supervise the Ping-Pong tourney. A little later he saw the three boys standing about disconsolately. There was little for them to do, among these adults who were drinking, eating, dancing, and talking endlessly about scripts and studios. Scott went up to them. "Would you boys like to see a wonderful card trick?" He dashed into the house, emerging with a deck of cards. "Only one other man in the world can do this," he said portentously. "And he's a lifer at San Quentin, who spent ten years in solitary where he thought up this trick." He rolled up his sleeves. "Watch!" He knitted his eyebrows, intoned a selpulchral "Abracadabra" and whirled three times with his eyes closed. Then he produced from the deck, on demand, an ace, a king, a ten, a four—all to the delight of his rapt audience.

He mystified them with half a dozen other tricks, showing a surprising sleight of hand. Then he brought string from one pocket and began making and dissolving intricate knots. I was as fascinated as the children. "Now," he said, "Aren't you kids thirsty? How about something to drink?"

Joe, Jr., spoke up politely. "I'd like a glass of champagne, thank you."

Scott stared at him, horrified. "Coming right up," he said. He immediately telephoned Mrs. Swerling. "Are you aware that your six-year-old son drinks champagne?" he demanded. Mrs. Swerling laughed. "We gave him ginger ale at his birthday party last week and told him it was champagne." Mollified, Scott emerged with a tray of ginger ale which he announced as champagne newly imported from France.

Meanwhile, everyone seemed to be enjoying themselves except Charlie Warren and Alice Hyde. Although at first they appeared to hit it off beautifully, now she seemed deliberately to avoid him. Scott came up to Charlie. "What's the matter, old man?" he asked. "Seems she can't stand you. You haven't said anything offensive to her, have you?"

"Oh, no, sir," said Charlie, woebegone. "I can't understand it."

Alice took me aside. She pleaded an excruciating headache. Would we forgive her if she left? She gave Charlie an icy good-by and was gone.

"Do you want me to try to fix things up, Charlie?" Scott asked, solicitously. "I see her at the studio. I'll talk to her."

Charlie said heavily he was afraid it would do no good.

Finally the evening drew to a close. There had been word games and charades and much drinking. I saw Scott taking couples to their cars. He seemed in excellent humor. He had been gay all evening despite his unhappiness at Metro. All at once I realized he had been *too* gay. *Of course. Gin, not water.* At this moment he was escorting Nunnally and Marion to the door. Suddenly, as they came opposite a bedroom, I saw Scott violently shove Nunnally into the room, slip in after him and slam the door. I heard the lock click—and then Scott's voice, raised in anger. Later Nunnally told me what had happened. Scott had locked the door, dropped the key dramatically into his shirt pocket and began to harangue him.

"Listen, Nunnally, get out of Hollywood. It will ruin you. You have a talent—you'll kill it here." He began to tick off on his fingers the friends he had known whose talent had been violated by Hollywood.

Nunnally protested. He liked Hollywood. "Look," he said, "I don't think I've been chosen by destiny to be a great writer, Scott. I haven't felt the call. I'm just a guy who makes his living writing and I make a better living writing in Hollywood than anywhere else. Why should I leave?"

This enraged Scott. "Why, you sonofabitch, you don't know what's good for you." Scott looked about wildly, as though seeking something to throw at him. "I'm warning you—get out of here. This place isn't for you. Go back to New York—"

Nunnally decided to reverse his field gracefully. "Come to think of it, Scott, you're right. Of course. Soon as I finish this script I'm working on, I'll go."

Scott glared at him. "Oh, no," he said. "Now you're lying." He advanced on him menacingly and Nunnally backed away. "You tell me the truth—"

"I am telling you the truth," Nunnally insisted, almost backed against the wall now and wondering how hard he would have to punch to render Scott harmless. "I promise, honest to God, Scott."

I pounded on the door. "Scott, everyone's leaving, they want to say good-by to you."

Finally the door opened. Nunnally skittered out with a belligerent Scott on his heels. He was quite drunk. Cameron and Buff Rogers came to say good-by. Scott tried to goad Cameron, who was a big man, into a fight. Cameron refused. Scott turned to Buff. "God damn that big Harvard lug—if he doesn't knock me out, I'll kill him. I got to be knocked out!" He squared off. "Come on, Cameron, put up your fists like a man!"

Cameron didn't know what to do. I fluttered about helplessly. Finally Cameron doubled up his right fist and tapped Scott in the stomach. Scott collapsed and we carried him to a sofa. He was mumbling bitterly to himself. "That big, hulking brute—and me dying of tuberculosis."

Buff, who felt like a sister to Scott, said, "Oh, be quiet, Scott. If he hadn't done it, I would have."

Minutes later Scott was up again, ordering everyone home. The last to leave were Nunnally and Marion. They had almost reached their car when Scott hurled a parting insult. "You'll never come back here. Never!"

Nunnally turned. "Of course I will, Scott," he said. "I want to see you and Sheilah again."

"Oh, no, you won't," roared Scott. "Because I'm living with my paramour! That's why you won't."

I could hardly believe my ears. I wanted to slap Scott, but, instead, I turned and ran from the room onto the beach. How dare he! Just then I saw him. He had dashed out of the beach house and was racing across the sand to the water. To my utter horror, as I watched him, he plunged, clothes and all, into the ocean and began swimming furiously, like a man about to swim the English Channel. "Scott!" I shrieked. "You'll die of pneumonia! Scott—"

He swam a few strokes, turned, swam back and emerged, dripping. He paid no attention to me. Instead, he trotted to his car nearby, got in, and drove off in a roar of gears.

He did not return until an hour later, with a bottle of liquor he had bought at the Malibu Inn.

I heard him tumble into bed in his room.

A few days later Charlie Warren called. He had a date with Alice Hyde. Everything was fine. He began to laugh. "Do you know why she walked out on me at your party?" In the course of the evening Scott had taken her aside. He felt a great responsibility, he said, because he had introduced her to Charlie. He must swear her to secrecy, but the fact was that Charlie, although a fine fellow, suffered from syphilis. He was slowly wasting away. It was all too tragic. His fingers were due to fall off any day. Even now the poor boy went about strapped tightly in a brace. Otherwise he would collapse. If she danced with him and surreptitiously touched his back, she would feel the brace that held him together. Scott had told her this ridiculous story with the most solemn mien. "Well," said Charlie. "She danced with me and that was it." He was indignant when he first learned Scott's joke—Scott had finally taken pity on him and told him—but now he thought it hilarious.

"I don't, Charlie," I said. "I don't think it's funny at all."

"Maybe it isn't," Charlie said. He laughed again. "But don't take it too seriously. That's Scott."

CHAPTER TWENTY-TWO

Paramour. Such a hard, such a cruel word. It haunted me. Each time my anger surged, I tried to calm myself. Yes, I thought, that is Scott, too. Scott the Puritan who lashes himself—and me. Who takes out his frustration on Nunnally and pleads with Cameron to knock him out and plays his pranks, just this side of cruelty, on those he loves.

Had I been more perceptive, I might have had a better understanding of Scott's struggle in Hollywood, of the dark night in his own soul. But in this first year or so, he hid much from me. He would not be pitied and I had too much respect for him to pry. And it was not easy to pity him: he dazzled me. I was overwhelmed by the excitement he engendered in me, by his infectious enthusiasm, by the delight he took in opening new horizons for me, by the intense interest he concentrated upon me.

I gave him every thought I had. I turned to him for every judgment, every standard of conduct. I wanted him to teach me, to open to me the intellectual treasures of the world he knew and enjoyed with such zest. What he enjoyed, what he delighted in, I wanted to enjoy and delight in.

And so, quite without knowing it, I found myself enrolled in the F. Scott Fitzgerald College of One.

It began with a poem.

We were driving back to Malibu from a preview in Hollywood when Scott began to recite:

> Fair youth, beneath the trees, thou canst not leave
> Thy song, nor ever can those trees be bare;
> Bold Lover, never never canst thou kiss,
> Though winning near the goal—yet, do not grieve;
> She cannot fade, though thou hast not thy bliss,
> Forever wilt thou love, and she be fair—

I put my hand on his. "I like that, Scott. Say the last line again." He repeated it. "Who wrote that?" I asked, dreamily. "Keats," he said. "It's from 'Ode on a Grecian Urn.' "

I said, softly, "I think that is the most beautiful line I have ever heard. 'Forever wilt thou love, and she be fair. . . .' "

"Would you like to hear it all?" he asked. "I have the book at the house." When we reached Malibu, we both eagerly searched through his books until we found his volume of Keats. He read the entire poem aloud to me.

He saw how moved I was. "Let me read something else, Sheilo," he said. "Listen to this. The title is, 'To His Coy Mistress.' " And while the surf rolled endlessly outside our window, Scott read in a voice which, when he wished, had the dramatic timbre of an actor's:

> Had we but world enough, and time,
> This coyness, Lady, were no crime.
> We would sit down and think which way
> To walk, and pass our long love's day.

.   .   .   .

But at my back I always hear
Time's winged chariot hurrying near;
And yonder all before us lie
Deserts of vast eternity. . . .

He read on:

Now therefore, while the youthful hue
Sits on thy skin like morning dew,
And while thy willing soul transpires
At every pore with instant fires,
Now let us sport us while we may,
And now, like amorous birds of prey,
Rather at once our time devour,
Than languish in his low-chapt power.
Let us roll our strength and all
Our sweetness up into one ball,
And tear our pleasures with rough strife
Through the iron gates of life:
Thus, we cannot make our sun
Stand still, yet we will make him run.

We were both silent when he had finished. Then Scott
said, "Andrew Marvell wrote that more than two hundred
and fifty years ago."

I was filled with an overwhelming sense of wonder.
That people so long ago should have been as interested in
love as I was interested in love! "Sheilo," said Scott. "That
is part of the beauty of all literature. You discover that
your longings are universal longings, that you're not lonely
and isolated from anyone. You belong."

I said, "Scott, you know I never went past the eighth
grade. But I don't think you really know the tremendous
gaps in my knowledge. I was so embarrassed when you
and Cameron and Buff were talking about the Thirty
Years' War. I'm English, and you were discussing English history, and I couldn't join in. That's why I brought

Proust out here—I wanted to prove to myself that I could still become educated." And I said to him, "Will you tell me what to read? Will you give me a course in poetry?"

His face lit up. "Sheilo, of course!" He was enthusiastic. Neither of us were aware, then, that I was resuming the education that had stopped the day I left the orphanage. For Scott treated his teaching of me—which was finally to grow into a project beyond anything either of us anticipated—as a challenge as exciting as screen writing. He made out careful lists of books and gave me daily reading schedules. I would arrive at the beach house to discover half a dozen books on my desk. He had gone through them and made scores of notes to help me. On the margin of one page he wrote, "Skip this—boring." On another: "Read this carefully, then read the marked pages in Plutarch's *Lives*. The two taken together—Matthew Arnold and Plutarch—will give you a good picture of the times." On the margin of Keats' "Eve of St. Agnes," I found, "When we come to read the Fifth Tale of Boccaccio's *Decameron*—one hundred magnificent short stories written nearly six centuries ago—you'll see where Keats got his idea for these lines." Again, it was as it had been with Proust: what had been only names mentioned in the conversation of Randolph Churchill and A. P. Herbert, Eddie Mayer and Dorothy Parker and Bob Benchley, suddenly took on the reality of living human beings—men and women who in their time had toiled over manuscripts and hunted an elusive word.

A new routine began for us. I set aside three hours each day to do the reading he assigned me. Each evening we discussed what I had read. Scott quizzed me: I answered his questions. Scott *was* a teacher. To be asked to explain was like a tonic to him, and I was athirst for everything he could tell me. "We'll begin from scratch," he said. "We must first create a façade for you so that you can handle yourself in company—at least you'll know the general subject if it comes up. Then we will go into detail."

He had always been interested in education, he told me. He felt most people stopped learning when they left college because they had not been taught properly. "The object of education is to provide you with a key to knowledge," he explained. But most people on leaving college, threw the key away. "Only those who are eager for it should have a college education. The schools are neglecting their most important responsibility: to make education interesting, to make you love and enjoy it, to apply it to your own life after you leave school." Someday, he said, he'd like to write a book on the subject.

My reading, as outlined by Scott, was anything but haphazard. He devoted hours to the job of working out schedules for me. When I read Shelley's poems, I read them with André Maurois *Ariel*—the biography of the poet—on the table. I had an assignment sheet on which Scott had written: "How to learn from a Frenchman about an exiled Englishman (by an American)." It specified the poems I was to read after reading selected chapters in the biography, so that I would know the genesis of each poem.

The same procedure was followed with Byron. Now I had Byron's collected works, *The Oxford Book of English Verse,* and other cross-references which Scott had read and marked for me. I had to read Keats in the 1910 Oxford Edition: *The Poetical Works of John Keats,* and here Scott separated the good from the bad. In the margin of "La Belle Dame Sans Merci," he wrote, "This is the *bad* form as edited by Leigh Hunt." Then: "See below,"—and here he had the poem edited to his satisfaction.

I remember looking up from my work one day to say, "I'm student one in your college—the F. Scott Fitzgerald College of One." Scott's fancy was caught by my words. "You do well and I'll give you a diploma," he said. I thought, I finally shall get one, after all.

I studied the Elizabethan poets—not only Marvell but Herrick, Donne, Jonson, men who so long ago had written so feelingly about love—and I took great joy in surprising Scott. I was the girl who could memorize verses faster than anyone in the orphanage. When Scott dropped in I'd say, "Sit down, Scott—" and I'd reel off an entire poem that he had assigned me to read only two days before. He sat there listening, quite pleased; his problems at the studio, his concern over Scottie, the upsetting letters from Zelda, all forgotten. "I like the truth of poetry," I told him. "I think it's the finest way of speaking the truth." He liked that.

Our reading stimulated me. I wanted to turn everything into words. Walking with him in the late afternoon, we stopped to watch the sun sink slowly into the Pacific. It was a moment of utter peacefulness, the sea calm, and I was moved. "Oh Scott, that sunset is so beautiful! Just like molten gold—"

He said, sharply, "Please be quiet. You don't have to say that."

I was hurt. Was my observation too commonplace? But I had no original observations of my own. I had to copy those in use. I told him so. "If I'm full of clichés, Scott, you mustn't be angry with me. I need them—they're my little stepping stones in conversation. I feel safe with them." And I said, "I come to you, I open myself completely to you—you shouldn't lash me with a whip like that."

He apologized. He was very contrite. "I'm sorry, Sheilo,

I was short with you and it wasn't fair of me. I won't do it again." Never again did he make me feel ashamed of my inadequacy. He encouraged me, rather, to speak up if I did not know. Before, if one used a word I did not understand, or made an allusion that was obscure to me, I remained silent, instead of asking simply, "What does that mean?" I thought it disgraceful to show my ignorance. Scott made me feel it was disgraceful not to speak up when I didn't know.

He taught me respect for books. When he found me folding down a corner of a page, to keep my place in a book, he scolded me. "I'll make bookmarks for you," he said, and he did. I was scolded again when he discovered that I sometimes skipped to the end of a book to learn how the story came out. "The author spent a great deal of time writing this book as he wanted it read," he said. "You must have respect for him. Read it the way he wrote it to be read."

We moved to current events. He brought me Hitler's *Mein Kampf,* and *Das Kapital* by Marx, and carefully went over them with me, chapter by chapter, explaining, clarifying, interpreting. "Scott, I feel as though you're pushing back the cuticle that's grown over my mind all these years," I said. "It's painful but if you don't do it now, it will never go back."

He prepared a full curriculum. I would study Literature Through the Ages, Politics, Modern and Ancient History, Philosophy, Religion, Art, and Music. In each course I would not only read the books assigned to me, with the required cross-references, but also novels and poems Scott chose for me dealing with the subject.

I began to have opinions. When I could not accept Scott's interpretations, I challenged him. We actually debated with each other. He knew I was honest with him—

and for the first time I was with a man I did not need to impress, nor agree with for ulterior motives of my own. Scott had put it simply: "Never say what you don't believe just to please someone." This was an intellectual freedom I had never known before. I gloried in it. I thought, where have I been all these years? This is as exhilarating, as exciting, as dancing or making love or being admired. I felt the golden haze again. Was this what I have been really thirsting for so long—to *know*? To use my *mind*?

And Scott understood. Until now I had felt I *had* to be beautiful: people would accept me for no other reason. The fear that I would be discarded when I grew old and lost my beauty hung over me like a frightening shadow. Now Scott held out new hope. He made me feel he was grooming me to become more interesting with the years, to become an attractive, charming, interesting lady with whom everyone would want to be. "Always remember, Sheilah. Once you know the pattern of history you will stop being apprehensive. You won't be an unattached unit in the world. You will be at home. You will have a place in life."

It was so warming and reassuring!

CHAPTER TWENTY-THREE

AT ENCINO, in the San Fernando Valley, Edward Everett Horton, the actor, had an estate called "Belly Acres." Here, in spite of Scott's dismay—"How can I tell anyone I live in 'Belly Acres'?" he had asked, outraged— I rented a house when Scott's Malibu lease expired. Malibu was too cold and damp for him in winter: the Valley was always some ten degrees warmer than the rest of the countryside. In addition, the new house was well suited to our needs. Nearby were woods of fir and birch; there was a rolling green lawn, a lovely garden of pink and yellow roses surrounded by a small white picket fence, huge magnolia trees with deckchairs in their shade, a swimming pool and tennis court. The house, one of three on Mr. Horton's estate, was a big rambling structure with a long balcony off Scott's bedroom on which he could pace to his heart's content.

At the beginning Scott was not particularly enamored of the place. Then Buff Cobb dropped in. He showed her around. "Don't you think this is a rather uninspired house?" he asked.

"I don't know," said Buff. "The garden is lovely—"

"Yes," said Scott, grudgingly. "The garden is kind of charming."

Buff went on, "And all those little pickets look like little gravestones in a Confederate graveyard."

Scott looked at her absolutely delighted. "Sheilah!" He ran inside. "She's made the place livable! We've got romance in the house." Now he was quite happy with it. He suggested that since it was large enough for both of us, I might as well give up my house and take a small apartment in town. I did so, renting a two-bedroom flat off Sunset Boulevard where Scott could work and stay when in town.

Scott helped me choose the furniture. Like newlyweds, we spent an entire morning wandering happily through Barker's Bargain Basement in Los Angeles inspecting carpets, desks, lamps: among the major pieces we selected were a green chintz sofa and a large green armchair, which Scott, with great seriousness, bounced in several times to see if it were comfortable.

In early January, 1939, David Selznick suddenly called Scott in to work on *Gone With the Wind*. For a week Scott toiled over the famous staircase scene, asking himself aloud, "What would she say to him? What would he say to her?" I became Scarlett O'Hara; he, Rhett Butler. I struck a pose at the top of our winding staircase at Encino, daintily holding the hem of an invisible evening gown. Scott, standing at the foot of the staircase, called out directions. "Now, slowly—keep your eye on me—"

Slowly, my head high, my skirts lifted from the stairs, I began to descend. From below, Scott looked up at me and smiled—the self-assured, half-provocative, half-disdainful smile of a great lover.

"Miss O'Hara—" he began silkily. I continued to de-

scend, languidly waving an imaginary fan. "Captain Butler, I believe—"

Scott couldn't contain himself. He burst into laughter.

I ran down the stairs into his arms. We were both laughing. "Am I really such an awful actress?" I asked. "I tried
to help—"

He said, "Sheilah, it might be better if I work it out on
paper."

But though he was determined to lick the script where
others had failed—Selznick had repeatedly brought in new
writers on his gigantic project—Scott lasted but two weeks.
Suddenly he was dismissed; Director George Cukor was no
longer on the picture; and Selznick was casting about for
another writer and another director. On the heels of this,
Metro failed to renew Scott's contract, so that *Gone With
the Wind* turned out to be Scott's final job for the studio
that had brought him to Hollywood eighteen months
before.

For the first time since he came west, he was without
salary. "Well," he said hopefully, "I'll just have to work
from picture to picture. Maybe I'll go ahead with my
novel. Try some short stories, too."

It was now that Walter Wanger, the producer, learning
that Scott was free, hired him to work with Budd Schulberg, a young screen writer, on a film about Dartmouth
College's Winter Ice Carnival, held annually in Hanover,
New Hampshire. Wanger was a Dartmouth alumnus and
Budd had graduated from Dartmouth a few years before.
If the idea of collaborating with a beginning writer—one
who admired him but did not conceal the fact that he
thought he had died long ago—was a blow to Scott's ego,
he did not show it. He liked young writers and he welcomed Schulberg cordially.

For days I watched Scott labor on the script with Budd. As always with a new project, he was full of enthusiasm: he worked to instill warmth and charm into this story of a college week end. Here were all the ingredients he had handled so superbly in the past. Yet I could not help thinking—how much hinged on his success here! If he failed on this assignment, too, where would his next job come from? Scott must have felt this concern: in the quiet of the Encino night I heard his endless pacing, back and forth. Sometimes sleep did not come to him until dawn. When he woke, his face was gray as clay. One morning he said in a matter-of-fact voice, "My T.B.'s flared up." He was running a low fever which gave him night sweats. It was sometimes necessary, I learned, to change his bed sheets two and three times during the night.

I was alarmed. Despite his annoyance I took his temperature. It was 101 degrees. "Don't worry about me," he said irritably. "I won't be babied. Forget it."

At this critical stage Wanger, who was in the East preparing to shoot the script, wired Scott and Budd to join him at once in Hanover. I protested to Scott. He was in no condition to fly to New York. "Not with a temperature—"

He said, reluctantly, he must go. He had to carry this project through. All right, I said finally. But if he went, I'd go with him. I had not been to New York for a long time. "It will be a change to write my column from the East for a week or two." Jonah Ruddy would cover for me here.

In our plane, Budd and Scott were busily discussing their script when I went to my berth. Next morning Scott had the grayness of death on him. I attributed this to a combination of temperature and insomnia. Only then I learned that Budd's father, B. P. Schulberg, a former producer, had presented Budd with a magnum of champagne before the flight. Scott had been up all night reminiscing with Budd, the two sustaining themselves on champagne. I was furious with them but there was nothing to do.

When we reached New York they dropped me off at the Weylin Hotel, met Wanger at the Waldorf, and went on by train to Hanover. They would be back in a week, Scott said. "Better not call me there. I'll be working. I'll phone you."

The call that came to me from Scott a few days later alarmed me. He was at the Hanover Inn with Budd: they were making wonderful progress. He bubbled over, he was uproariously funny—I knew then that he was still drinking. Liquor plus his illness—*anything* could happen. "Be back in town Friday," he said expansively over the phone. "I'll call you."

The second call never came. Nor was Scott back on Friday. I waited in my room at the Weylin, growing more frantic as my imagination conjured up every possible tragedy. Saturday came, then Sunday. I put in a call for Scott at the Hanover Inn. Mr. Fitzgerald and Mr. Schulberg had checked out days ago. I telephoned every hotel in the vicinity without success.

On Monday evening the telephone rang. I leaped at it. It was Budd. "What happened?" I demanded. "Where's Scott?"

Budd's voice was shaky. "I've got bad news, Sheilah—"

"Scott's dead!" I cried.

"No, no, no. But he's sick. I've been taking care of him. He went on a terrible bender—" Budd began to blame himself. "I should never have given him that champagne." Scott had been drinking for days, he had made a spectacle of himself at Dartmouth, he'd gotten into an argument with Wanger, Wanger had ordered them both out of Hanover, it was a sorry, awful mess—"

I broke in. "Where's Scott now?"

"I can't tell you," Budd said evasively. "He made me promise not to. I'm just to say that you'll see him very soon. I'm sorry I can't tell you more, Sheilah." He hung up.

I sat at the telephone. Poor Scott! I blamed Budd for the champagne but I blamed myself for not insisting that Scott remain in Hollywood. What would this *do* to him?

The telephone rang again. "Hello, Sheilo—" It was Scott. He had checked in at the Weylin a few minutes ago. I hurried down to his room. He was slumped in a chair, unshaven, exhausted, his face with the ashen pallor that terrified me. He had had "the most awful time" in Hanover. "I was never so cold before." He was running a temperature of 102 degrees, he said, when he had to join Wanger and Budd as they climbed a snow-covered hill leading to a ski jump. "It was agony, Sheilah. I plowed through that snow thinking I'd die." Every step had been a stab of pain. He made a grimace. "I shouldn't have left Hollywood. But I needed the money." It was the first time Scott had admitted his financial difficulties.

"Get into bed, Scott," I said gently. "I'll call a doctor and nurse—"

He began to push himself out of the chair. "Must have something to drink," he said. "Got to have a bottle."

"Just get into bed, Scott," I said. "I'll run out and get you a bottle."

I went to the bed to turn back the covers—and Scott scuttled out the door and down the service stairs. "Scott, Scott!"—I shouted after him. But he was gone. Almost distraught, I found my way back to my room. How would

I get him in condition to return to the Coast? I telephoned a physician who had treated me when I lived in New York. "You need a psychiatrist to handle this," he said. He recommended Dr. Richard H. Hoffman.

Scott had not yet returned when Dr. Hoffman, a soft-spoken man with piercing dark eyes and great charm, arrived in response to my telephone call. He listened while I told him about Scott. Then, with a smile, he said, "I know Mr. Fitzgerald and admire him very much." He had met Scott and Zelda in Paris in 1925, and had often come upon them at parties given there by mutual friends. "Then you know about his drinking?" I asked. Dr. Hoffman nodded. He had followed Scott's career through the years. He would do his best to help him.

At this moment, Scott, bottle in hand, came in unsteadily. I introduced them, a little apprehensive because I knew how Scott resented interference. "This is Dr. Hoffman," I said. "He is a psychiatrist and you met him before, in Paris, years ago—"

Scott, with exaggerated politeness, took Dr. Hoffman's hand. "Yes, of course," he said. It was obvious he did not remember. He looked at him impishly. "A psychiatrist, eh?" He indicated a chair and slid into one himself. "Sit down, Doctor." He unscrewed the top of his bottle, put his head back and took a long drink, replaced the cover and stuffed the bottle into his pocket. "Now, what is it you'd like to know about me?"

I excused myself and left the room.

That night Dr. Hoffman moved Scott to Doctors Hospital and placed him on a strict regimen. He visited him daily; at the end of a week Scott was back at the Weylin where I cared for him. Dr. Hoffman continued his daily treatment.

At the end of two weeks we returned to Hollywood.

I had not talked to Dr. Hoffmann alone since our first meeting. That I must not discuss him with the psychiatrist outside his hearing became almost an obsession with Scott. "Anything Dr. Hoffmann has to say about me, I want to know," he said. "There'll be no whispering in corners." He pledged me on my word of honor. It was as though Scott feared Dr. Hoffmann might reveal something to me that would make me pity him: and this he could not bear.

Not until many years later did Dr. Hoffmann, at my request, tell me what he had found about Scott, and what he had told him in their many sessions. Scott, he discovered, suffered from hyperinsulinism, a rapid burning away of body sugars, which might be described as the reverse of diabetes. This condition, although it might have been created by his drinking, now contributed to his need for alcohol. Scott was sugar starved, and alcohol was one of the quickest ways the body could replenish sugar. I thought, this explained his craving for Coca-Cola, his heavily sweetened coffee, his addiction to fudge.

Dr. Hoffmann had treated Scott with medication and made use of psychotherapy—spending an hour a day helping Scott analyze his attitude toward himself and his future. Scott, Dr. Hoffmann said, was then in despair. He believed he was finished as a writer. "I don't have it any more," he told the psychiatrist. "It's gone, vanished." Dr. Hoffmann said to him, "This is not your death, it is the death of your youth. This is a transitional period, not an end. You will lie fallow for a while, then you will go on." He quoted Emerson to him: "'On the debris of your despair, you build your character.' Not on your despair alone. First you destroy your despair, and on its debris you begin to rebuild." Later, when Scott wrote him, asking for a bill, Dr. Hoffmann waived the fee and, in his letter, replied, "Let's buy a wreath for the grave of your adolescence, and then go on from there."

But none of this I knew as Scott and I flew back to Hollywood, Scott wan but outwardly cheerful, I wondering, when will this end?

CHAPTER TWENTY-FOUR

Back in encino, Scott tried to follow a careful regimen. It was too much for him. He had no contract; there were no screen-writing jobs; there was no money coming in. The difficult months began. Before the year was over Scott and I were to have our most anguished times together.

I was never sure when he drank. Scott, sober, could be so ebullient that one could not tell. Now, casting about, speaking one moment of getting into his novel, the next of whipping out a short story that might sell for $3,000, as he had done in the past, he grew increasingly nervous. The Hanover episode had shaken him. He wrote endless letters to Scottie at Vassar, to his agent, Harold Ober, to his editors in New York, asking if reprints of his books might not be put out to bring in revenue. I suspected that he was drinking and I became angry with him for concealing it. Gin has the faintest of odors. I would maneuver myself as close to him as possible to see if I could detect it, and when I did, I could not contain myself. "Are you drinking?" I demanded. "I'm sure you're drinking."

"That is none of your business," he replied stiffly.

"I hate you when you drink," I burst out. "You're not

the person I like then. Why do you drink? When I fell in love with you you weren't drinking. Why are you doing it now?"

"I'm not drinking," he retorted, and walked away.

One afternoon when he left for the barber I went through his bureau drawers. I found eleven empty gin bottles. On his return I accused him. "You said you're not drinking—how do you explain these bottles!"

I know now that I was doing all the wrong things. I was like a bull in a china shop. I had no idea how to handle him; my reaction was always anger.

His features seemed to crowd to the center of his face. "What's that to you?" he demanded. He strode to a cupboard, stuck his hand into a far corner and brought out a bottle he had hidden there. As I watched, he unscrewed the top and, putting the bottle to his mouth, drank heavily from it as he had done in front of Dr. Hoffman.

I began to shout at him as I had never dared before. "Why don't you stop it? Any idiot can laugh at you! Why are you doing this? You don't know how silly you are! You're a good writer, why are you wasting your talent? You'll die. You'll drop dead. You'll have a stroke. You'll be through in Hollywood, through for good—then what will you do?"

He cast a glance of deep injury at me, turned, and made his way to his room. I thought, *I will do something about this.* In Chicago, Arnold Gingrich had told me of a remarkable new pill he had used on another *Esquire* writer whom he had tried to discourage from drinking. I had only to drop it surreptitiously in Scott's drink: he would become so ill that even the thought of liquor would nauseate him. There was only one drawback. Liquor treated with the pill turned blue in a few minutes. I would have to work swiftly.

I planned it carefully. Each night after the eleven P.M. news—these were the days of the Spanish Civil War, which Scott followed with great interest—he usually came into the kitchen where he kept a bottle of gin in the cupboard for a nightcap. One week-end I bought six bottles of gin and secreted them in the kitchen. A few minutes after eleven o'clock I emptied one to the level in Scott's bottle, dropped in a pill and substituted it for his bottle. Then I waited, nervously, in the dining room. Minutes passed— but no Scott. I dashed to the cupboard: the gin had become a rich, laundry blue. I poured it into the sink, swiftly prepared a second, and dashed back to my hiding place. Again, no Scott. In the cupboard the second bottle was slowly turning blue. Almost in panic now lest Scott walk in on me, I rushed through the same procedure with a third bottle. And so, in the next half hour, dashing in and out of the kitchen, I used up all six—and still Scott had not appeared. Now only his bottle remained. There was nothing to do but drop a pill into it. Perhaps he'd show up before it changed color; perhaps he'd take his drink in the dark and notice nothing. I went to bed.

Late that night Scott came into my room, glass in hand. "Funny," he said puzzled. "This gin is blue."

Suddenly I was terrified at what I had done. "Don't drink it, Scott! Maybe it's poisoned!"

He looked at me and tossed it down with one gulp, then stumbled to bed. All night I remained awake, tiptoeing fearfully into his room every few minutes to see if he still breathed. Strangely enough the pills had no effect on him then or later.

He tried to take himself in hand. "I've started my novel," he announced expansively one April afternoon. He had hired a secretary—Frances Kroll, a slender dark-eyed girl just out of college. When she came for her interview she found Scott in his faded, slate-blue bathrobe, the inevitable pencil over his ear. He questioned her gently, quizzically, asking with a smile which belied his words, "How do I know I can trust you?" He explained that he was writing a novel about Hollywood. No one must know about it. "I don't trust the secretaries in the studios," he said. "They're always telling each other what they're working on. This must be kept absolutely secret. If you take the job I don't want you talking to other writers' secretaries." She promised. He looked at her thoughtfully. "I want to put your name down, Miss Kroll," he said. "Would you get me my notebook in that top bureau drawer?" She opened the drawer to see the notebook lying next to half a dozen bottles of gin neatly placed side by side. When she looked up, Scott was watching her intently. His eyes asked, "What do you think of that?" Frances, who assumed the liquor had been stocked for a party, obviously thought nothing of it. She had passed her test and Scott hired her.

Each day, now, he dictated for a few hours. This was one stage of his writing process. He preferred to dictate dialogue and write narration in longhand. Though he was still drinking, he seemed to have himself under control. He was trying to get along on one beer a day, he explained. I tried to become resigned, but I could not. I managed to get him to agree that if he became too drunk I was to take away his car keys and wallet. I did not want him driving in that condition, nor did I want him distributing fifty-dollar bills to waiters as he had done in the past. There was nothing else I could do about the situation. This was part of the package. If I wanted Scott, I had to take him as he was. Perhaps, as he got deeper into his novel he would find less need to drink.

It was not to be so. As the days passed, his T.B. flared up. With it came the steady fever, accompanied by night sweats and a hacking cough. He put himself in care of a physician, Dr. Lawrence Wilson, and hired a nurse; yet he drank, not beer now, but gin, as much, finally, as a pint a day. Once a week Frances Kroll gathered the empty bottles, placed them in a burlap bag in the back of her car when she drove home, and under cover of darkness tossed them into Coldwater Canyon. Scott did not want the bottles showing up in the rubbish at Belly Acres.

One morning, after a feverish, impossible night, he woke to find himself unable to move his arms. He was entangled in his pajamas, but in his drugged, half-sleeping state he knew only that his arms refused to obey his command. "I can't move my arms!" he gasped. The nurse took in the situation. "Oh, Mr. Fitzgerald!" she exclaimed in a tragic voice. "Has it come to this?"

Scott stared at her, frightened. "What do you mean?"

"Has all that alcohol caught up with you? It's paralyzed you!"

Scott was almost overcome. She must call Dr. Wilson instantly. "Good work," the physician told her. "Just fine. Say I'll be there at once."

While they waited, the nurse slowly disentangled Scott and he began gingerly trying his arms, discovering to his enormous relief that he could use them. When Dr. Wilson arrived, he examined Scott with great care, then sat down and talked with him.

"Scott," he said, "there is no doubt this was due to the alcohol. You're lucky you got out of it so easily this time. You can continue drinking and it may never happen again. But, then again—it can. One drink might do it. And this time it could paralyze you for life."

Scott said belligerently, "I'd just blow my brains out then."

"Ah, it's not that easy," said Dr. Wilson. "Who's going

to hold the gun?" he rose. "The Good Lord tapped you on the shoulder, Scott. Let it be a warning to you."

Scott seemed to take the experience to heart. Months later he wrote Scottie that he had suffered "a nervous breakdown of such severity that for a time it threatened to paralyze both arms—"

The warning halted him only temporarily. Soon Frances was once more driving home each week with a burlap bag of bottles. I could not stand the situation. Despite my determination to be resigned, despite my promise not to make a scene, I alternately raged and wept. Sometimes for days I would not see him.

At four o'clock one morning Scott telephoned me. He was alone. Frances had not been there all week, he said. He had told her not to come unless he called her. He had been drinking around the clock. Now he had to get out of it. "I'm really going to sober up, Sheilo," he said. "I mean it. I've called the nurse. But I've taken so many pills, I might fall asleep before she gets here. Would you come over and let her in?"

I dressed and in the chill darkness drove the twenty miles to Encino. Scott was in bed. I sat on the edge of his bed and talked with him. He was very gentle. He had given all of us a hard time in recent weeks. "Dearest, I'm sorry I woke you up and made you come over."

I held his hand. "I'm so glad you're going to stop, Scott. It's really no good, your going on like this—you're not helping yourself. You're only making things worse."

He nodded. "I know." He was grateful that I was staying with him until the nurse came. He did not want to be alone. We talked until the birds woke and began singing in the magnolia trees outside his window. It was nearly six o'clock. "I'll go downstairs and make you some breakfast," I said. "She ought to be here very soon now."

I passed his dresser. My photograph stood on it. My eyes dropped to the bottom drawer. It was ajar and I saw a pistol, half covered with a handkerchief. Scott had told me about his gun. He had had one in Baltimore when he lived far out of the city. There were many wealthy homes in the Valley: Scott suspected the presence of prowlers and he liked the assurance of a weapon.

As I passed the dresser, almost in a reflex action—*He's been drinking, he shouldn't have a gun*—I stooped and extracted the pistol from the drawer.

"Give me that gun!" It was Scott. I turned just as he flung himself on me. We both crashed to the floor. "Give me that gun!" he shouted. I was momentarily dazed, but I clutched it tightly. "No, no, you can't have it. You might—"

We struggled wildly. Scott was like a madman. He grabbed at the gun, cursing as he pried my fingers loose. I gasped in pain. My fingers had been caught in the trigger guard and he had pulled them away so violently the flesh tore. Blind rage flooded me. With a tremendous effort I jerked the gun away and hurled it at the opposite wall. "Take it!" I screamed. "Shoot yourself, you son of a bitch! See if I care!" I was hysterical. I pulled back my right hand and slapped him with all my might on the side of his face. It stunned him. I had no idea what I was doing. "I don't care what happens to you! You're not worth saving, you're not worth anything!" I scrambled to my feet. I screamed at him, "I didn't pull myself out of the gutter to waste my life on a drunk like you!" I rushed downstairs and into my car and drove home. I drove recklessly over the Canyon, sobbing to myself. "I'll never see him again. Never. I don't care. I can't take it any more. I just can't!"

But overnight my anger evaporated. How could I remain at odds with Scott? He didn't know what he was doing. He was drunk. And I had gone there to comfort him. How could I have said such terrible things to him? By noon I could not help myself: I telephoned him. The nurse answered. "Mr. Fitzgerald left this morning for New York."

As swiftly as my anger had vanished it returned. *He had abandoned me. Gone to Zelda.* All right, I thought. See if I care. Cecil B. DeMille had invited me to go to Omaha for the première of *Union Pacific,* starring Barbara Stanwyck. I was to share his private car with Miss Stanwyck and others of the cast. I had said no. Now I accepted the invitation.

The trip acted as a great salve to my self-esteem. In Omaha I was feted, interviewed and treated like a celebrity. I thought, I *have* a career of my own, I've neglected it for Scott for too long. Let him go where he wants.

But I could not wait to return to Hollywood. When I arrived there, Scott was still away. It was nearly two weeks before he returned to Encino. Then the maid he hired was evasive. He was busy; he was writing; he could not come to the phone—

"You mean he doesn't want to talk to me?"

She said, reluctantly, yes.

Now I pursued him. After refusing for two days to phone me back, he relented. His voice was cool and impersonal. "I'm returning your call because I remembered how miserable you are when people don't call you back," he said. "I didn't want to put you through that."

"Scott," I said, "I want to see you. Can I come to see you?"

On his balcony overlooking the rose garden with its little white pickets, I apologized to him. "I'm sorry I slapped you," I said. "I didn't mean it. I didn't mean all those awful things I said. You know that, don't you, Scott?"

He was quite sober. He said, "We won't talk about it any more." There was a pause. Neither of us spoke. Then, almost slyly, he remarked, "That gun was loaded."

My face registered such shock that he burst into laughter and the barrier between us was broken. He proceeded to tell me in great detail, and with an impish gleam which led me to wonder how much was true, a long, bizarre story. Furious with me, he had packed, flown to Asheville, and taken Zelda to Cuba—to get away from everything. "I didn't want to take her out because I knew I was drunk, but I did." In Havana, Zelda was in a state of religious fervor, endlessly praying or reading the Bible. She refused to leave their hotel. He wandered out one afternoon and by nightfall unaccountably found himself in a little court-yard watching a cockfight. There had been intense betting all around him. Then the fight began. He was horrified. "One cock was slashing the other to bits and those men were egging them on," he said. "I couldn't bear it." He vaulted the guardrail into the pit and tried to separate the birds. This precipitated a riot. The spectators pounced on him and he escaped with a painful beating. When he finally found his way to the hotel, Zelda was sitting on the bed, in the darkness, praying.

They returned to New York and registered at the Algonquin Hotel, managed by our Malibu landlord, Frank Case. "We raised so much hell there"—Scott's macabre sense of humor was at work. He fought with a waiter, there were complaints by guests, and he woke up one morning in the alcoholic ward at Bellevue. Somehow he managed to get his clothes and sneak out. Zelda had gone back to the sanitarium. Scott signed himself into Doctors Hospital, sobered up and returned to California.

I simply did not know how much to believe.

During this difficult summer and autumn of 1939 there were considerable periods of time when Scott had himself in hand. Then I was utterly content. In addition to making voluminous notes for his novel, he turned out short stories for *Esquire*. At the same time he worked on my education. He sent Frances Kroll into the city to scour secondhand bookshops for the editions he preferred of Chaucer, Cervantes, and Melville. The reading lists expanded. Now in the margins of my books, he translated foreign phrases, identified proper names, explained allusions. Thus, in a volume of Balzac, Lucullus was underlined, and in the margin Scott wrote: "gave great feasts in ancient Rome." In similar fashion: Panurge—"character in Rabelais. We'll read his great work, *Gargantua and Pantagruel* next;" Carlist—"supporter of a monarchic coup in Spain"; De Viris illustribus—"about illustrious men;" Bossuet—"a famous preacher of the 18th century." Beside a paragraph in Matthew Arnold's "Essay on Wordsworth;" "This is Arnold at his best, absolutely without preachment," and again, "Pretty daring for this old boy! !"

One day he appeared, holding something behind his back. "When I was little," he began impressively, "if I was bad my mother called me a bad Brownie. If I was good, I was a good Brownie. If I was *very* good"—with a flourish he produced a gaily wrapped package—"she gave me a lollypop. Here is a lollypop for doing your Darwin so well." We had spent the night before discussing *Origin of Species*. I unwrapped the gift to find a volume of *Bleak House*. "This is the best of Dickens," Scott said. "I know you'll enjoy it." Thereafter, each time I completed a difficult assignment—Plato's *Republic,* for example—I received as a lollypop an easy-to-read book: Sinclair Lewis' *Babbitt,*

Thackeray's *Vanity Fair,* James Joyce's book of short stories, *Dubliners.* For every three of Plutarch's *Lives* I read and could discuss in detail with him, I received a novel by Dickens. By now I owned many books. With scissors, glue pot, and a roll of heavy brown wrapping paper, Scott made book jackets for me. On the spine of each he lettered in India ink, "ENCINO EDITION," and under it, the book title. I was very proud of my Encino Edition. There was none rarer anywhere.

Now, in the autumn of 1939, Scott began putting his notes together for his novel, *The Last Tycoon. Collier's* was interested in printing it before book publication. If they bought the novel, they were prepared to run eight, ten, or even twelve installments—depending on its length. At $2,500 an installment this could mean as much as $30,000 to Scott—money he needed desperately, for since his Wanger assignment he had earned nothing save a few hundred dollars from *Esquire.* Kenneth Littauer, the editor at *Collier's,* wanted to see at least 15,000 words before making a decision.

Nursing his T.B., Scott wrote mainly in bed. Frances bought him a writing board and, sitting up in his bathrobe, he worked furiously, the yellow sheets piling up on the floor on either side. Dr. Wilson, making frequent visits to give him vitamin injections and medication, marveled at Scott's power of concentration. The physician would climb the stairs to his room, pick his way through the paper on the floor, and sit down while Scott continued to write busily, completely impervious to anything around him. After perhaps five minutes he would look up. "Oh, hello," he'd say. "Been waiting long?" "No," Dr. Wilson would reply. "Only a minute or two." Then Scott would put down his pencil and launch into a long discussion, ranging from Hitler's *blitzkrieg* in Poland to the role of medicine in the modern novel.

The pages mounted. Each evening Scott read me what he had written that day. "That's terribly exciting," I'd say. "What happens next?" He would refuse to tell me. He did not believe in talking a story out beforehand. "You lose the freshness," he said.

Unexpectedly, I received word from John Wheeler in New York that he had booked me for a two-week lecture tour on behalf of the North American Newspaper Alliance. In November, I was to visit major cities in which my column appeared, so my readers could meet Sheilah Graham and hear first hand the truth about Hollywood. Scott approved the idea, as he encouraged any project he thought would help me. I welcomed it, too, not only because I would receive two hundred dollars a lecture, but because Louella Parsons was also going on a tour through the country. I would be keeping pace with the dean of Hollywood columnists. I painstakingly prepared a draft of my lecture and showed it to Scott for his opinion. He read it, frowning. "You don't believe this, do you?"

Entitled "Now It Can Be Told," it was a gossipy, behind-the-scenes recital in which I painted a conventional picture of Hollywood, glamor city of the world, related the Cinderella stories of the stars as invented by press agents, and told a few scandalous tales.

"No I don't, Scott—but it's what they expect to hear."

"If you don't believe it, don't say it." He studied my speech again. "This really isn't very good. I can't let you do a lecture like this." He became the schoolmaster. "Now, who is the most important man on the Hollywood scene?"

"The writer?" I ventured.

"No. The writer can be destroyed by the actor and the actor can be destroyed by the director. We start with this thesis—that the director is the most important man in Hollywood. Let's give your audience an honest picture of what goes on. Making films is a serious business and the people who make them are serious people who are prepared to meet their responsibility if moviegoers will only demand it of them."

He sat down and edited my speech. As usual, before he was finished he had written a completely new lecture. We read it together. "Now, isn't this better? Isn't this what you really believe?"

I agreed. "Good," said Scott. He gave it to Frances to type. "Don't memorize it, but study it until you almost know it by heart."

Overnight my lecture became a joint project. I brought home books dealing with the latest film techniques, memorized the names of Oscar winners of the last decade, and even learned the parts of a movie camera, in case I should be asked. One evening I returned to Encino to find a raised wooden platform with a music stand perched on it, set up in the middle of the living room. Scott had borrowed the stand from Frances' brother, Herman, an orchestra conductor, and had constructed the platform from packing cases he found in the cellar. "We're going to rehearse you, Sheilo," he said. "We'll find out if you can project, too. We don't want any ladies in the rear piping up to say that they can't hear you."

At Encino the living room led to the dining room, which led to the kitchen, which opened in turn on to the back porch, creating a straight vista some sixty feet long. Scott placed three chairs on the porch and seated Frances, the maid, and himself. I was to take my place on the platform. "Go ahead," Scott called out. "Let's have your lecture. Be sure we can hear you back here."

I stood on the platform, my script on the music stand,

and began. After the first sentence I broke into a nervous giggle. "Stop that!" Scott's voice was sharp. "You mustn't even think that way. You are an authority on Hollywood. You have something to say and your audience has come to hear it. Don't be apologetic. You're Sheilah Graham. Now, begin again."

I read my lecture with my eyes glued to the page.

"Look up, Sheilo," came his voice. "There are people seated in front of you. You're a pretty girl, and they want to see your face: look up now and then."

I did. I tried a few jokes Scott had salted among the paragraphs. My audience of three laughed politely. When I came to the end, there was loud applause from the back porch.

Scott put up his hand. I nodded to him. "Yes?"

He stood up. "Miss, I'd like to know—is it true that Shirley Temple is really a midget?"

I thought seriously, as Scott had advised me. Never laugh at any question, however foolish. "I have heard those rumors, sir," I replied. "But they are not true. I can assure you from personal knowledge that Shirley is a bright, normal little girl who happens to be extremely intelligent for her age."

Scott said, "Thank you, Miss Graham," and sat down.

I went off on my tour. Scott's parting gift was his briefcase in which to keep my notes. "For good luck," he said, kissing me. I did not tell him that, facing thousands of miles of air travel, I had made a will leaving everything I possessed to him.

CHAPTER TWENTY-FIVE

IT WAS ALMOST as though Scott were at my side. A telegram from him—amusing, or serious, but always encouraging—awaited me at each city. In the course of the next two weeks I spoke in seven cities, beginning in New York and concluding in Kansas City. Despite my rehearsals, I read my first lecture without looking up once. There were no questions from the audience. Going down in the elevator with some of them I overheard one woman ask another, "Don't you miss John Mason Brown?"

In my room I found Scott's cheering wire:

KENNY WASHINGTON RUNNING WELL TODAY
I THINK OF YOU

SCOTT

Kenny Washington was the great Negro quarterback of U.C.L.A. Friday evenings Scott and I used to go to the Coliseum to watch the football games so that Scott could cheer Kenny, who was his favorite player, and work out intricate football strategy on the back of his program.

In Cleveland I did better, managing to take my eyes off my script long enough to flash a smile at the audience, and even to ad-lib a joke. Again, a telegram from Scott:

REMEMBER YOU ARE GIVING YOUR AUDIENCE A CHANCE TO KNOW DIFFICULTIES FACING PICTURE PEOPLE. AT SAME TIME YOU ARE TELLING THEM THAT IF THEY WANT PICTURES TO BE HARDER HITTING IT MIGHT BE ARRANGED. DO THEY WANT TO BE ENTERTAINED OR INSTRUCTED? THE TWO THINGS ARE POSSIBLY COMPATIBLE BUT EXTREMELY DIFFICULT. CAN THEY HELP?

YOUR HOLLYWOOD ADMIRER SCOTT

In Louisville the telegram delivered to me read:

COUNTRY IS BEHIND YOU STOP RELAX AND DO YOUR BEST STOP WE ARE ROOTING FOR YOU SIGNED CONSTANCE, LOUELLA, HEDDA. I STILL MISS YOU TERRIBLY.

SCOTT

In St. Louis I went into my lecture bolstered by Scott's final message:

AM SO VERY VERY VERY ANXIOUS FOR YOUR RETURN LOVE

SCOTT

In Kansas City I reached the top of my form. There had been a flattering interview and picture of me on the front page of the *Kansas City Star*. I felt I had mastered platform technique: I paused at the right places, my jokes were well timed, and my audience seemed taken with me. When I finished, the applause was the most generous I had yet received.

Then a woman rose. "Is Shirley Temple's hair blond?"

I replied that it was light brown but had to be lightened up for the films. I knew this because Shirley and Mrs. Temple and I often met at the same beauty parlor— Westmore's—in Hollywood.

"What is Loretta Young like?" another listener asked.

I kept Scott's advice in mind. Be serious, never flippant, think carefully. "Loretta is the most charming person," I said. "She always presents a happy appearance to the world. I have never known her to lose her temper. An excellent actress, a very pleasant woman." I added, in a burst of confidence, "But, of course, it's always hard for one woman to know another woman. If you really want to know what she's like underneath, you must ask a man."

There was a moment's silence, then a roar of laughter. Suddenly I realized what I had said. "Oh, my God!" I exclaimed, aloud. The audience found that even funnier. I sat down, blushing, and they were still laughing as they filed out.

I telephoned Scott that night just before taking the plane to Hollywood. I bubbled over. Everything had gone beautifully. The farther west I went, the better I had done. And tonight, in Kansas City—"I had them in the aisles, Scott!" "Wonderful!" he said. "I knew you'd be a success, baby!" He sounded light-hearted. I hung up, wondering, has he been drinking?

Scott greeted me warmly at the airport. He seemed tense, but I was so exhilarated with my triumph that I could only talk about myself. After breakfast, he took me to my apartment so I could get some sleep.

A few mornings later I opened *The Hollywood Reporter*. There, on the front page, was an editorial signed by the publisher, W. R. Wilkerson, whom I had offended during my first weeks in Hollywood by writing so disparagingly about his Trocadero Restaurant. I read with mounting disbelief:

The two junkets, headed by prominent motion-picture columnists, now visiting various key spots throughout the country—Louella Parsons and Sheilah Graham—are having a good and very bad effect on this picture business.

Miss Parsons will, unquestionably, do the business good . . . she should be commended and thanked and helped. . . . But the case of Sheilah Graham is another thing altogether.

Then Mr. Wilkerson quoted from a report written by Jack Moffitt, *The Reporter's* Kansas City correspondent, who had not attended my lecture:

Sheilah Graham got $200 for a one-night stand at the Kansas City Woman's Club. The studios could have paid her two thousand to stay in Hollywood, and made money. The lecture was a dirt-dishing session that left none of the movie mighty unsmeared. Even Shirley Temple and her mother were exposed as having their hair dyed in Sheilah's shellacking. The nocturnal pastimes of an adult star were hinted at with Groucho eyebrows and stream-lined innuendo. . . .

Mr. Wilkerson continued:

Miss Graham's speaking tour was arranged by her newspaper syndicate, the North American Newspaper Alliance, which serves a very important group of news-papers throughout the U.S., each of which gets quite a bit of motion picture advertising. . . . Hollywood, its players, producers, writers and directors should tell Miss Graham they won't countenance her further "dishing" to the ticket buyers on this "lecture tour" and the industry should remind her papers such "dishing" is NOT CRICKET.

The Parsons tour is a cinch to be a great success. . . . Lolly herself does not "dish" from the hip, but spreads news and gossip from her rostrum that help the picture business.

I was beside myself. I telephoned Scott and in a choking voice read it to him. "That's the most shocking thing—" he began. "Sheilah, don't do anything. I'm getting a copy. They are going to give you an apology and a retraction."

I could only wail, "Oh, those awful people!"

"Wait," Scott said, ominously. "Wait."

I learned later what had happened. Scott drove immediately into Hollywood, to Schwab's drugstore where *The Hollywood Reporter* was on sale. He stood at the cigar counter reading it. Sidney Skolsky, the columnist, strolled by. Scott turned to him, brandishing the rolled-up newspaper in his fist. "Did you see this? Have you read this?" He was white with fury, his voice trembling. Then he turned and strode from the store.

A few minutes later Scott was on the telephone to John O'Hara. Had he read the attack on Sheilah in the *Reporter*? "It's so damn unfair!" Scott exclaimed. "Sheilah did a beautiful job and this man Wilkerson— John, I'm challenging him to a duel. I want you to be my second."

O'Hara tried to placate him. Scott couldn't do that. People didn't fight duels any more. It would be silly.

"Oh, no, oh, no," said Scott. "I'm challenging him to a duel. He can choose any weapon he wants. Will you come along with me?"

O'Hara said no.

"All right," said Scott. "I'll call up Eddie Mayer. He's a gentleman—he won't let me down."

O'Hara telephoned Eddie to warn him that Scott might be calling on him. But instead, Scott drove direct to *The Hollywood Reporter* offices on Sunset Boulevard, stormed into the reception room and roared that he wanted to see Mr. W. R. Wilkerson. A wary secretary said that Mr.

Wilkerson was not in. Scott paced up and down for nearly an hour before he gave up and drove back to Encino.

I caught up with him there, after Eddie telephoned me. Scott was raging. I managed to calm him down. I had telephoned Roy Roberts, editor of the *Kansas City Star*, who had attended my lecture. He promised to wire an immediate protest to Wilkerson. The prestige and respectability of the *Star* were unassailable. This was the best—the only—way to handle it.

Only now, seeing Scott, did I realize the extent of his agitation. My distress had only served to intensify his own difficulties. He had been drinking—I should have recognized it at the airport—and he was under great stress. A few days before he had completed the first chapter of *The Last Tycoon*. He had been so anxious to get it off to *Collier's* that Frances had driven to the airport and mailed it from there. But the manuscript ran only 6,000 words instead of 15,000. Littauer had wired him he must defer his decision until he had seen more. Scott, bitterly disappointed had immediately had a copy mailed to *The Saturday Evening Post*. *The Post,* too, had refused to commit itself.

This twofold rejection by magazines which in the past had been proud to print almost anything he wrote, overwhelmed Scott. He fell into despair such as I had not seen before. "They don't want anything by F. Scott Fitzgerald," he said, bitterly. "I'm not in fashion any more. No matter what I write, they don't want it."

He drank steadily. There was no stopping him. Frances and I were alarmed. We slipped his gun out of the kitchen-table drawer where he now kept it, wrapped it in newspaper, and hid it far back on a high shelf in the pantry.

Several nights later I came to Encino to find Scott

entertaining two strangers. They could have walked out
of a hobo scene on a movie set: they were filthy, unshaven,
and drunk. Scott, in his bathrobe, was pressing on them
his pink shirts, his ties, and handkerchiefs. One man already had two of Scott's Brooks Brothers' suits draped
over his arm.

"Meet my friends," Scott said expansively. He had come
upon them thumbing their way on Ventura Boulevard.
He had invited them to stay for dinner. Poor fellows, they
hadn't even a shirt to their name—

I said, "Don't you boys think you ought to go? And
leave Mr. Fitzgerald's clothes here, please."

Scott focused on me. "Why should they go, Sheilo? I
told you they're my friends." The two men smirked at me.

I paid no attention to Scott. "Will you please put down
those clothes and go? Immediately? Get out of here!"

Scott interrupted me. "Don't talk like that to my
friends." There was a warning note in his voice that he
had never used before to me. "*You* go. These are my
friends. Old friends."

I said to them again, as though Scott were not there:
"I warn you. If you don't leave at once I will call the
police."

They saw I meant it. They made an elaborate ceremony
of depositing the suits and haberdashery on a chair. "The
lady says go, I guess we better go," one remarked. He
waved at Scott. "So long, old fellow. Be seeing you." They
left.

Scott stared after them. He seemed lost.

I knew that Miss Steffan, his nurse, was somewhere
around. "Scott, I'm getting you some food," I said. I heated
a can of tomato soup in the kitchen, poured it into two
bowls and brought them into the dining room. I set a

table for two. "Come on, Scott—hot soup will do you good."

He refused. He sat slumped in an easy chair, mumbling, "Being rude to my friends—never so insulted in my life—"

I began sipping my soup, thinking, if he wants it he'll come to the table.

Suddenly, with the surprising agility he showed when one least expected it, he leaped from his chair, pounced on his bowl of soup, and hurled it across the dining room. It smashed against a wall, splashing over everything. "Oh, Scott!" I groaned. I got a dishtowel and started mopping up. I was going to the kitchen with the broken china when Scott stood in my way. "Scott, stop being silly—" I began.

He pulled his right hand back and slapped me with all his strength. The blow struck the left side of my face with stunning impact. My ears rang, and tears started in my eyes. I stood there, stunned and deafened, the broken pieces of china in my hands, staring at him. Could this be happening? Was this the gentle lover, the tender confidant, the infinitely understanding Scott . . . ? Then I saw him winding up to strike me again. I backed away.

Unexpectedly Miss Steffen appeared. She took in the scene. "Mr. Fitzgerald, please—" She advanced on him.

He wheeled on her. "Oh, you think she needs protection, eh? You think she's somebody worth protecting? If you knew what she really is!" He took a step toward me, then back toward her. "She's a fake! She's right out of the slums of London, she was raised in an orphanage, her name's not Sheilah Graham, it's Lily Sheil. Lily Sheil!" He began hopping around like a frenzied Rumpelstiltskin, chanting, *"Lily Sheil, Lily Sheil, Lily Sheil. . ."*

The nurse, aghast, said, "Mr. Fitzgerald—"

He kicked her hard, on the shins, and she fled in tears.

I was almost in a state of shock. Was he dangerous? I could not think of him as dangerous. This was Scott, the bad Brownie—putting on a melodramatic act. There was nothing for me to do but leave. He would wake up in the morning contrite. . .

I backed away. With as much dignity as I could command, I turned and walked into the kitchen on the way to my car parked in the back. Scott suddenly sprinted around me and stood against the door blocking my way. "Oh, no you don't. You're not leaving this house."

"Why not?" I demanded icily. "I want to go."

"You're staying right here—Lily Sheil. You'll go when I say you can go."

I stared at him. How could he hurt me so? I burst out, "I hate you! I don't love you any more! I don't respect you!"

He pulled out a cigarette and managed fumblingly to light it. "You're not going," he said. "I'm going to kill you."

I did not panic. Suddenly I knew that to panic now might lead to real tragedy.

"All right, Scott," I said, conversationally. I hoisted myself on the low cupboard and sat there swinging my legs as though this were a schoolgirl conversation. "If you don't want me to go, let's talk. What would you like to talk about!"

He repeated, "I'm going to kill you." He pulled open the table drawer. "Where's my gun?" He cast a suspicious glance at me. "Where's my gun?" He began ripping out pantry drawers. I thought, I might make it through the door but he'd catch me long before I reached the car. I sat, silent. Finally he said, almost to himself. "Frances. She'll know." There was a telephone on the cupboard a few inches from me. He dialed his secretary's number.

"Frances"—his voice was gentle—"I've been hearing suspicious noises around here. Have you any idea where my gun is?"

I held my breath. Then, with vast relief, I heard Frances' reply: "No, I haven't, Mr. Fitzgerald." He had not fooled her.

"Did you see me put it anywhere? Maybe I hid it."

"No, Mr. Fitzgerald, I'm sorry, but I didn't."

"All right," he said, and hung up. He began searching for the gun again, rummaging amid the pots and pans. I said, "Scott, are you going to let me go? I want to go, Scott."

"No, you're not going. You're not getting out of here alive."

"If you don't let me go, Scott," I went on, quite reasonably, "I will call the police and there will be a frightful scandal. You wouldn't like that for Scottie, would you? You wouldn't like that at all."

He only mumbled to himself, "Where is that Goddamn gun!"

He began searching through drawers at the end of the kitchen. I seized the telephone and got the operator. I said aloud, "Get me the police. If I am cut off, this is my number." Scott whirled around, but made no move to stop me. I was amazed at my own calm. To the sergeant who replied, I said clearly, "I am being kept against my will at this address." I told him the address. Scott was staring at me with a baffled expression, but still made no move. The sergeant's voice was loud in the receiver. "We'll be right over."

I said to Scott, "Now, Scott, you heard me call the police. I think you heard what they said. It will be very bad if they find me here. I think you'd better let me go now."

I slid down off the cupboard and walked to the door.
Scott did not stop me. I walked out the door and got into
my car. I had trouble starting it, for now hysteria was
coming on. I cried all the way home. I was still crying
when I entered my apartment to hear my phone ringing.
It was Scott.

"What do *you* want?" I sobbed.

He said, "I just wanted to be sure you got home safely."

"Huh!" I cried. "That's a joke!" And I hung up in
tears.

But there was to be no sleep for me that night. My
telephone rang steadily. I answered once: it was Scott. I
hung up. Every few minutes he tried. *Let him ring. I am
finished with him. I'll never see him again.*

At seven A.M. I was awakened from a tortured dream
by a special-delivery letter. It was addressed, to my consternation, to Lily Sheil Graham. Scrawled on it were the
words: "Get out of town, Lily Sheil, or you will be dead
in 24 hours." And for the remainder of that day, every
few hours, a new special delivery arrived: "Leave town
or your body will be found in Coldwater Canyon. . . Get
out of Hollywood or you know what to expect. . ." My
telephone rang repeatedly. My secretary answered. Each
time it was Scott. "Is Lily there?" he would demand. She
hung up. Once I took the call. "Oh, Lily?" It was Scott
at his most dramatic. "You haven't left town yet? You'll
be dead in 24 hours!" He slammed down the receiver.

A few hours later John Wheeler was on the tele-
phone from New York. "What kind of a jam are you in?"
he demanded. He had just received a telegram from
F. Scott Fitzgerald which read: SHEILAH GRAHAM
TODAY BANNED BY EVERY STUDIO STOP SHE
IS RUINING NANA IN HOLLYWOOD STOP SUG-

GEST YOU SEND HER BACK TO ENGLAND
WHERE SHE BELONGS STOP DO YOU KNOW HER
REAL NAME IS LILY SHEIL? With some difficulty I
explained this away as one of Scott's practical jokes.

For the next two days Scott bombarded me with letters
and calls. In desperation I consulted a lawyer. "I can't
work, I can't sleep, this man is driving me out of my
mind." What could I do?

I could go to court or, if I wished to avoid publicity,
for $500 two policemen could be persuaded to call upon
Scott and threaten his arrest unless he stopped annoying
me. I agreed—anything to end this ordeal. How would
they go about it? "They'll pound on his door about five
A.M. one morning." The lawyer explained. "We've found
that a police visit just before dawn is pretty effective."

"Oh, no, you can't do that," I heard myself saying. "He
sleeps so badly. He'd just be falling asleep about that
time."

The lawyer looked at me, and shook his head. We gave
up the idea.

A letter came from Scott:

Dear Sheilah:

I went berserk in your presence and hurt you and Jean
Steffan. That's done.

But I said things too—awful things and they can to
some extent be unsaid. They come from the merest fraction of my mind, as you must know—they represent nothing in my consciousness and very little in my subconscious.
About as important and significant as the quarrels we
used to have about England and America.

I don't think we're getting anywhere. I'm glad you no
longer can think of me with either respect or affection.
People are either good for each other or not, and obvi-

ously I am *horrible* for you. I loved you with everything
I had, but something was terribly wrong. You don't have
to look far for the reason—I was it. Not fit for any human
relation. I just *loved* you—you brought me everything.
And it was very fine and chivalrous—and you.

I want to die, Sheilah, and in my own way. I used to
have my daughter and my poor lost Zelda. Now for over
two years your image is everywhere. Let me remember
you up to the end which is very close. You are the finest.
You are something all by yourself. You are too much
something for a tubercular neurotic who can only be
jealous and mean and perverse. I will have my last time
with you, though you won't be here. It's not long now.
I wish I could have left you more of myself. You can have
the first chapter of the novel and the plan. I have no
money but it might be worth something. Ask [Leland]
Hayward. I loved you utterly and completely. I meant to
send this longhand but I don't think it would be intel-
ligible.

Scott

I was touched very deeply. I saw Scott, in a moment of
frightening sobriety, writing this letter, then having it
typed so I would know exactly what it was he wanted
to say. Yet I could not bring myself to call him. I
steeled myself. He was not going to die—not Scott. And I
simply could not face going through such agony again.

For the first time I accepted dates from other men. I
dined with Louis Meltzer, a screenwriter I'd known before
Scott. I went to the theater with Garson Kanin, the director. I attended parties with Victor Mature, John Mc-
Clain, John O'Hara. "I've returned to circulation," I told
them. When they pressed me I said only that Mr. Fitzgerald was a closed chapter in my life.

Then, one day, my secretary told me Scott had appeared at my apartment, insisting he wanted to see me.

He had wandered aimlessly from room to room, and disappeared. A few days after his visit Marc Connolly invited me to dinner. I had not been out with Marc since the Writers Guild dance at which Scott and I had first spoken to each other. Marc, gay, witty, and extremely charming, called for me, and I thought as I went to my closet for my silver-fox jacket, there *are* other men in the world.

The jacket was not there. I looked everywhere. It was gone. A great light struck me. *Scott!* I remember rushing into the sitting room and sputtering to an astonished Mr. Connolly, "That man—" I was so furious I could not utter Scott's name. "That man stole my fur jacket!"

My insurance agent called on Scott the next day. Scott admitted he had taken it. He had only lent the jacket to me, he said. "You have five days to return it," the agent told him. "Then we—not Miss Graham—will start criminal action." Scott capitulated. It might take more than five days, he said, heavily. He had mailed the jacket to his daughter at Vassar as a Christmas present. Now he would have to write that he'd sent her the wrong jacket. She must return it and he would replace it with another.

I was not sorry for Scott's predicament nor, at this moment, for Scottie's disappointment. *Let Scott suffer.* The more I thought about it the angrier I became. *I'll fix him.* I took the first editions he had given me of his books —each with an inscription in it—and deliberately tore them from cover to cover. I ripped out the title pages. I threw everything into the rubbish. *I don't want to see his name again, I don't want to hear his name again, I don't want to be reminded of him.* I hated this man. He had betrayed me. He had revealed my most secret confidences—my name, the orphanage—my background. He had struck me; he had threatened to kill me; he had tried to make me lose my job; and most infuriating of all, he had stolen my precious silver-fox jacket, the first real fur I had ever had, so dear to me that I dared not even lean back in it!

I told my secretary that if there were any calls from him, I had left town. I could not be reached.

A week later, a letter, quite formal, from Frances Kroll:

Dear Miss Graham:

Mr. Fitzgerald is himself again after six days in bed and everything he did seems perfectly abominable to him. He wants to know if there is any material way in which he can partially atone for the damage. He will, of course, replace anything, and more particularly he wants to know if it will be any help if he leaves Hollywood for good.

He has no idea where you are nor has he any intention of trying to see you. He merely wants to remove as much of the unhappiness as is possible from what he did to you.

Sincerely,
Frances Kroll.

I told Frances I wanted nothing from him. I wanted only to be left alone.

The note was in pencil. It arrived several days after the letter from Frances Kroll. Written on one of his yellow sheets, it was wrapped around a little notebook in which I had entered addresses and telephone numbers. The note read:

When I came to myself last Tuesday I found this, which seems to be yours. It is very quiet out here now. I went into your room this afternoon and lay on your bed awhile to see if you had left anything of yourself. There were some pencils and the electric pad that didn't work and the autumn out the window that won't ever be the same. Then I wrote down a lot of expressions of your face, but one I can't bear to read, of the little girl who trusted me so and whom I loved more than anything in the world—and to whom I gave grief when I wanted to give joy. Something should have told you I was extemporizing wildly. . . . It was all fever and liquor and sedatives— what nurses hear in any bad drunk case. I'm glad you're rid of me. I hope you're happy and the last awful impression is fading a little till someday you'll say, 'he can't have been that black.' Goodbye, Sheilo, I won't bother you any more.

Scott

CHAPTER TWENTY-SIX

A HUGE BOUQUET of American Beauty roses was delivered to my apartment. The card read simply, "Scott." The flowers were magnificent. It would be a pity to throw them away. I arranged them in a vase.

The next day Frances Kroll called on me with a small suitcase of my belongings—the last of my things from Encino. Scott was working hard, she remarked. He was well through Chapter II of the novel. And he had stopped drinking. When I looked at her she said, "I mean it. It's true." "Good for him," I said indifferently. We chatted a little longer and then she left.

At Encino Scott waited impatiently for her. "Well?" he asked. Frances smiled. "They're there, Mr. Fitzgerald," she reported. "I saw them in a lovely vase on her desk."

Scott's face lit up. "I've got her!" he said triumphantly. He had, too, although I did not know it.

I had not seen or talked to him for five weeks. He had apologized to John Wheeler in a telegram which my employer forwarded to me:

I SENT YOU THAT WIRE WITH A TEMPERA-
TURE OF 102 DEGREES AND A GOOD DEAL OF

LIQUOR ON BOARD. THERE IS NO REASON TO
WORRY ABOUT SHEILAH IN CONNECTION
WITH THE STUDIOS. WE HAD SOME PERSONAL
TROUBLE IN WHICH I BEHAVED VERY VERY
BADLY. PLEASE CONSIDER THE TELEGRAM AS
THE MUMBLINGS OF A MAN WHO WAS FAR
FROM BEING HIMSELF.

SCOTT FITZGERALD

I read it with a curious apathy. It all seemed remote to
me now. It was pleasant, those first days of 1940, to be
free to enjoy all that Hollywood had to offer—to go out
again with young men, to be once more a part of the movie
colony. My column now appeared in sixty-five newspapers
in the United States and Canada, and on occasion even
in the London *Evening Standard*. Johnny, who through
the years remained a faithful correspondent, sent me clippings when Sheilah Graham's HOLLYWOOD TODAY
appeared there. Early in January, 1940, *Look* magazine
asked to do a picture story on me as the prettiest columnist
in Hollywood. The project fell through when I demurred
at posing in a bathing suit. "That's not my type of thing,"
I protested. "I'll pose for you playing tennis—" When
nothing developed, I did not feel too badly. I had come
far since my Cochran days.

I had a new assurance. It was pleasing to know the
admiration of the men I went out with—even to dismay
them, sometimes, with my ability to reel off entire stanzas
of Andrew Marvell or Robert Herrick, or point out that
Keats had borrowed from Boccaccio, or discuss Matthew
Arnold's influence on English prose. To have as literate
and talented a writer as Irwin Shaw say, "It's amazing how
well read you are," was enormously flattering. And it was
fun to flirt again, to dine each evening at another restau-

rant, table-hopping and gratifyingly conspicuous, to dance each evening at different nightclub. . . .

One Saturday night I joined a group of friends for an evening of fun. We had dinner at Lucey's, went on for dancing and entertainment at Ciro's, the Mocambo, the Coconut Grove. At the end of the evening I was dropped at my apartment. I entered and switched on the light and sank down exhausted on the sofa just as the telephone rang. It was Scott. "I'd very much like to see you, Sheilo," he said. "May I see you tomorrow?"

For a moment I did not reply. Suddenly, sitting there on the sofa he and I had bought together at Barker's Bargain Basement, wearing a frothy rose and blue hat he had always admired, I thought, I cannot bear it. Not the dancing nor the dining nor the flirting nor the empty, empty conversation. I want Scott. I don't want these other men. They are sweet and charming and personable and tremendously successful, but they are not Scott. I don't care, I have no pride, I want Scott. His voice came again, softly: "Are you there, Sheilo?"

I said, "Yes, Scott. I'm here." And I added, "Of course you can see me."

"All right," he said. "I'll pick you up early in the morning—nine o'clock. I want to drive somewhere so we can talk."

At nine the next morning, an astonishingly early hour for him, he called for me. We were both reserved, even formal. I sat silently beside him as his little car slowly climbed the winding, curving road to the top of Laurel Canyon, high above the city. At this early hour on a January Sunday morning, it was utterly silent. There was a lonely, dreary quality to the hills about us and the cold blue sky overhead.

We left the car and I walked with him to the rim of a small knoll. We sat down on the grass, on the edge of the Canyon. Far in the distance glinted the thin silver line of the Pacific; a little nearer the Malibu mountains, blue and smoky in the morning haze, and here and there on the hills between, patches of purple bougainvillaea. Far below to the left the roofs and spires of Los Angeles lay spread out before us like a painting.

Scott began to talk, slowly. He spoke about himself, about Zelda, about his drinking—he knew he could not drink. He knew that when he was drunk he was unfit for human association. He had begun drinking, as a young man, because in those days everyone drank. "Zelda and I drank with them. I was able to drink and enjoy it. I thought all I needed anywhere in the world to make a living was pencil and paper. Then I found I needed liquor too. I needed it to write." The day came when he realized he was drinking to escape—not only to escape the growing sense of his wasted potentialities but also to dull the guilt he felt over Zelda. "I feel that I am responsible for what happened to her. I could no longer bear what became of her. I could not bear what had become of me. But liquor did not help me forget. In these past years the escape has been more awful than the reality." He was finished with this form of escape. He felt stronger, now, than he had felt in a long time, though he still had his T.B. and insomnia to contend with. He looked forward hopefully to the future. He had hired another agent who might find screenwriting jobs for him. He had gotten well into his novel. He knew he could write a good book. He wanted me back, very, very much. "I am going to stop drinking, Sheilah. I have made a promise to myself. Whether you come back to me or not, I will stop drinking. But I want you back—very much."

He became silent. We were utterly alone in a remote, isolated world of our own. Scott had uttered his last words with such solemnity. I thought, he has never unburdened himself like this before; he has never opened himself like this to me before; he has never before promised he would stop drinking. This might have been an enormous church and I, here, with Scott in a confessional. . . . For a moment I almost shivered. I knew I would take him back but I had to be sure.

"Scott—" I began. I searched for the words. "How do I know I can believe you? *Can* you stop drinking, Scott? Do you really mean it?"

"I mean it," he said. There was a long pause. We looked at each other. "Don't just take my words, Sheilah. Test me."

I went back to him, and everything fell into place once more.

Scott did not drink. Early in 1940, for the first time in months, he worked on a script again, adapting his short story, "Babylon Revisited," which Producer Lester Cowan bought from him for a thousand dollars. Cowan paid him an additional five thousand dollars to turn it into a screen play. One thousand dollars was a ridiculously low price for an F. Scott Fitzgerald movie property; five thousand dollars for the sixteen weeks he was to spend on the script was also far below Scott's rate of payment. But he was grateful for the opportunity. Once more he was gainfully employed, he enjoyed working on his own story, and his morale was high.

We lived very quietly in Encino, now. At noon each day, when I had finished my column, Scott would come down to the pool and give me swimming lessons. While

I floundered in the water, Scott, in a sweater and hat, coached me from the side, careful to keep out of the sun no matter how exasperated he grew. After lunch, we each went to our own rooms. Scott to work on the script, I to read steadily whatever book he had assigned me. I was deep in Renan's *The Life of Jesus;* at the same time Scott had me read the Gospels of St. Mark and St. Luke; then I began Calverton's *The Making of Society.* After dinner we took long walks and Scott discussed with me in detail what I had read. Or, in the evening, we sat like an old married couple on his balcony, sometimes not exchanging a word for a long time. Somewhere in the vicinity but out of sight was an RKO Western lot and in the hush of the Encino night, broken only by the singing of crickets, we would suddenly hear a distant voice: "Ev'ry-body-quiet! Camera—shoot!" And then the thunder of horses' hoofs and the crack of guns in the night air. It was strange, weirdly theatrical—and we were content.

Once we drove down to Tijuana for a day and, on impulse, had a picture snapped of us by a sidewalk photographer. I sat beaming on a sleepy burro and Scott, in a sombrero and with a colorful serape tossed over one shoulder, stood beside me, every inch the cabellero. It was the only photograph we had ever had taken together.

Because Encino, warm as it was in winter, became insufferable during the summer, in April Scott gave up his house. I found him an apartment in Hollywood on the street next to mine. To economize, we shared the same maid, each paying half of her salary. We dined at each other's apartment on alternate nights: one night she cooked his dinner and I was his guest, the next, she cooked mine and he was my guest. Again, like a married couple, we went shopping at night in the supermarkets on Sunset

Boulevard, or spent an hour in Schwab's drugstore, five minutes away, browsing among the magazines and ending our visit sipping chocolate malted milks at the ice-cream counter. On the way home we chanted poetry to each other, swinging hands as we walked in the darkness, Scott declaiming passionately from Keats:

> What leaf-fringed legend haunts about thy shape
> Of deities or mortals, or of both,
> In Tempe or the dales of Arcady?"

And I would reply with equal fervor:

> What men or gods are these? What maidens loth?
> What mad pursuit? What struggle to escape?
> What pipes and timbrels? What wild ecstasy?

Sometimes a passerby stared at us and I would burst out laughing, but Scott would maintain a stern demeanor.

Could either of us have known, this summer of 1940, that Scott was in the last year of his life? There were no signs. In fact, everything underlined his own hopeful words—he had become a new man. He was not drinking; and now that he was not, I marveled at how much work he accomplished. He worked on his script, on his novel, on short stories for *Esquire;* at the same time he wrote endless letters to his daughter, his editors, his friends, dramatically describing his nightsweats and temperature.

He found time to follow every detail of the war in Europe on a map in his study, working out his own ideas of military strategy on paper, as he used to plot football plays on the backs of our U.C.L.A. programs. On May 31, we were on a train bound for a two-week vacation at San Francisco and the World's Fair when news came of the British evacuation from Dunkirk. Scott almost did a jig in the aisle as Anthony Eden's voice came over the club-car radio announcing the rescue of three-fourths of the British Army. Until then, despite my outraged arguments, Scott had predicted Britain's defeat. "Scott, you don't know the British!" I'd say hotly, and he would reply, "Oh, Sheilah, they can't possibly win." Now, he said jubilantly, "You're going to win! You've saved your soldiers to fight another day!"

The fall of France was reported on our return to Los Angeles. It threw Scott into mourning but overnight his natural buoyance reasserted itself and he came hurrying into my flat with a long poem he had just written. "Here," he said, "you're always complaining history confuses you. Memorize this and it will fix French history—at least the highlights—in your mind for good." There was a mischievous gleam in his eye as he gave it to me.

Among the verses were these:

LEST WE FORGET

(France by Big Shots)

Frankish Period   500—1000

Clovis—baptized "en regnant"—
Was ancestor to "rois faineantes"

Hammer! Hammer! Charles Martel!
At Tours he sent the Moors to Hell
Mayor-of-the-Palace, Boss of the Gang
He cleared the way for Charlemagne

Charlemagne stands all alone
One pine in a burned-over zone.
He passed—and Europe should cry "Merde!" on
The fatal treaty signed at Verdun. . .

The House of Valois   1350—1600

For Charles the Wise and Charles the Mad
And Jehan's Charles the times were bad;
But Jehan and the Bastard met
And glued that dome on Charles-le-sept.

Life was no heaven seventh
For foes of Louis Eleventh
With marriage, guile and hate
Created he *The State*

The Renaissance—France sings and dances
Fights and fails with handsome Francis

Catherine de Medici
In fifteen hundred seventy-three
With her sons (two lousy snots)
Massacred the Hugenots. . .

The Revolution

Mirabeau the swell began it
Then Citoyan Marat ran it
      Hey! Hey!
      Charlotte Corday

They didn't let Danton rant on.

Robespierre was a sea-green incorruptible
They broke his jaw to prove he was interruptible. . .

The Nineteenth Century

The Consulate and Empire blaze:
  And freeze at last at Borodino
Then Elba and The Hundred Days
  And Waterloo—and St. Helena

The Monarchs of The Restoration
Were not favorites of the nation

But even more did Fat Cats hate
The Barricades of Forty-eight

Republic Two was soon to falter . .
The Décor, now by Winterhalter,
Starred Napoleon the Little
Bluff—a bushel, brains—a tittle

The Prussians take Sedan and Metz
The commune dies on bayonets
The Third Republic comes to *stay*
—or rather ended yesterday.

VIVE LA FRANCE!

This was our happiest time. My books were piling up
by the score now; Scott appeared with a tape measure
and carefully measured my walls for bookcases. When
they came, covering one entire wall, we spent several days
cataloguing the volumes which once more included his
own first editions. (He had replaced them, a little ruefully,
inscribing each to me as he had inscribed them before.)
Scott sat cross-legged on the floor arranging and checking
the books so that fiction and non-fiction, American authors
(headed by Dreiser, whom he considered his greatest con-
temporary) and foreign authors, all had their place. Now
and then, in the middle of the day, he would grow tired
and have to rest from whatever he was doing, but nothing
stopped the eagerness of his mind. Even Cowan's decision
at this time not to use his screenplay of *Babylon Revisited*
was not the crushing blow it would have been six months
before. Instead, he asked his agent to see what other jobs
were available and devoted more time to his novel. He was
full of projects for me. I must start making notes for my
autobiography, he told me. "Your story is fascinating,
Sheilah," he said. "Some day you must do it. It should be
a book."

"Oh, Scott," I'd say. "You should do it—I wish you'd write my story."

"No," he would say. "That will be your project. But I'll help you. I'll show you how to start." He brought home a huge leather-bound ledger, the kind used by accountants, that must have cost him twenty dollars. "You must begin by making notes. You may have to make notes for years." He drew up a rough outline, dividing my life into seven parts: the orphanage, my strolling at night on Piccadilly; my dilemma in choosing between Johnny and Monte; my stage career; my society career; journalism in New York; and Hollywood. "When you think of something, when you recall something, put it where it belongs," he said. "Put it down when you think of it. You may never recapture it quite as vividly the second time."

I had put an iron door between my past and myself. I had opened it only once—when I revealed the truth about myself to Scott. Now, with his encouragement, I began to revisit my childhood. I began to remember smells—the musty horsehair odor of my mother's flat, the fragrance of Ginger's hair pomade, Monte Collins' talc. I began to remember how I felt the first time I sat opposite Johnny at his desk, licking envelopes; I recalled the golden haze at the Pavilion. "That's good," said Scott. "Put it down." And he kept after me. "Make notes, always make notes." I had noticed, proudly, that some of my observations were in his notebooks. Once, sitting on the balcony at Encino, in the dark, I had said, "The Ping-pong balls on the grass look like stars." He put it down. One night when the rain drummed on the roof, I said, "It sounds like horses weeing." Scott like that, and into his notebook it had gone.

Though I jotted down notes whenever I thought of them, I did not neglect my education. I had moved into Scott's music course. Scott made a present to me of a record player and then, admitting that his knowledge of music was limited, called in Frances Kroll's brother to help plan the curriculum. Now Scott brought me albums of records instead of books. I was to play each record repeatedly until I was thoroughly familiar with the music. I began to realize that what I had always thought of as great, blaring batches of sound had a tune, a melody, a pattern, hidden in them. We both listened, we read the biographies of the composers, and we studied music criticism recommended by Herman Kroll. My apartment was filled with music.

Then we took up art. We spent each Saturday afternoon at a gallery or museum. Under Scott's watchful eye I learned how to look at pictures, to see what Goya and Brueghel and Paul Klee, were all about. The Huntington Library in Pasadena had outstanding canvases by England's great painters: portraits by Gainsborough, Reynolds, and Romney, breath-taking landscapes by Constable and Turner. We would pause before each picture and ask ourselves what the artist intended, then check our interpretations with those in the best books of art criticism we could find.

One August day as we strolled through the Huntington Library I said to Scott, half-teasingly, "How well has the best and worst student in the Fitzgerald College of One done so far?"

"Very well, Sheilo," he said. "I'm quite proud of you—you've worked hard."

"Do you think I'll be ready to graduate soon?"

"Well, let's see," he said, seriously. "You've been studying about a year and a half. Now, if you were going to Vassar, like Scottie, it would take you four years. But ours is a very concentrated curriculum—" At this rate, he said, I should be ready to graduate next June. I should consider myself a member of the Class of 1941.

"And you'll really give me a diploma?"

He laughed. "In your cap and gown. I promise." I would have to pass a complete written final examination. He would arrange it all. We would conduct appropriate graduation exercises and he would present a hand-lettered diploma, the only one of its kind, to me.

So we planned it.

CHAPTER TWENTY-SEVEN

THAT SCOTT was not drinking—that Dr. Wilson, dropping in on him unexpectedly, could always assure me that Scott had taken no alcohol—was the overwhelming fact of that idyllic summer and autumn of 1940. Almost as overwhelming to me was my discovery that I was in Scott's novel.

He had never told me that he was writing about me—that Stahr, the central character of the book, would fall in love with an English girl who was based on me. Her name was Kathleen. She spoke like me. She used my phrases. Telling Scott how I had sold tooth brushes at Gamage's, I had said, "I have nice teeth for an English girl." Now Kathleen, in *The Last Tycoon,* made that observation to Stahr. When Scott read to me, night after night, what he had written during the day, I began to realize that the love affair between Kathleen and Stahr—the very heart of the novel—was *our* love affair.

I had the weirdest sense of unreality as Scott read to me. Was this not our encounter at the Writers Guild dance, as magically recreated by Scott.

> . . . he saw Kathleen sitting in the middle of a long white table alone.

Immediately things changed. As he walked toward her, the people shrank back against the walls till they were only murals; the white tables lengthened and became an altar where the priestess sat alone. Vitality welled up in him, and he could have stood a long time across the table from her, looking and smiling.

The incumbents of the table were crawling back—Stahr and Kathleen danced.

When she came close, his several visions of her blurred; she was momentarily unreal. Usually a girl's skull made her real, but not this time—Stahr continued to be dazzled as they danced out along the floor—to the last edge, where they stepped through a mirror into another dance with new dancers whose faces were familiar but nothing more. In this new region he talked, fast and urgently.

"What's your name?"

"Kathleen Moore."

"Kathleen Moore," he repeated.

"I have no telephone, if that's what you're thinking."

"When will you come to the studio?"

"It's not possible. Truly."

"Why isn't it? Are you married?"

"No."

"You're not married?"

"No, nor never have been. But then I may be."

"Someone there at the table."

"No." She laughed. "What curiosity."

But she was deep in it with him, no matter what the words were. Her eyes invited him to a romantic communion of unbelievable intensity. As if she realized this, she said, frightened:

"I must go back now. I promised this dance."

"I don't want to lose you. Couldn't we have lunch or dinner?"

"It's impossible." But her expression helplessly amended the words to, "It's just possible. The door is still open by a chink, if you could squeeze past. But quickly—so little time."

"I must go back," she repeated aloud. Then she dropped her arms, stopped dancing, and looked at him, a laughing wanton.

"When I'm with you, I don't breathe quite right," she said.

She turned, picked up her long dress, and stepped back through the mirror. Stahr followed until she stopped near her table.

"Thank you for the dance," she said, "and now really, good night."

Then she nearly ran.

How he had taken our meeting at the Coconut Grove, and our dance a few nights later at the Clover Club, where Eddie and Jonah sat patiently at the table waiting for us— how he had taken these and worked magic on them!

Listening, I was deeply moved, thinking, is this how he saw me? Is this what I mean to him? I was proud and humble that he should invest me with such beauty, such desirability, such power to make him vital and whole. And I was embarrassed, as if Scott had nakedly revealed a part of himself that even I should not know.

Then I made another discovery. Stahr is a lonely man, still in love with his dead wife, Minna. When he first sees Kathleen she vanishes before he can speak. He sets out in search of her, only to discover the girl he thinks is Kathleen is really someone else. So, I recalled, it had been at Benchley's party, when Scott returned, hoping to find me— and instead had found Tala Birrell. When, in the novel, Stahr does find Kathleen, she is standing in the doorway of her house:

There she was—face and form and smile against the light from inside. It was Minna's face—the skin with its peculiar radiance as if phosphorus had touched it, the mouth with its warm line that never counted costs. . . .

Was this how he saw me? If I was Kathleen, Minna was Zelda. How much I must have reminded him of Zelda! Was this how I had appeared that night, when he stood at my door saying good-by, and I had not wanted to let him go and I had asked him in, and he had come in?

Had he—has he—been reliving with me his life with Zelda? Once, I recalled, he had said that I looked like her. I had not thought so. I listened to his reading, caught up in a waking dream, trying to understand the mystery of love, of the yearning that draws two people to become one.

When he finished reading as far as he had written, I said, "Scott, I think that is so beautiful—"

He put the manuscript down and looked at me for a long moment. He smiled and said, softly, "Sheilo—"

Wordlessly, I went into the circle of his arms. I possessed something precious and irreplaceable in this man, and I loved him deeply.

Strange, I thought. The people in Hollywood do not exist save as paragraphs in my column. There is no reality but Scott and me. We see no one; we do not entertain; we do not go out; we live in a world bounded by our apartments and Schwab's drugstore. Seldom was our routine broken—once when I went to Dallas for the world *première* of *The Westerner,* and again when Scott spent several weeks adapting Emlyn Williams' play, *The Light of Heart,* for Darryl Zanuck.

By October, he was again reading *The Last Tycoon* to me. I discovered new, and fascinating, parallels between our story and that of Stahr and Kathleen. I had been engaged to a marquess: Kathleen had been engaged to a king.

I was being educated by Scott: in the book, Kathleen had been educated by the king. At one point Stahr remarks to her, "You know a lot, don't you?" She replies, "I never went to a university, if that's what you mean. But the man I told you about knew everything and he had a passion for educating me. He made out schedules and made me take courses at the Sorbonne and go to museums."

It became a delightful game for me, waiting each night, to hear more of the story Scott wove from us into the novel he hoped would restore him to his rightful place among his contemporaries.

I did not hear Scott return. "I'm going to Schwab's for cigarettes," he had said, twenty minutes before. It was a Thursday afternoon in November, a dull, gray day, and I was curled up on the sofa, listening to the massed voices lifted in the stirring chorus of Bach's cantata *Singet dem Herrn*. Then I looked up. Scott was there, gray and trembling, letting himself slowly into his easy chair. Alarmed, I asked, "Is anything the matter, Scott?" I hurried to turn down the music. He lit a cigarette carefully before he spoke. "I almost fainted at Schwab's," he said. "Everything started to fade." He had never felt quite like that before. "I think I'd better see Dr. Wilson in the morning."

"Scott, I wish you would," I said, thinking, *Scott and his hypochondria*. I tried never to comment on his aches and pains because he was so quick to resent my concern.

In the morning he drove downtown to Dr. Wilson's office. He was back an hour later, his face solemn— He said, "I had a cardiac spasm."

A great pang of fear shot through me. "Is that a heart attack?"

Scott was vague. "No—"

"Did he say you must stay in bed?"

"No," said Scott. He lied, and I did not know. "But I must take it easy. Stairs are out."

I was relieved. Dr. Wilson had not put him to bed. I had read about heart attacks. If you had one, you were sent to bed at once and kept there, flat on your back. Yet Scott must take care of himself. His apartment was on the third floor, mine on the first. "All right," I said. "You move in with me right away." Frances and I would look for a suitable ground-floor apartment nearby. Until then, he would stay with me.

Scott was a difficult patient. As had been the case in New York, he made me promise I would not talk to the doctor alone. "I don't want him telling you anything he wouldn't tell me," he explained. On Dr. Wilson's visits, I was not to take him aside. I never questioned Dr. Wilson about the condition of Scott's heart.

In late November we attended a preview at Metro. As Scott brought his little car to a halt in the parking lot, I suddenly recalled that Metro's projection room was at the top of a long flight of steps. Scott, I knew, would disdain any show of weakness: I had to do something—and I did it. As I got out of the car I cried sharply, "Oh!" and almost fell. I held my ankle. "I've turned it, Scott," I groaned. I played my role well. He helped me as I limped to the stairs and I went up them slowly, one at a time, Scott holding my arm as I rested on each step. We took about five minutes to reach the top. If Scott knew that I pretended for his sake, he never let me know.

Most of the day he took it easy, remaining in bed, writing steadily, keeping Frances busy typing his material. Then he labored over the typed pages with infinite care, revising, rewriting, polishing. He was in excellent spirits. At night I lay awake, thinking. If only the novel could go on forever! I had never seen him so content before. And then I worried. If it was a success, would he drink, to celebrate? If it was a failure, would he begin to drink again, to forget?

Sometimes, however high in spirits, he became unexpectedly, unpredictably, irritable. Once a week I brought fresh flowers to the apartment, filling the vases industriously as I had done at Malibu. One afternoon, as I came in with an armful of flowers from the florist, Scott said, sharply, "Take those flowers away!"

I stared at him. He said, still sharply: "I hate cut flowers!"

"But at the beach—" I began.

"I couldn't stand them there, either."

I was perplexed, but I said nothing. I thought, and all that time at the beach he never said anything.

One afternoon, two weeks before Christmas, I returned from a shopping spree ecstatic over three dresses I had bought. "They're so heavenly!" I described them in detail. "Of course, they're terribly expensive, but they're worth every penny—" I prattled on and he snapped, "Oh, stop talking about it! I don't want to hear about your dresses and what they cost!"

I was taken aback. A moment later he apologized but I had begun to think. I had bought the dresses with my own money. Why should he be annoyed? There had been such anguish in his voice—the words seemed to burst forth despite himself. I asked myself, was it money? Was Scott in financial difficulties? Until he became completely well again, he could not accept any screen-writing jobs. Had he enough money to keep going until he finished his novel? I questioned Frances. And Frances, who paid all of Scott's bills, admitted reluctantly that he had only enough funds to carry him for three months. He would have been in

even greater straits had he not had several weeks' work on
The Light of Heart.

That night I made notes for a letter I would send, when
the time came, to Maxwell Perkins, Scott's editor at Scribner's. I had nearly $3,000 saved. I would give $2,000 to
Scott, but in such a fashion that he would not know it
came from me. I would give it on condition that Scribner's
advance $3,000, making $5,000 in all, the entire sum to
come from Scribner's in the form of an advance to Scott so
that he could finish the first draft of his novel.

My notes for the letter to Perkins read:

> Scott never to know, even if book brings back millions.
> He would never forgive me. If book a success, naturally
> I'll be happy to get the money back; if not, that is all
> right, too. Important thing is for him to finish this book.
> No mention ever to be made of this correspondence—he'd
> be too humiliated, and might take to drink again, just
> to prove something. No drinking since last December—
> more than 12 months now. Been working steadily on
> book for five months, in addition to what done last year.
> It would be criminal for him to be forced to go back to
> a studio which destroys his confidence and may mean he'll
> never finish book. But all money must come from you.
> Query: Is it best to wait until Scott asks you for an
> advance? Or offer it before, in case he doesn't ask? Some
> tactful way of giving him $1,000 a month for five months.
> This is better than a lump sum. Use my $2,000 first, so if
> anything goes wrong, I inform you and you needn't send
> the rest. At worst I lose two, you lose three. At best, a
> good novel, Scott reclaims his position as writer and
> person, and we get our money back. My honest conviction
> this will be best of all his writing.

Scott struggled with *The Last Tycoon.* He was in the
middle of a difficult chapter. The solution he sought would

not come. He had been in bed all morning, it was mid-afternoon, he wanted to dictate, and Frances was not there. He was fretful.

I sat on the edge of his bed and stroked his forehead and pushed the hair out of his eyes. "You go to sleep now, and I promise you that when you wake up, Frances will be here and things will seem a lot better." I sat there talking quietly until he became drowsy and fell asleep. I tiptoed out and closed the door behind me.

I phoned Frances. "Please come over. Scott needs you."

He slept for about two hours while I worked on my column. "Sheilo—" he called. When I came into his room he was like a new man, yawning and stretching. "I've had a wonderful sleep," he said. Frances had arrived and waited, ready for dictation.

They were closeted about half an hour; then she left. Scott set up his writing board and began to write energetically. Dr. Wilson was due in an hour to take a cardiogram. Would I telephone him, Scott called, and tell him to come tomorrow? His work was moving too well to be interrupted now.

Not until seven o'clock did Scott rise and join me for dinner. He read me the last paragraph of what he had written. "I've solved it," he said with satisfaction. He was elated, almost exhilarated.

I said, "You see, by just not fretting and taking it easy, you work better."

He kissed me. "Let's celebrate." He was in high spirits. "Let's go out."

I had tickets to a press preview of *This Thing Called Love*, a comedy starring Rosalind Russell and Melvyn Douglas. I hadn't gone to a preview in weeks. A comedy would be just the thing.

Scott dressed. He stood before the mirror fixing his bow

tie. He gave it a final tug at both ends and threw a puckish glance at me. I was waiting at the door. "I always wanted to be a dandy," he said, with a grin. That night, Friday night, December 20, we went to the Pantages Theatre and saw *This Thing Called Love*.

When the film was over and the house lights came on, Scott stood up to let me by him into the aisle. I looked back just in time to see him stagger, as if someone had struck him off balance. He had to lean down and grab the arm rest for support. I thought he had stumbled. I hurried back and took his arm. He said, in a low, strained voice, "I feel awful—everything started to go as it did in Schwab's." I held his arm tightly. He said, "I suppose people will think I'm drunk." I said, "Scott, nobody saw it." I held him under his arm, supporting as much of his weight as I could without drawing attention, and we moved slowly up the aisle. A chill went through me as I realized that he had not pushed my hand away as he had done each time I had tried to help him in the past. I tried to appear in animated conversation with him as we made our way. I thought, furiously, he hasn't taken a drink in a year and now they'll all think he's drunk again.

We walked slowly to his car. The air revived him and he breathed deeply. "How do I look?" he asked. In the powerful lights of the Pantages, I could see him clearly. I said, "You look very pale. Shouldn't we call the doctor?"

Scott said no. Dr. Wilson was coming tomorrow, anyway. Let's not make any fuss.

He drove home slowly and by the time we had arrived, he felt better. He took his sleeping pills, went immediately to bed, and fell asleep.

I went into his room, later, and looked at him. He slept very peacefully, like a tired child.

I did not know that he would die the next day.

CHAPTER TWENTY-EIGHT

A BRIGHT NOON-DAY sun shone through the window of my sitting room. I sat at the typewriter. Scott, comfortable in slacks, slippers, and a sweater over his shirt, paced up and down, dictating. It was a letter to Scottie from me, informing her that for Christmas I was sending her my fox-fur jacket and an evening dress. I knew Scottie, now in her junior year, could make good use of them. I felt a pang at giving up my jacket—but I wanted to please her. I had said to Scott, "I don't want her to think I'm patronizing her or sending cast-off clothes—will you tell me just what to write?"

I wrote as he dictated:

December 21, 1940

Dear Scottie:

I bought this dress to go to Dallas for *The Westerner*. The winter is slipping away and because of natural unpopularity, I find no reason to use it. So there it sat in my closet, losing style week after week. I mentioned this to your father and he told me that you burned up dresses at the rate of one a month and suggested that instead of selling it down the river, I contribute it to the conflagration. The coat also seems to have been waiting in my closet for the victory celebration and I don't think now we will win before 1943. By that time it will be unusual for English people to wear furs.

Why don't you send your father a picture of how you look now, or he won't be able to recognize you when you meet again. I hope you have a very happy Christmas and everything you want in the New Year.

Yours,

Sheilah.

P. S. Your father has not been well, but he's getting better now. He hasn't had a drink for over a year.

Scott had awakened only a little before, having slept well. I brought him coffee as he sat up in bed, making notes for a new chapter. Then, restless, he had gotten up and dressed. Dr. Wilson was to come after lunch.

Frances dropped in, bringing Scott's mail, which still went to his apartment. There were a few bills, several advertisements, and the current issue of *The Princeton Alumni Weekly*. I gave Frances my dress and jacket which she promised to pack and mail. She left.

It was a little after two o'clock.

I prepared sandwiches and coffee for lunch while Scott glanced through the newspapers. I heard an exclamation. He began to read aloud: Germany, Italy, and Japan had signed a mutual-aid pact. He shook his head as he read. Though he was contemptuous of Mussolini, he respected Japan as a fighting power. This would force the United States into the war. Sooner or later we would be in it. If his book was a success, he went on, he would like to go to Europe and write about the war. And with a rueful smile, "Ernest won't have that field all to himself, then." Hemingway had written brilliantly about the Spanish Civil War: now he was sending special dispatches from Europe. And after the war, Scott was saying—if *The Last Tycoon* was a hit—I would give up my job, we would both live in the East and travel a great deal. He would care for me. Once before he had said, "If ever I get out of this mess, I'll make it up to you, Sheilo—"

After lunch he was restless. He went into the kitchen and I heard him moving around, opening cupboards. Then he reappeared. "I'm going to Schwab's to get some ice cream," he said.

"But you might miss the doctor—if it's something sweet you want, I've got some Hershey bars."

"Good enough," he said. "They'll be fine."

I brought him two chocolate bars from the box I kept by my bedside table. He picked up *The Princeton Alumni Weekly,* sank into his green armchair next to the fireplace, and began reading. As he read, he munched on the chocolate. I picked up one of my music books, curled up on the settee, and began reading about Beethoven.

Every little while we looked up and exchanged smiles. I noticed that Scott, with one of his stubby pencils, was making notes on the margin of an article about the Princeton football team. Again our eyes met: he grinned as he deliberately licked the chocolate from his fingers and bent down to his magazine again. I turned back to my book.

I saw, out of the corner of my eye—as you see something when you are not looking directly at it—I saw him suddenly start up out of his chair, clutch the mantelpiece and, without a sound, fall to the floor. He lay flat on his back, his eyes closed, breathing heavily.

When he stood up so unexpectedly I thought, *oh, he's stretching.* When he fell I thought, *oh, he's stumbled.* And then: *he's fainted!*

In the split second of that realization, as I sat there, willing myself to rise, yet not able, there was a choking, gasping sound in his throat.

Then I was up, and kneeling on the floor beside him, saying, "Scott—Scott—"

My mind whirled with thoughts. He's fainted. What do you do when someone faints? You pour brandy down his throat. But Scott's not been drinking—won't the taste of brandy start him off again? In the movies they loosen the collar—yes, that's sensible. That's harmless. I loosened his collar.

I was on my knees, looking at him.

I thought, *this faint has lasted a long time*.

His body seemed to heave gently. I ought to do something. I'll call Dr. Wilson. No, he'll be here any minute. No, I must call him, I can't wait. What doctor *will* I call? No, the brandy. It must be brandy, right away.

I clambered to my feet and rushed into the dinette and found the brandy bottle and poured some into a glass and rushed back and poured some into his mouth. His teeth were clenched. I poured the brandy between his clenched teeth. It spilled over on his face and ran down his chin and neck. I felt embarrassed. This was sacrilege—it was taking advantage of Scott. He wasn't there to wipe it off. I wiped it off with my hand.

I found myself at the telephone, calling Dr. Wilson. There was no answer. I ran my finger down the list of doctors and called one. "Someone's very ill—he's unconscious—can you come right over?"

Then I rushed out of the apartment and pounded on the door of Harry Culver, the manager of the building. "Come quickly—Mr. Fitzgerald has fainted and it's lasted so long, I'm getting frightened."

Mr. Culver was at my heels as I ran back. He knelt beside Scott and felt for his pulse. He looked up at me. "I'm afraid he's dead."

I thought, oxygen. I was at the telephone calling the fire

department. Then the police. The door opened and Pat Duff, my secretary, entered. Then everything became confused. It seemed that I was still at the telephone when the apartment was full of people and soft voices and firemen with a Pulmotor were working over Scott and I heard myself saying again and again, "Hurry up, please, hurry up, please save him." Unexpectedly Buff Cobb was holding me close to her, the firemen were gone, and a white sheet covered Scott's body. I became hysterical. "Take that away, he won't be able to breathe, he'll suffocate, please, please!" Buff was leading me into another room. "You'll stay with us tonight," she was saying gently. "We'll take care of everything—" I broke away to rush into the sitting room and Scott's body was not there.

I began to cry. I cried but no sound came. The tears rolled down my cheeks but I made no sound.

Buff Cobb said, "We're going to take you to a doctor, Sheilah." Then time passed, and it was night, and I was in her home, at the table, and her father, Irvin Cobb, at the head of the table, was addressing his remarks to me. I have no idea what he said or I said. I sobbed without a sound. Sometimes I stopped and talked but most of the time I was shaking and sobbing. I slept in Buff Cobb's room that night.

Then it was the next day and Scottie was on the telephone from Harold Ober's home in Connecticut, where she had gone to spend Christmas. Her voice was broken. How had it happened? I told her. There was a strange calm upon me. We talked for some time. "Poor Sheilah," she said at one point. "How awful for you!" And she said, it must be a comfort to me to know that I had made her father's last years happy—and that this should be my solace. I was grateful for her words. Then she said she would leave school as soon as possible. Oh, no, I replied, she must not. "Scott's dearest wish was that you complete your schooling." She said, "No, I want to quit and earn my living. I don't think there's much money."

She must not do that, I repeated. She must stay at Vassar. She must not worry about the money. It would be found, somehow.

"Well, I'll think about it," she said.

Then, in her eighteen-year-old voice she went on, "By the way, Sheilah—we're going to bury Daddy in Baltimore. I don't think it would be advisable for you to come to the funeral, do you?"

I had never intended to go to the funeral. I would not have gone to the funeral. I was able to choke out, "No, of course not—good-by." I put down the phone and for the first time I began to cry aloud. I sobbed loudly and could not control myself. I had had Scott, he had belonged to me, and now he was dead and everyone had taken over, they had taken him away and I had nothing. I thought, if he were alive, he wouldn't have allowed them to do this to me. Yet I knew if he were alive he, too, would have said to me, Sheilo, you cannot come to my funeral.

I remained in my apartment. I could not bear to leave it. Friends came. How can you stay here? they asked. Get out. Go somewhere. It's morbid. Don't stay in this room where he died.

Why? I asked. This is where Scott is. Why should I leave Scott?

People were kind to me. I was invited to three Christmas parties. I was in a whirl: people took me and spun me around and when I stopped they thrust a turkey leg in my mouth. I had three dinners and ate none of them.

I drove to a Christmas party at Dorothy Parker's. On the way a strange thing happened. Suddenly my car would not go forward. It went only backward. Sitting there, I began to cry. I put on the brake in the middle of the street and got out and said aloud, "Will someone please help me?"

A man approached. "What's the trouble?"

"My car keeps going backward," I said, crying.

He got behind the wheel and tried it. "What direction are you going?"

"That way—to six-o-two North Bedford."

"If you get in, I'll drive you there."

I got in, the tears running down my cheeks. I thought, he probably thinks I'm on a drunken crying jag, but I don't care what he thinks. I almost said to him, "The man I loved has died," but I managed not to let the words escape.

We drove past the house. "This is six-ten," he said.

"I want six-o-two," I said.

He turned the car around and stopped on the far side of the street. "I'll walk across," I said. I was weeping hysterically. "Thank you."

"Oh, that's all right." He watched me take a few steps. They were so uncertain, now, that I was sure he thought I was drunk. Again I almost told him about Scott. But it seemed undignified to tell him, and Scott would have thought that, too. Yet Scott's heart would have been torn to see my misery. He would have comforted me and we would have been very close.

The man gently took my arm and walked with me across the street. And carefully and stumblingly I found Dorothy's house and walked inside. I could not bear the laughter and the talk. I went into her bedroom and lay on her bed. I lay there, crying. "I've had such a loss," I said, over and over. "I've had such a loss." I was full of poetry. I recited Christina Rossetti's "When I am dead, my dearest, sing no sad songs for me." I recited, "Bold Lover . . . do not grieve, She cannot fade, though thou hast not thy bliss, Forever wilt thou love, and she be fair—"

And then I wept again. "I've had such a loss, Oh, such a terrible loss."

And Dorothy sat with me, and wept with me.

EPILOGUE

I sɪᴛ in the quiet study of my home in Beverly Hills. It is September, 1958, and the autumn out the window is the autumn Scott knew, and loved. How many years have passed, and still I feel his presence. Before me on my bookshelves, their paper covers faded by time, are row upon row of the Encino edition. I open one volume at random. It is *Outline for Review: Greek History*. On the flyleaf there is written:

For S. G. For her proficiency in pre-Socratic philosophy, Hellenistic anthropology, and Trojan archeology
from
Her Loving Prof
T. Themstocles Smith
Olympic Games, 1910

Here, folded in the pages of Palgrave's *The Golden Treasury*, is a poem Scott wrote to me—when, I do not know:

SOME INTERRUPTED LINES TO SHEILAH

Once you were so far away
Nothing was so far
On the edge of space you lay

Like an outer star
Even your most tender word
    On that week we met
Was a station dimly heard
    On a short-wave set
Was a lost imperilled boat
    Sending far alarms
Oh, so infinitely remote
    Even in my arms.

Now you are so near, so near
    That no furth'rest wing
Takes you where I cannot hear
    Your faint whispering
Hear the clamor of your hands
    Thunder of your eyes
Your most far-sent wish commands
    Me to Paradise—
—There! You've phoned—ten minutes late
    Driving me insane
Why'd you make a down-town date?
    I'm stood up again!

I think, how do I grasp the essence that is Scott, the
charm, the tenderness, the quick, alert, infinitely sensitive
mind, the integrity that was the very measure of the man?
What had he done for me that keeps him so alive for me?
He taught me, above all, what no one else had ever taught
me: that I am valuable: that every human being has value.
He enlarged my capacity for every experience—for joy, for
suffering, for understanding. When he died, I thought, I
have been greatly honored: I shall wear my four years
with Scott like a crown.

If Scott were sitting beside me in my study on this September day, what would he think, how would he feel, to
know his high estate in the world of letters today? That he

has been the subject of critical studies, of a biography, a novel, and a play; that his own stories have been dramatized for audiences of millions; that college students read him today not only because he is required reading in the universities but because they love his writing. He would have been delighted to know this, for they were the audience he believed he had lost, the audience of young people. He thought they considered him too old fashioned. He thought, nobody ever reads F. Scott Fitzgerald any more.

He is a myth and a legend: his fame is secure. The other day a book dealer came to buy cartons of old books from me. Among them were first editions of Faulkner and Hemingway and Dreiser and Dos Passos—Scott's contemporaries. The dealer said, "I see you have first editions of Scott Fitzgerald. If you care to sell them, I'll give you as much for them as I've given you for all the rest put together." Scott would have taken his own ironic enjoyment from this. What would he say if he knew all this, if he knew that were he and I to wander into a bookstore today, his books might be unavailable not because no one wants them but because there is so great a demand for them?

I see him now. He'd square his shoulders, like a boxer who has been tired, and has suddenly renewed his strength. He'd walk to the window and look out with a happy smile —he'd regained his position. I can almost hear him say, "Yes, they've come around at last."

He would be so pleased.